T0367870

A Covenant
PEOPLE

Israel from Abraham to the Present

JAMES P. ECKMAN

WESTBOW°
PRESS
A DIVISION OF THOMAS NELSON
& ZONDERVAN

WestBow Press books may be ordered through booksellers or by contacting:

WestBow Press
A Division of Thomas Nelson & Zondervan
1663 Liberty Drive
Bloomington, IN 47403
www.westbowpress.com
1 (866) 928-1240

ISBN: 978-1-4908-2137-5 (sc)
ISBN: 978-1-4908-2138-2 (hc)
ISBN: 978-1-4908-2136-8 (e)

Library of Congress Control Number: 2014905034

Printed in the United States of America.

WestBow Press rev. date: 3/24/2014

Maps, charts, and graphs by Greg Thompson

This book is dedicated to my beloved wife, Peggy, whose encouragement and prayer support have been indispensable. Next to Jesus, she is God's greatest gift.

I also extend profound thanks to my dear friends, David and Lori Scott and Gary and Marsha Marron, whose support made this vision become a reality.

Contents

Introduction

It has been said that to truly understand modern Israel, one must come to terms with Masada, the Wailing Wall, and Yad Vashem, the Holocaust Museum in Jerusalem. Masada is the plateau in the Judean wilderness where, in AD 73, a small band of Jewish zealots committed suicide rather than submit to the oppression of the conquering Romans. The Wailing Wall (actually the western retaining wall) is the only remnant of the Second Temple in Jerusalem—the holiest site of Judaism. Yad Vashem documents the horrors of the Nazi Holocaust that directly led to the creation of the modern nation-state of Israel in 1948. Each has symbolic power to the modern Jew, and each plays a role in the remarkable history of the Jewish people.

This book is the story of the Jewish people—a story filled with promise, hope, and redemption but also with despair, judgment, and oppression. It begins with the astonishing promises God made to the patriarch Abraham over 4,000 years ago. It ends with the creation of Israel by the United Nations in 1947–8 and the subsequent wars that the Jewish people have fought to preserve Israel as the Jewish homeland. There are about 18 million Jews in the world today, and over 6 million of them live in Israel. (The United States has the other largest concentration of Jews—about 5.8 million). The survival of the Jewish people over these 4,000 years is a miracle. This book seeks to tell the story of that miracle.

I begin with a review of certain basic assumptions, rooted in Scripture, which inform this history of Israel:

1. The Bible presents accurate and trustworthy history. Our God is a God of history, and Scripture documents

his redemptive work in history. That redemptive story is revealed in the history of Israel, in the early church, and of course most importantly in Jesus Christ. The Old Testament historical books are authentic accounts of actual historical events, many of which have been validated by archeology. The hundreds of prophecies about the first advent of the Messiah were fulfilled in space-time history by Jesus.

2. There are three important biblical covenants that define God's relationship with the Jewish people: the Abrahamic covenant, the Davidic covenant, and the new covenant. God promised Abraham descendants as numerous as the sand of the seashore and the stars of the sky, land, and blessing—that in him "all the nations would be blessed" (Genesis 12:1–7). Because of Genesis 15:9–21, we are to understand these covenant promises as eternal and unconditional. God promised King David an eternal throne, dynasty, and kingdom (succinctly summarized in 2 Samuel 7:16). The Old Testament prophets, major and minor, are filled with hundreds of promises about the coming Son of David who will rule and reign. The New Testament declares Jesus to be that King. Finally, the new covenant contains God's promise of spiritual blessing and renewal energized by the coming of His Holy Spirit. (See Jeremiah 31:31–33 and Ezekiel 36:24–29.)

3. The Mosaic covenant was a conditional covenant, added to the Abrahamic promise (see Galatians 3:19–22), which defined how Israel was to walk with God. The God of the Bible is the Sovereign Lord who chose Israel to be a vehicle to reveal His holiness and His righteous character to the nations. As the major and minor prophets indicate, when God disciplined His people, He did so on the basis of the curses and blessings of the Mosaic covenant. (See Deuteronomy 28.) But His ongoing promise to restore them and renew them was always on the basis of His covenant commitment to Abraham.

4. I believe that God will keep His covenant promises to Israel; indeed, when His Son returns, a national regeneration of

Israel will occur. With clarity, Paul declared in Romans 11:26 that there is coming a day when "all of Israel will be saved." This remarkable event will be preceded by the regathering of the Jewish people to their homeland. God promised this regathering throughout the Old Testament but most clearly in Ezekiel 36–37. In these vital chapters, God declares that He will bring His people back to their land, renew them spiritually, and fulfill completely the promises He made to Abraham and David. He will then implement all the dimensions of the new covenant. (See especially Ezekiel 37:15–28.)

Israel's Strategic Location

The land God promised to Abraham in Genesis 12 was actually a land bridge between two great river valleys—the Tigris and Euphrates valley, the center of the great Mesopotamian civilizations (e.g., Assyria and Babylonia) and the Nile valley, the center of the famous Egyptian civilization. With the Arabian Desert to the east and the Mediterranean Sea to the west, Israel provided the natural location for two international highways that connected Mesopotamia and Egypt—the "way of the sea" (Via Maris) along the Mediterranean coast, and the King's Highway along the mountains of Jordan. Hence, throughout its history, Israel was often a battleground between the warring civilizations of these two great river valleys, a reality that is central to understanding the background of the Old Testament.

Israel was a part of what many have called the "Fertile Crescent," a band of often rich, arable land that stretches from the Persian Gulf, north through the Mesopotamian valley, west through southern Turkey, and then south to Israel's Dead Sea. There is generally adequate rainfall, and thus significant agricultural development occurred in this strip of land. For that reason, several of the oldest human settlements on planet Earth are located in this crescent. Israel is thus in the center of one of the most important sections of land in the world.

Israel's Geography

For a relatively small section of territory, Israel has more geographical diversity than any other comparable place on earth. Bounded on the east by the Syro-Arabian Desert, on the west by the Mediterranean, and on the south by the Negev Desert, Israel is about 150 miles north to south and about 60 miles east to west. There are several distinctive features of Israel's geography:

1. *The Jordan Rift.* Stretching from Central Asia deep into Africa is a fissure in the earth's surface, much of which in Israel is below sea level. Large, rugged mountains on both the east and the west sides of the rift accentuate the significance of this topographical distinction in Israel. As you move from the north to the south along this rift, the Hulah Lake (now drained by modern Israel) is about 210 feet above sea level, followed by the Sea of Galilee (13 miles long and 7 miles wide), which is about 690 feet below sea level. The sea empties, via the Jordan River, into the Dead Sea (50 miles long and 10 miles wide), which is about 1,300 feet below sea level. The rift continues south of the Dead Sea in what is called the Arabah (a dry, desolate area) to the Gulf of Aqaba and the important port city called Elath.

2. *Transjordan.* To the east of the rift rises a series of high plateaus that drain into the rift. To the east of the plateau is the Syro-Arabian Desert. Important biblical locations are associated with Transjordan. Beginning from the north is Bashan (the Golan Heights), a rich, fertile area due to past volcanic activity. Next is Gilead, a heavily wooded area in the ancient world. The Ammonites lived in this area, much of which the Israelite tribes of Gad and half of Manasseh claimed. Next is Moab, east of the Dead Sea and the home of the Moabites. Finally, south of the Dead Sea is Edom, home of Esau's descendants, the Edomites.

3. *The Central Mountains.* West of the rift are the central mountains of Israel, which are divided into three regions. In

the north is Galilee, separated from Samaria by the Jezreel Valley, which is a rugged, elevated plateau in the north but a smaller series of east-west hills that contain productive, rich soil. The hills of Samaria south of the Jezreel Valley contain important cities and villages associated with the northern kingdom of Israel (e.g., Shechem and Samaria) and Mounts Ebal and Gerizim. Finally, the southern hills are those of Judah, which contain the important city of Jerusalem.

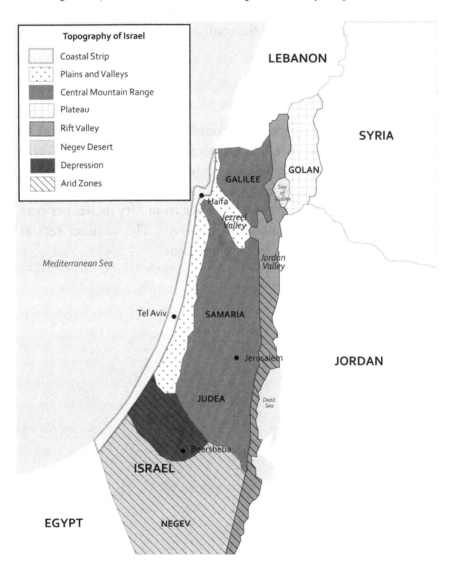

4. *Shephelah.* West of the hills of Judah are the Shephelah, foothills that run to the coastal plain, which are rich in both moisture and good farmland. In ancient Israel, the Shephelah formed an important natural boundary protecting Judah from the coastal plain inhabited by the Philistines.
5. *The Coastal Plain.* Stretching from ancient Lebanon down into Egypt, the coastal plain was important for the international highway (Via Maris) and contained rich soil and adequate rainfall. Throughout much of ancient Israel, the Philistines controlled the southern part of the plain, in what is today called Gaza.[1]

Israel's Climate

Essentially, there are only two seasons in the subtropical climate of Israel: summer and winter. The winter season (November to April) is the wet period when Israel receives virtually all of its rain. The northern sections receive much more moisture than the extremely arid south. Those rainfall amounts range from fifty inches per year in the north to virtually none in the south. The summer season (May to October) receives little if any rain.

Chapter 1

The Patriarchs: The Founding of the Nation

The history of Israel begins with Abraham. Since the Bible singularly focuses on the redemptive purposes of God in history (see Genesis 3:15), choosing one man—Abraham—as the channel for that purpose is extraordinary. Indeed, the apostle Paul, in his commentary on Abraham's life in Galatians 3, argues that God's promise—"In you all the nations will be blessed" (Genesis 12:3)—is in effect the promise of salvation. Before Abraham, God dealt with all of humanity, making no covenant distinctions. His judgment for sin in the flood extended to all of humanity, and He chose to repopulate the earth with Noah and his descendants (Genesis 6–11). But in choosing Abraham, God determined to focus His redemptive plan on one man and his descendants. God's redemptive program, then, is inextricably linked to Israel, the descendants of Abraham.

Abraham

According to Genesis 12, Abram lived in Ur of the Chaldees, an important, cosmopolitan Sumerian city. Ur was the central hub of Sumerian city-states in southern Mesopotamia, the land between the Tigris and Euphrates Rivers. A professor of Semitic studies, Eugene H. Merrill, argues that Abram was born in 2166 BC.[2] According to the biblical genealogy of Abram (Genesis 11:10–32), Abram and his family were Semitic peoples, but the Bible does not detail when or why they settled in Ur. Joshua 24:2 indicates that Abram, his father, Terah, and the family worshipped the gods associated with Ur. More than likely, this included the moon god, Sin, and his many associates in the Sumerian pantheon. Evidence of this worship could be reflected in the names Sarah (Abram's wife) and Milcah (his brother's daughter), both of which derived from Babylonian titles. Milcah means "princess," the daughter of the moon god, and Sarah means "queen," the wife of the moon god. Indeed, Terah is a Hebrew form of the term *moon*, which is another indication of the family's pagan worship.[3] Yet Genesis 31:53 explains that Abram worshiped the true God. What caused the change?

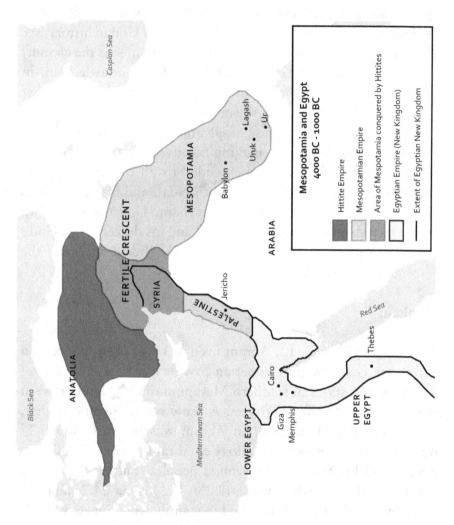

Abram responded in faith to God's call to leave Ur and found a new nation that would bless the entire world. What makes Abram's response more remarkable is that Abram's conversion and response of faith was the response of a pagan. Also, he was old, more than likely prosperous, and well established in Ur. The nation of Israel was founded by Abram, the man of faith, and it was rooted in God's will—He chose Abram!

God's promise to Abram (Genesis 12:1–7) was threefold: his descendants would be as numerous as the stars and the sand, He would give him land, and He would bless the world through Abram. This promise is called the Abrahamic covenant, and it provides the key framework for explaining how God has dealt with Israel throughout its long history.

Connecting Genesis 15:17–21 to 12:1–7 is critical, for these verses describe how God "cut a covenant" with Abram. In the ancient world, especially the ancient Akkadian world from which Abram came, animals were killed and cut in two, and their respective parts were laid opposite one another. The parties making the covenant walked between the parts together, signifying that if either party broke the covenant, that party would become as dead. However, in this narrative, God (in the symbolic form of the oven and the torch) walked between the severed animals alone. God, who is holy and perfect, was binding Himself to this covenant. He would fulfill His unconditional and eternal covenant promises, for His promises to Abram and his descendants are forever.[4] In the narrative, it says, "Abraham believed God and it was counted to him as righteousness" (Genesis 15:6). As the New Testament affirms (Romans 4 and Galatians 3:6–9), here is where Abram was justified by his faith.

Returning to the narrative of Abram's life, Genesis explains that Abram, Sarah, Terah, and Lot (Abram's brother Haran's son) left Ur and traveled to Haran, undoubtedly following the Euphrates River north about six hundred miles. Haran was apparently the ancestral home of Abram, and Genesis 11:32 explains that Terah died there.

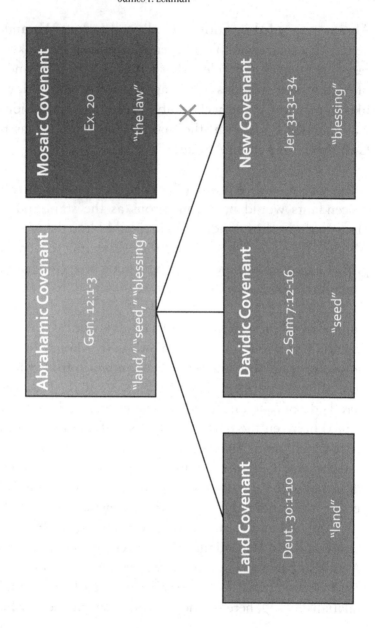

The Covenants of the Old Testament

In 2091 BC, Abram proceeded to Canaan, the land that God had promised him. He no doubt entered Canaan from the east, along the Jabbok River, and camped in Shechem, where he built an altar. He then traveled south along the hills, settling for a time near Bethel, and then traveled down to the Negev. (See Genesis 12:6–9.)

Why did Abram meet no Canaanite resistance in his sojourn? The Canaanites had settled in the valleys and the coastal plain, while the hills and mountains west of the Jordan Rift were virtually unsettled. In the hill country, Abram was thus able to move about and settle down at will.

A severe drought and famine in the Negev caused Abram and his family to seek relief in Egypt, where, because of the Nile Valley, there was normally an abundance of food. While in Egypt, he would no doubt have the viewed the great pyramids near Memphis. He was welcomed by the pharaoh (perhaps Wahkare Achtthoes III), to whom he lied about his wife, Sarah. Despite Abram's duplicity, God blessed him with abundant sheep, cattle, and camels. Abram returned to the Negev a wealthy man.[5]

Genesis 13 mentions that Abram traveled throughout the land of Canaan, following an alternation between the hill country and the southern desert lands. During the winter months, Abram and his clan grazed their animals in the Negev, where winter rains provided grass for the herds. During the hot summer months, they traveled to the hill country (Shechem, Bethel, and Ai), where the grazing lands were cooler.[6] So wealthy had Abram become that he and Lot decided to separate. Lot chose the area in the southern Jordan Valley in Transjordan, while Abram chose the hill country south to Hebron. The Genesis text makes no significant reference to any resistance from the Canaanites, who inhabited the valleys and coastal plan. Abram was now living in the land God had promised him, and he was referred to as "Abram, the Hebrew" (14:13).

The remaining narrative of Abram's life (Genesis 14–23) takes on an entirely different tone in the text. The results of Abram's settling in Canaan are detailed. Each part of this narrative expands upon Abram, the founder of the nation, as a man of extraordinary faith. First is the story of Lot's kidnapping in Genesis 14 by powerful kings of the east. The difficult names of the eastern kings cannot yet be identified with known rulers from this period in history.

However, the place names can be: Shinar, Elam, Arioch, Tidal, and Zoar are all identifiable locations in the ancient Near East. The five kings of the Jordan Valley had apparently been vassal states paying tribute to these eastern kings. When they rebelled, Chedorlaomer of Elam led the other eastern kings in an effort to crush the revolt. The result was the battle of Siddim, in which Lot was captured. Abram then assembled an army of 318 men who chased the enemy as far as Dan (then known as Laish). During a nighttime raid, Abram rescued Lot, his possessions, and his family.

The text makes clear that Abram's victory was by the power of God. The land God promised him had been plundered, so Abram, trusting in God, vanquished his enemies, proving the outworking of the covenant promises of God. Abram refused to accept anything from the pagan king of Sodom (14:22–24), for he relied on God to keep His promises and depended on His blessing, not those of a pagan king. For that reason, Abram received the blessing from and paid tithes to the mysterious Melchizedek, a priest-king linked to Jerusalem. The contrast between Abram's response to the king of Sodom and to Melchizedek heightens the message that Abram is a man of faith in God: he waits for God's blessing.

Second, the debacle with Hagar in Genesis 16 illustrates how the founders of Israel often exhibited impatience as they waited for God to fulfill His promises. When barrenness occurred in the ancient Near East, it was a common practice for a maidservant to bear a child in place of the wife. Hence, Sarah suggests that Abram take her servant Hagar. The result is Ishmael and an unbelievably complicated legacy. As Allen P. Ross suggests, the lesson of this passage is to "trust God's Word and patiently wait for His promises. Foolishly to adopt worldly customs and expedients will only complicate matters and bring greater tensions. Any people who owe their existence to divine creation and election must live by faith."[7]

Third, in chapter 17, thirteen years after Ishmael was born, Abram was ninety-nine years old and God appeared to him again. God declared Himself to be "God Almighty" (El Shaddai in 17:1) and affirmed the unconditional nature of the covenant. God declared that Abram would be "the father of many nations," and He changed his name from Abram, an old West Semitic name (a "father of distinguished birth"), to Abraham (a "father of a multitude"). By renaming him Abraham, God was giving him a pledge of His promise. God then instituted the sign of the covenant: circumcision. As Ross argues, "With this symbol God instructed his people regarding the joining of faith with the act of reproduction. The sign was sexual—the promise was for a seed."[8]

Fourth, God's covenant with Abraham is recorded five times in Genesis: 12:1–3, 13:14–17, 15:1–21, 17:1–22, and 22:15–18. Each one of these iterations of the promise was conditioned on Abraham having a son, but Abraham had no son. When Abraham entered Canaan, he was seventy-five, and he was eighty-five when Ishmael was born. Finally, in 2066 BC,[9] Sarah, at age ninety, gave birth to Isaac, the covenant son, when Abraham was one hundred years old (Genesis 21:1–7).

Why did Abraham and Sarah need to wait twenty-five years for Isaac? The Bible is silent on this, but it seems reasonable that the delay was a significant test of Abraham's faith. Could he trust God and His promises? Despite Ishmael, Abraham did trust God. But another reason is certain. Because Abraham was one hundred and Sarah was ninety, Isaac's birth was a miracle, and it was imperative for Abraham to understand that. Further, the ongoing fulfillment of God's promises to Abraham would also be miraculous. The people of Israel, Abraham's descendants, could only be explained as supernatural—the very conclusion God wanted them to draw.

Finally, due to his treaty with Abimelech, Abraham settled in Beersheba in the northern Negev (Genesis 21:22–34). In Beersheba, the greatest test of Abraham the man of faith, is recorded. He had waited twenty-five years for Isaac, and then God tested his faith. Would Abraham be willing to give his son back to God?

The command was to offer Isaac on Mount Moriah, about for-ty-five miles north of Beersheba. The narrative presents Abraham as a man of unwavering faith, arising early in the morning to obey God's command (v. 3), even declaring to his servant who accompanied him that both he and his son would return, implying God would restore his son's life (vv. 5-8; Hebrews 11:17–19). Because of Abraham's faith, God provided a substitute, a ram, which was sacrificed in Isaac's place (v. 13).

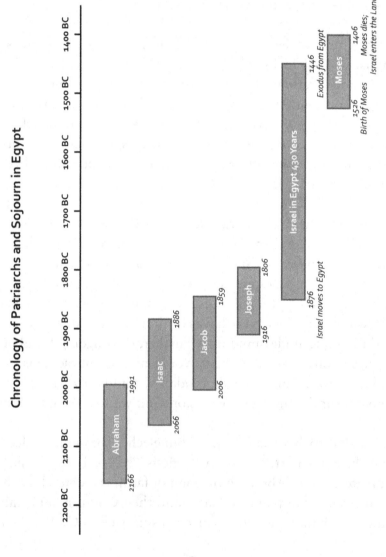

For Abraham, God was Jehovah Jireh, the Lord who provides. God, in the language of a vow, then reiterated His covenant promises to Abraham (vv. 15–18). Since 2 Chronicles 3:1 explains that Solomon built the Temple on Mount Moriah, the connection between Isaac and Jesus cannot be missed. Two thousand years later, another Father and Son would walk up that same Mount Moriah, but there would be no substitute for that Son, for He was the substitute (see Isaiah 52:13–53:12). The New Testament constructs the intertextual link between Abraham's offspring and Jesus Christ quite clearly. Jesus is the Seed of Abraham who would die for sin and provide the offer of justification by faith (Galatians 3:16).

Throughout the Bible, Abraham, as the founder of the Jewish nation, is presented as a paradigm of faith, the father of all those who believe. Despite his moments of doubt, he was called a "friend of God" (James 2:23). For the people of Israel, Abraham was not only their father, but also their model of how to walk with God.

Isaac

Compared to Abraham and Jacob, the Bible has comparatively little to say about Isaac. In fact, in terms of the fulfillment of the covenant promise, there are only two aspects of Isaac's life that are important. The first relates to the celebration surrounding the weaning of Isaac, when his brother Ishmael mocked him. The term "mock" and the story with Ishmael in Genesis 21:9 illustrate the truth that faith and unbelief are incompatible. As Ross comments, "That which trifles with God's work must be removed so that faith can prosper under God's blessing."[10] Hence, Hagar and Ishmael were banished from the family and from the land, but God promised Abraham that He would still protect and provide for them.

Regarding the covenant promise, the second dimension of importance was Isaac's marriage. Through Isaac the line of promise was to be maintained, so it was quite important whom he married. Abraham feared he would marry a Canaanite, so Abraham sent

Eliezer his servant to his homeland, Haran, to find a wife for Isaac (Genesis 24:2–6). The text emphasizes that Eliezer was the instrument God used to secure a bride for Isaac, and God superintended everything about his journey. So God's sovereignty and providence are the main themes of the narrative. Even Rebekah's father, Laban, recognized God's providence (Genesis 24:50). Isaac and Rebekah were married in 2026 BC.[11] Hence the covenant line was preserved, and God was the reason for the preservation.

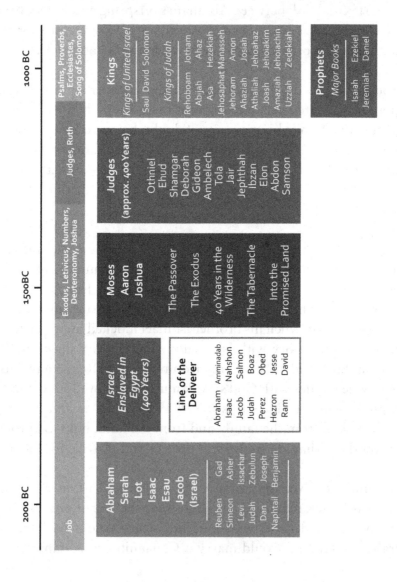

Jacob

Abraham's grandson, Jacob, was the actual father of the nation of Israel, via his twelve sons, and from him came the actual name of the people, "Israel." Even while Jacob and Esau were in Rebekah's womb, God declared by divine election that the elder, Esau, would serve the younger, Jacob. Jacob would thus be the heir to the covenant promise.

But Jacob, with the help of his duplicitous mother, secured those blessings his way. Because he was holding on to his brother's heel as he came out of the womb, Jacob was called the "heel-catcher, the supplanter."[12] Because Esau was dismissive and indifferent to his position as the firstborn, he sold his birthright to Jacob for a bowl of red stew (25:29–34). Jacob leveraged that indifference. Further, he secured the special blessing of Isaac by deceptive means. Driven by Rebekah, Jacob tricked Isaac into thinking Jacob was Esau. So Isaac blessed Jacob, and that blessing, along with the birthright, were irrevocable (27:1–45). For fear of Esau, Jacob fled Canaan to Paddan Aram, where he lived for twenty years. Although by nefarious means, Jacob became the bearer of the covenant blessing and the heir to Canaan. Esau inherited what became known as Edom.

Because about one-fourth of Genesis is devoted to Jacob, there are four elements of Jacob's life important to the history of Israel. First is the dream/vision he received at Bethel (28:10–22). Because of his duplicity and sin, Jacob was a fugitive from his brother Esau. At Bethel, God intervened in his life. As he slept, he saw a ladder connecting heaven and earth. At the top of the ladder, the Lord stood. God confirmed there that the covenant promises he had made to Abraham and Isaac would be applied to Jacob's life as well. God would not abandon him but would fulfill all of the covenant promises He had made to Abraham.

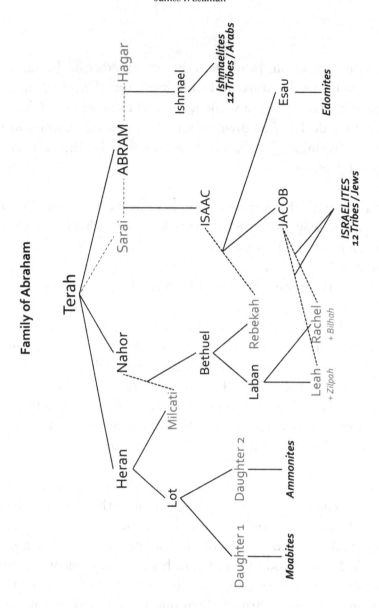

Family of Abraham

Second, from Jacob came his twelve sons, each of whom would found one of the twelve tribes of Israel. Within the context of a virtual contest of childbearing between Rachel and Leah, the two wives of Jacob, Genesis 29–30 records the birth of Jacob's sons. The first four sons were born to Leah—Reuben, Simeon, Levi, and Judah. Meanwhile, Rachel, envious of Leah, contrived to have

Jacob sleep with her servant girl, Bilhah, who bore Jacob two sons, Dan and Naphtali. Leah then had her servant, Zilpah, sleep with Jacob, and Zilpah bore him two sons, Gad and Asher. God granted Leah two more sons, Issachar and Zebulun. Then God "remembered Rachel", and she bore Joseph (Genesis 30:22). Finally, Rachel died giving birth to Jacob's youngest son, Benjamin (Genesis 35:18).

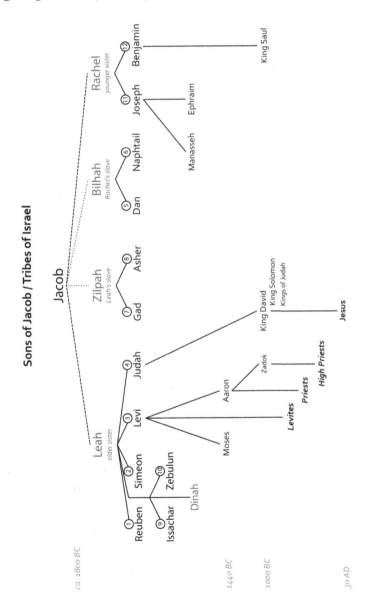

Jacob's Twelve Sons: Birth Order and Names' Meanings

1. Reuben—the Lord sees affliction
2. Simeon—the Lord hears
3. Levi—hope for attachment
4. Judah—praise for the Lord
5. Dan—vindication
6. Naphtali—that which struggles
7. Gad—prosperity
8. Asher—happiness
9. Issachar—reward or man of hire
10. Zebulun—endowed me
11. Joseph—fruitful or addition
12. Benjamin—son of the right hand

Third, Jacob's name was changed to "Israel," which became the name of the nation itself (Genesis 32:28). The context for this significant event was Jacob's return to Canaan. In Paddan Aram, Jacob had worked for Laban, his uncle, for twenty years. Laban's treachery was worse than Jacob's, for he tricked Jacob into serving him to attain the right to marry Rachel. First, however, Jacob was forced to settle for Leah. In addition, during his time with Laban, most of Jacob's sons were born.

Jacob fled Laban and prepared to enter Canaan, where he knew he would meet his brother Esau, whose murderous threats still echoed in his mind. All of his life, Jacob had manipulated people and events to get what he wanted. He tricked his foolish brother twice, his father, and, in the end, even his uncle Laban, for he left Paddan Aram a wealthy man. But as Jacob wrestled with God at Jabbok (there is wordplay in Hebrew between these key words), he was broken by God. The Assailant crippled Jacob (Genesis 32:25) and changed his name from Jacob, the heel catcher, to Israel, "he strives, fights with God."[13] He entered the Promised Land limping, a powerful symbol of his dependence on God (32:31).

Jacob's struggle with God reached its apex at the Jabbok River. Jacob was a changed man. The God of his father and grandfather was now his personal God. He had wrestled with God and, as the name Israel implies, was now ready to "wrestle" with Esau. The name Israel became a metaphor for the nation. They would strive with God throughout their history, but, in that striving, they were always ready to strive with others. As Ross comments, "The story of Israel the man serves as an acted parable of the life of the nation, in which is here presented its relationship with God almost prophetically. The patriarch portrays the real spirit of the nation to engage in the persistent struggle with God until emerging strong in the blessing."[14] Perhaps that is why, throughout the rest of Scripture, the people are referred to as either "Israel" or "Jacob." For the people of Israel to be strong in their faith, they needed to empty themselves of their self-sufficiency.

Finally, the Genesis cycle dealing with Jacob's son Joseph explains how Jacob's clan entered Egypt—and how that clan grew into a nation (Genesis 37–50). This unit on Joseph is rich in wisdom and applicational teaching that invite comparisons and contrasts between Joseph and the nation and between Joseph and Daniel, as well as redemptive hints of God's grace.

However, for this book, the focus on Joseph is to explain why Jacob's clan journeys to Egypt. The chronology of Joseph that fits best with the evidence is the one adopted by Merrill: Joseph was born in 1916 BC, entered Egypt in 1899, came to power in 1866, and died in 1806 BC.[15] Thus, Joseph's entire life was contemporaneous with the twelfth dynasty of Egypt's Middle Kingdom. During the reign of Pharaoh Sestoris II (1897–1878 BC), land reclamation projects and flood control projects abounded, some of which correspond with the biblical record of projects Joseph supervised as the vizier (prime minister) of pharaoh. Indeed, one was a canal connecting the Fayyum Basin with the Nile River, which is called the River of Joseph.[16]

Because "the Lord was with Joseph," God's sovereignty explains Joseph's rise to power in Egypt. God's providence explains Joseph being sold to the Ishmaelites by his brothers, Potiphar buying him as a servant, his time in an Egyptian prison, and his elevation to the position of vizier to the pharaoh. Joseph adapted to this new role well, taking an Egyptian name, Zaphenath-paneah, and taking an Egyptian woman, Asenath, as his wife. She was the daughter of a priest of the god Ra. She bore him two sons, Ephraim and Manasseh. Joseph was thus fully integrated into the Egyptian court and society. When his brothers come to him due to the famine in Canaan, his authority in Egypt was recognized. After he revealed himself to them, he authorized their move to Goshen (Genesis 45:10), and Jacob and his entire clan of seventy entered Goshen in 1876 BC.

Goshen was in the eastern Nile delta region where the clan herded their animals and where some of them cared for pharaoh's flocks as well (Genesis 47:6).[17] Because the Egyptian capital was in Memphis, they would also be close to Joseph, for Goshen was only about fifty-five miles away. They would be in Egypt for four hundred years.

Before Jacob died in 1859 BC, he called his sons together and blessed them (Genesis 49). The language of the blessings is poetic and metaphorical. But the blessing on Judah was the most profound. Jacob declared that "the Scepter shall not depart from Judah" (v. 10). This phrase plus the entire blessing (vv. 8–12) stressed the qualities of leadership Judah had already exhibited and which his descendants would demonstrate as well. Of course, the rest of Scripture indicates this prophetic blessing was fulfilled in King David and ultimately in David's greater son, the Lord Jesus Christ. The redemptive theme of Scripture thus continues to unfold, and we leave Genesis with the hint that Judah's line was the most important for these redemptive purposes.

Israel was now a clan in Goshen, but the promises God had made to Abraham, Isaac, and Jacob remained unfulfilled. The patriarchs had demonstrated that faith in God brings blessing. As the clan of Jacob grew into a nation over the next four hundred years, they would need to apply those lessons of patriarchal faith to get from Goshen to the Promised Land.

Chapter 2

The Birth of Israel as a Nation

The exodus from Egypt is the most profound event in ancient Israel's history. God delivered His people from slavery into freedom, from oppression to liberation, and from a people of promise to a nation. The exodus from Egypt led to the formation of the theocracy of Israel, with God as their ruler and with the Law as their constitution. God manifested astonishing power in the ten plagues by which He made war on the gods of Egypt. He demonstrated to the Egyptians, but much more importantly to the people of Israel, that He was the Sovereign Lord of His world, able to muster all power needed to accomplish His ends. Egypt let God's people go.

Chronological Challenges

For an event so momentous in Scripture, the controversies surrounding its chronology are significant. There are two primary challenges, neither of which minimizes or affects the truth of the exodus event itself.

First, was Israel in Egypt 430 years or 215 years? Exodus 12:40 declares that Israel was in Egypt 430 years. In addition, Genesis 15:13 prophesied that the Egyptian oppression would last 400 years, a round figure similarly used in Acts 7:6–7 by Stephen. The argument for 215 years in Egypt hinges primarily on Paul, who, in Galatians 3:17, connects the Abrahamic promise to the giving of the Law—"the law introduced 430 years later." This declaration would seemingly make it impossible for there to be 430 years

17

between Abraham and the giving of the Law, because indisputably there were 215 years between Genesis 12 and Jacob moving his clan to Egypt, which would leave only 215 years for the stay in Egypt. However, since the Abrahamic covenant was renewed with each patriarch throughout Genesis, the last renewal of the covenant was with Jacob in Genesis 46. From Genesis 46 to the giving of the Law in Exodus 20 is exactly 430 years, thereby confirming that Israel was in Egypt exactly 430 years as Exodus 12:40 declares. There are no significant reasons to set aside the conclusion that Israel was in Egypt for 430 years.[18]

The second chronological issue is more difficult. When did the exodus occur—1446 BC or 1290 (or 1260) BC? This book argues for a 1446 BC date for the exodus. The most important biblical evidence is 1 Kings 6:1, which declares that the exodus occurred 480 years prior to the laying the foundation of Solomon's Temple. Since we know this event occurred in 966 BC, 1446 BC would be the date for the exodus. Jephthath's message in Judges 11:26 gives further support to the 1446 BC date. Further, the historical events recorded in the book of Judges require about 350 years, which, if there was a late exodus in the thirteenth century, results in only 170 years for the period of the judges, which is not reasonable. Archeological evidence points to the destruction of key Canaanite cites (e.g., Jericho, Ai, Hazor) in the late fifteenth century BC, quite consistent with the 1446 BC exodus date. In fact, there is no evidence of Jericho being even occupied in the thirteenth century BC, the late exodus date. For these reasons, this book assumes an exodus date of 1446 BC.[19]

The Population of Israel

According to Exodus 38:26 and Numbers 1:46, the total number of men twenty years and older who left Egypt was 603,550. With women and children added to this total, the number of Israelites leaving Egypt could have reached several million. This is an astonishing number simply because the human effort to manage, feed, care for, and lead that many people seems impossible. For that reason, some have suggested that the Hebrew word 'elep should not be translated "thousand," but should be understood as a social unit such as a clan. It is so used in several Old Testament passages (e.g., Judges 6:15; 1 Samuel 10:19). However, the difficulty with this interpretation is that you would then have 603 clans, which does not harmonize with other biblical figures. Hence, it seems wisest to understand this biblical number from the census in Numbers literally, and to understand that God supernaturally provided for the people of Israel as they left Egypt.[20]

Historical Background

Assuming a 1446 BC exodus, what were the conditions in Egypt? Who was the pharaoh? When was Moses born, and who was his Egyptian mother? The Bible is clear that Moses was eighty years old at the beginning of the exodus (Exodus 7:7) and that he died at one hundred and twenty years of age (Deuteronomy 34:7). Thus, given a 1446 BC exodus date, Moses was born in 1526 BC, meaning that he was born during the New Kingdom in Egypt and during the last year of Pharaoh Amenhotep I.

Since Amenhotep I died in 1526, Thutmoses I (1526–1512 BC) was the pharaoh who issued the infanticide decree, which caused Moses' mother to place him in the Nile River to save his life. The pharaoh's daughter who rescued Moses was Hatshepsut. As Merrill comments, "Only she of all known women of the period possessed the presumption and independence to violate an ordinance of the king."[21] As the daughter of Thutmoses I, she became the wife of Thutmoses II (1512–1504 BC), who died mysteriously in his late twenties. As the power behind the scenes, she dominated the first twenty years or so of the reign of Thutmoses III (1504–1450 BC), the most powerful pharaoh of the New Kingdom. Thus Moses was raised by Hatshepsut in the pharaoh's court and would have no doubt known and perhaps played with the young Thutmoses III.

There are several additional possibilities concerning the connections between Moses and Thutmoses III. According to the Exodus narrative, the pharaoh who tried to kill Moses and the one whose death caused Moses to return to Egypt from Midian reigned for at least forty years. Of all the pharaohs of the Eighteenth Dynasty during the New Kingdom, only Thutmoses III ruled that long.

As Moses and Thutmoses were both being raised in the court, rivalry and even animosity would naturally have resulted. Since Hatshepsut had no natural children, was Moses a potential candidate for pharaoh? This is possibly the background for the new pharaoh, Thutmoses III, taking such a keen interest in Moses' killing of an Egyptian (Exodus 2:11–16) in 1486 BC.

Thutmoses viewed this murder as a means of ridding himself of Moses. Hatshepsut had died in 1483, so there was no one left to protect Moses. Moses therefore fled to Midian in the Sinai. When Thutmoses died, Moses was free to return to Egypt. He had been in Midian forty years.[22]

Amenhotep II (1450–1425 BC) was the next pharaoh, and thus the pharaoh of the exodus. Most pharaohs of the Eighteenth Dynasty resided in Thebes, considerably south along the Nile River. But Amenhotep II resided in Memphis, quite close to the Israelites in Goshen. Moses and Aaron, therefore, would have had no difficulty making their numerous excursions to Pharaoh's court. We also know that Amenhotep's oldest son did not succeed him; rather his younger son, Thutmoses IV, did. Amenhotep's older son presumably had died. Merrill suggests an untimely death: "This is at least implied in the so-called dream stela found at the base of the Great Sphinx near Memphis. This text, which records a dream in which Thutmoses IV was promised that he would one day be king, suggests ... that his reign came about through an unforeseen turn of fate such as the premature death of an elder brother" (the tenth plague in Exodus 12:29?).[23] It is a tantalizing piece of speculative evidence connecting the Eighteenth Dynasty to Moses and the exodus.

Assyrian Empire, 650 BC

Israel Enslaved and the Deliverer Identified

The Exodus narrative establishes two prominent facts about Israel in Goshen: there was a population explosion (1:7) and that Pharaoh, "who knew not Joseph" (1:8), enslaved them. The harsher Pharaoh's affliction, the more Israel increased in population (1:12).

Who was Pharaoh? Between the death of Joseph and the birth of Moses, the Hyksos (a Semitic group of invaders from Southwest Asia) occupied the Nile Delta region and ruled Egypt from 1720 to 1570 BC. Hyksos rule extended as far south as Memphis. The successful use of the war chariot explained their military success. It was ultimately Pharaoh Ahmose (1570–1546 BC) who freed Egypt completely from Hyksos rule (what is called the Second

Intermediate Period in ancient Egyptian history). Ahmose introduced the Eighteenth Dynasty and hence the New Kingdom
period.[24]

Because the Israelites were Semitic peoples, similar to the Hyksos,
it is logical that Pharaoh Ahmose chose to enslave them. That their
population was increasing was undoubtedly a perceived threat to
his new kingdom, and the New Kingdom pharaohs used enslaved
Israelites to build many public works projects (Exodus 1:11–14).

So serious was the threat of Israel to this dynasty that Pharaoh
Amenhotep I launched a policy of genocide: Hebrew midwives
were to kill Hebrew boys at birth, followed by an order to kill all
male Hebrew children (Exodus 1:15–22). To spare her son from
certain death, Jochebed placed him in a basket of bulrushes in the
Nile River, where Pharaoh's daughter found him. As argued above,
Hatshepsut adopted him, named him Moses, and took him into her
court. *Moses* was both an Egyptian name and a Hebrew name; it
means "drawn out of water" (2:10). As an Egyptian name, it could
also be related to the Egyptian word for "son."[25]

Moses' education in the Egyptian court was comprehensive and
was, therefore, an important indicator of how God was preparing
him to be Israel's deliverer. He would most likely have learned the
languages, both conversational and written, of the day—Egyptian
hieroglyphics and the languages of Canaan— as well as the geography of both. In the court he would have enjoyed archery and
horseback riding.[26] Undoubtedly, he was taught by Egypt's finest
tutors, such that the early church leader, Stephen, declared, "Moses
was instructed in all the wisdom of the Egyptians, and he was
mighty in his words and deeds" (Acts 7:22 ESV).

According to Hebrews 11:23–26, at age forty Moses rejected his
Egyptian training and life of privilege, including being "the son of
Pharaoh's daughter," choosing to identify with his people Israel.
His newfound zeal and enthusiasm for his people caused him

to murder an Egyptian official, which in turn resulted in Moses fleeing the wrath of Pharaoh Thutmoses III.

During his forty years in Midian, Moses tended the flocks of a Midianite priest named Reuel (also called Jethro) and married one of his daughters, Zipporah. While caring for Jethro's flocks, Exodus 3 explains that, via a burning bush, the God of Abraham, Isaac, and Jacob called Moses to be Israel's deliverer. In Exodus 3:14, God declared Himself to be YHWH (Yahweh), the "I am that I am," indicating that He is the self-existent, self-sufficient creator and sustainer of all things. Further, YHWH reminded Moses that He would liberate Israel from Egyptian bondage, thereby fulfilling the covenant promises He had made to Abraham (see Exodus 2:24; 4:22–26).

After forty years of the best education the ancient world could offer and another forty years of learning utter dependence on God, Moses was now ready to lead Israel out of bondage and into the land God had promised to Abraham.

The Deliverance from Egypt: YHWH Declares War on Egypt's Gods

To truly understand the significance of the ten plagues God sent upon Egypt, one must have a rudimentary understanding of the ancient Egyptian worldview. Of all the ancient world's religions, Egypt's was the most multifaceted, difficult, and complex, for it evolved over the nearly 2,500 years of its history. By the time of the Eighteenth Dynasty of the New Kingdom, several important points about the Egyptian worldview are clear.

1. The core spiritual ideal of Egypt was *ma'at*, the cosmic harmony, justice, order, and peace of the universe. It was the universal order evident in the predictable flooding of the Nile. *Ma'at* was thus the model for human behavior. Everyone and everything was a part of this balance. For

example, when they died, Egyptians believed they became a part of that cosmic order. Life was thus preparation for death—almost an obsession in ancient Egypt.[27] As Henri Frankfort argues, "A collapse of the established order would leave the Egyptian totally disoriented ... When the established order from which the Egyptian way of life derived its orientation was destroyed, life became meaningless and, therefore, unbearable."[28]

2. The pharaoh was an incarnate god (of the gods Horus and Ra), and his principal duty was to maintain *ma'at* on earth. As both the chief priest of the temple cult and the head of state, pharaoh was regarded as supreme over all things.[29]

3. The Nile River was the celestial stream of Egypt: Egypt's life blood, the key to sustaining *ma'at*. Since many gods were associated with the Nile (e.g., Hapi, Osiris), numerous hymns were written to the Nile celebrating its blessings of fertility and happiness. It was the "Father of Life" and the "Mother of all Men."[30]

4. The sun god, Ra (Re) nourished all life on earth with the light of his heart. Egyptians called Ra the "King of the Earth, Master of the Universe."[31] By the New Kingdom, the worship of Ra had merged with that of Amon—hence Amon-Ra, Amon as the breath of life in all things, and Ra, the sun god, as the sustainer of all things.[32]

The ten plagues God sent upon Egypt undermined this entire worldview, demonstrating that Yahweh was the one true God. He desired that both His people Israel and the Egyptians would conclude that He alone was the Sovereign Lord—the Master of everything. The plagues were thus polemical in nature.

When Moses returned from Midian, God instructed him to confront Amenhotep II with the demand to "Let my people go." Exodus 7 through 12 is the account of this remarkable confrontation between Moses and Amenhotep II. In the cycle of ten plagues, there was an increasing intensity to each plague and an increasing hardening of Pharaoh's heart. In the end, Amenhotep II released Israel from its 430 years of bondage.

Old Testament scholar John D. Currid argues persuasively that the ten plagues were actually God's "De-Creation," for the Exodus was a "second creation. It was a new conquest of chaos, another prevailing over the waters of the deep, and a redemptive creation of the people of Israel … God took the creation order of Genesis 1 and reversed it in Exodus 7–12 for the purposes of reducing order to chaos and bringing judgment upon Egypt."[33] Plagues one and two (Exodus 7:14–8:15) focused on the Nile and its centrality to Egypt's fertility and blessing from the gods. Plagues three through eight (Exodus 8:16–10:20) upset the entire perception of order, harmony and stability so central to *ma'at*. Chaos triumphed over order. Plague nine (Exodus 10:21–29)—darkness—directly challenged Amon-Ra, the chef deity of the Egyptian pantheon. Finally, plague ten (Exodus 11:1–10) challenged the deity of Pharaoh and his role as the guardian of *ma'at*. Before Almighty God, Pharaoh was declared impotent and void of any power; he was not a god and could not preserve the order and balance of the Egyptian world.

The ten plagues undermined the entire worldview of ancient Egypt. With great power, Yahweh manifested Himself as the Sovereign Lord. Thus, in 1446 BC, powerless Amenhotep II "let God's people go."

The Gods of Egypt and the Plagues: A Polemic

Plague 1—Nile to blood	7:14–25	Egyptian god Hapi
Plague 2—Frogs	8:1–15	Egyptian goddess Hekhet
Plague 3—Gnats	8:16–19	Egyptian gods Geb, Kheperer
Plague 4—Stinging flies	8:20–32	Egyptian god Kheperer
Plague 5—Death of livestock	9:1–7	Egyptian gods Ptah, Re, Isis, Hathor

Plague 6—Boils	9:8–12	Egyptian gods Imhotep, Isis
Plague 7—Hail	9:13–35	Egyptian gods Nut, She, Tefnut
Plague 8—Locusts	10:1–20	Egyptian gods Seth, Senehem
Plague 9—Darkness	10:21–29	Egyptian god Amon-Re, chief deity of the Pantheon
Plague 10—Death of firstborn	11:1–10	Pharaoh as a god[34]

An important aspect of the final plague was the Passover. Each Israeli household was to kill an unblemished male lamb or goat and sprinkle its blood on the two side posts and lintel of the house. They were then to eat the roasted animal along with unleavened bread and bitter herbs, dressed in attire ready to leave Egypt immediately. When the tenth plague came, Israel was spared. This momentous event was institutionalized as the Passover Feast and the Feast of Unleavened Bread.

The Route of the Exodus

The journey of Israel from Egypt to Canaan is recorded in several places in the Pentateuch: Exodus 12–18, Numbers 11–12, and Deuteronomy 10. But it is Numbers 33:1–49 that provides the definitive record of the exodus from Egypt, the wilderness wanderings and the preparations to invade Canaan. Indeed, Moses wrote down this itinerary in Numbers 33 "by the command of the LORD" (v.2). Currid concludes that this passage "appears to be a uniform, consistent, complete itinerary" of the Hebrew journey.[35] The greatest challenge of Numbers 33 is that most of the sites listed cannot be identified today with certainty.

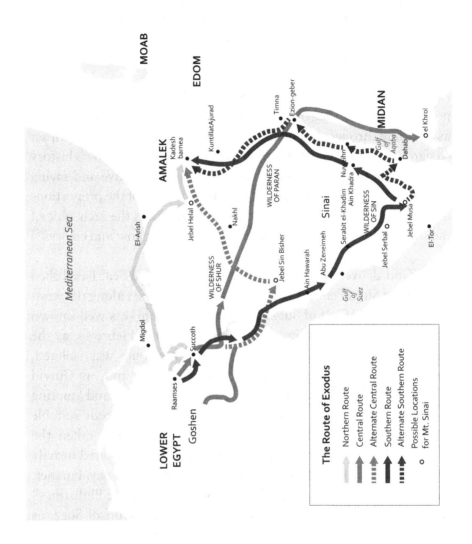

Exodus 14 records that God delivered Israel supernaturally at the Red Sea (*yam suph* in Hebrew, which could mean "Sea of Reeds," Exodus 13:18 and 15:4). It is possible that *yam suph* refers to the northern edge of the Gulf of Suez, the northern part of the Red Sea, or it could refer to Lake Ballah, Lake Timsah, or the Great Bitter Lake. However, every biblical reference of *yam suph* refers to the Red Sea or its northern extensions in the Gulfs of Aqaba or Suez (see 1 Kings 9:26; Jeremiah 49:21). Further, Currid shows quite convincingly that *suph* is derived from the Semitic root *soph,* which means "end." Therefore, the Hebrew *yam suph* literally means "sea of the end," which refers "to the waters of the far south, the waters of the end of the land. And that, of course, would be the Red Sea."[36]

As Eugene Merrill argues, "The crossing of Israel, which immediately preceded the drowning of the Egyptian chariotry, cannot be explained as a wading through a swamp. It required a mighty act of God, an act so significant in scope and meaning that forever after in Israel's history it was the paradigm against which all of his redemptive and saving work was measured. If there was no actual miracle of the proportions described, all subsequent reference to the exodus as the archetype of the sovereign power and salvific grace of God is hollow and empty."[37]

After God delivered them miraculously at the Red Sea, Israel then entered the Sinai Peninsula, turning south-southeast along the western coast of the Gulf of Suez. This southern route was well-known during the New Kingdom, probably even to the Hebrews, as the route for Egyptian mining expeditions. This route was isolated, covering land not under Egypt's direct control, and, as Currid demonstrates, had a reasonably adequate water supply and (quoting I. Beith-Arieh) "a seasonable cover of grasses and weeds suitable for pasturing sheep and goats."[38] Had the Hebrews taken the northern route into Canaan, they would have encountered heavily garrisoned Egyptian fortresses along the coastal highway. Further, God warned them not to go "by way of the land of the Philistines" (Exodus 13:17). They continued south along the Gulf of Suez, as God directed them, ending at Mount Sinai, probably modern-day Jebel Musa (7,363 feet in altitude). There God gave Moses the Law.

The Mosaic Covenant: The Constitution of Israel

The exodus from Egypt was the most important event in Israel's history. As a result of the exodus, Israel became a nation, a community of people. They received their "constitution" at Mt. Sinai and would soon occupy their own land—the Promised Land. In effect, God was now creating a theocracy in which He ruled Israel through His Law as mediated by the priesthood and made possible by the sacrifices. He would manifest Himself (His *shekinah* glory) in His tabernacle (and later the temple).

As Israel gathered at Mount Sinai, God declared that they were to be "a kingdom of priests and a holy nation" (Exodus 19:6). As Old Testament scholar Bruce Waltke explains, "The metaphor [of priests] likens Israel's relationship to the world to that of a priest who serves society and mediates God's blessing by being set apart to him ... They mediate God's blessings to others according to the divine intention for Abraham and his seed to be a missional nation from the beginning."[39] By walking in obedience with God, Israel was to show the world what the living and only true God was like.

The covenant God made with Israel at Sinai (in its entirety from Exodus 20 through Leviticus) was in the form of an ancient suzerain-vassal treaty, in the "forms of ancient near Eastern laws from the third/early second millennium and of vassal treaties from the late second millennium ... [and parallels] the vassal treaties the Hittite king authored and issued to his vassal kings."[40] This typical Ancient Near Eastern (ANE) covenant treaty had several key parts:

1. A *preamble* identifying the author and His magnificence. "I am the LORD your God" the preamble declares (Exodus 20:1; Deuteronomy 5:23–27).
2. A *historical prologue.* God reviewed His faithfulness in having brought Israel "out of the land of Egypt, out of the land of slavery" (Exodus 20:2), but He also identified himself as the Creator, the sustainer of Israel and their faithful God (see Deuteronomy 2:7; 4:32–38; Exodus 20:8–11).
3. *Stipulations* of the covenant. Obeying these stipulations would advance the kingdom of Almighty God (Exodus 20:3–23:33; Deuteronomy 4:12–11:32; 12:1–26:15).
4. Provisions for the *deposit* of the covenant and its *public reading.* These occurred in Deuteronomy 10:1–5 and 31:9–13, 24–25.

5. *Divine witnesses* to the covenant (Deuteronomy 30:19–20).
6. *Blessings and curses* (Leviticus 26 and Deuteronomy 28).[41]

However, unlike the pagan ANE kings and their treaties, the covenant treaty God made with Israel was different. Waltke observes, "Israel obeys the law on the basis of God's authority, who claims her allegiance by his virtue, not on the basis of royal power to coerce her obedience, nor on the basis of custom in the popular *ethos*."[42]

God established and consecrated the priesthood as a key element of the theocracy (Exodus 29; Leviticus 8–10). The theocracy's structure was simple but is essential in understanding the covenantal duties of sacrifice and worship of God by the people of Israel (Leviticus 1–7).

The Structure of Israel's Theocracy

God (Yahweh)

Levitical Priests

People

As an important aspect of the theocracy, God gave meticulously detailed instructions to Moses about constructing the *tabernacle*, or tent sanctuary, the center of worship and the place where God's presence was manifested (Exodus 25–31, 35–40). He would be present in the tabernacle (Exodus 40:34-38) and He would walk among His people (Leviticus 26:12). The tabernacle was intended to be a replica of heaven itself, "so that the people might understand what heaven was like."[43] (See Exodus 25:40; Hebrews 8:5; 9:23.) In the Holy of

Holies stood the ark of the covenant, which included the tablets containing the Ten Commandments, which in Waltke's words is "the eternal moral law of God, an expression of God himself. They are part of God's identity, a central part of God's self-revelation. God's moral attributes are summarized in these ten 'words.' They give insight to the heart and eternal character of God."[44]

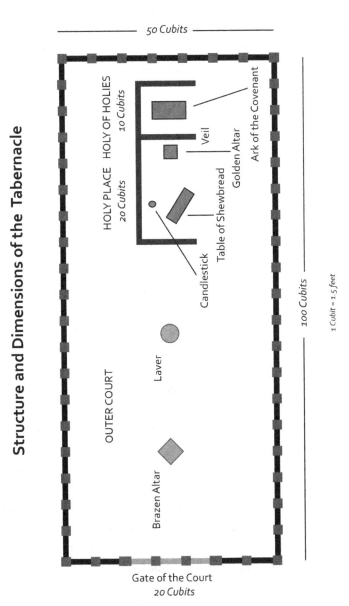

Structure and Dimensions of the Tabernacle

50 Cubits

HOLY OF HOLIES
10 Cubits

HOLY PLACE
20 Cubits

Ark of the Covenant

Veil

Golden Altar

Table of Shewbread

Candlestick

OUTER COURT

Laver

Brazen Altar

100 Cubits

1 Cubit = 1.5 feet

Gate of the Court
20 Cubits

Kadesh-Barnea and the Wilderness Wanderings

After nearly one year at Sinai, the people of Israel were now a theocratic community, with a constitution, a priesthood, and a tabernacle. They were ready to claim their land, so God directed them north to Kadesh-Barnea in the wilderness of Zin, about 150 miles from Sinai (Numbers 33:36). Kadesh-Barnea (most likely either Ain el-Qudeirat or Ai Qedeis, both of which have important springs) was positioned at the intersection of two important roads, one that linked Egypt with Edom, and the other that linked the Gulf of Aqabah with the hill country of Canaan.[45]

Several significant events occurred at Kadesh-Barnea:

1. Moses dispatched the twelve spies to investigate Canaan, with the purpose of plotting the invasion of the Promised Land (Numbers 13).
2. Despite the pleas of Joshua and Caleb that the land could be seized, the people believed the worst and rejected even Moses' leadership. God then condemned the people to thirty-eight years of fruitless wandering until that entire generation of Israel had died (Numbers 14:1–38).
3. Despite the silly attack against the Amalekites and Canaanites (Numbers 14:39–45), which resulted in a humiliating defeat, and the additional rebellions led by Korah, Dathan, and Abriam (Numbers 16), God affirmed the leadership of Moses.
4. Miriam, Moses' sister, died at Kadesh-Barnea.
5. Moses' defiance of God (Numbers 20) resulted in God's declaration that Moses would not enter the Promised Land.

In the fortieth year after Israel had left Egypt, they began to plan the invasion of Canaan. Denied access through Edom (Numbers 20:14–21), Moses led Israel through the Transjordan region, defeating the kings of Sihon and Og (Numbers 21). Because of his failure to trust God, Moses died and the mantle of leadership was passed to Joshua (Deuteronomy 34). Israel was now ready for the conquest of Canaan, the fulfillment of the covenant promise made by God to Abraham, Isaac, and Jacob.

Chapter 3

Israel Claims Its Covenant Land

God had freed the people of Israel from their harsh taskmaster, established the framework of His theocratic rule with a constitution, and declared them to be His "son." He was now ready to fulfill the promise He had made to the patriarchs to give them the land of Canaan. This was their land by promise, a land flowing with milk and honey, which would give them physical and spiritual rest, refuge, and riches. Under Joshua's leadership, they would need to trust Him to secure that promise. Thus, God made a stupendous promise to Joshua: "Just as I was with Moses, so I will be with you" (Joshua 1:5). Joshua, therefore, was to be strong and courageous, and nurture both by meditation upon and obedience to God's Law (vv. 6–9).

Historical Background of the Conquest

As with the exodus event, the date of the conquest is difficult. Assuming an exodus date of 1446 BC, then the conquest occurred, according to Deuteronomy 1:3, forty years after the exodus and lasted seven years (see Caleb's testimony in Joshua 14:7–10), which means that the conquest occurred from 1406 to 1399 BC.

The conquest dates of 1406–1399 fit well with the historical details of this period. To Canaan's north, the three major powers balanced one another. Mesopotamia, the land between the Tigris and Euphrates Rivers, saw invasions from the Kassites in the southern part of Mesopotamia, while the Assyrians were consolidating their power in northern Mesopotamia. There is no historical record of any significant interest in Canaan from either the Kassites or the Assyrians during this period. In fact, there would be no real Assyrian involvement in Canaan until the reign of Tiglath-Pileser I (1115–1077 BC) near the end of the period of the judges. Further, Mitanni, the kingdom of the Hurrian peoples, served as a buffer state between Assyria and the Hittites of Anatolia (modern Turkey). They were never a threat to Canaan. Finally, the Hittite Empire was coming into a position of prominence in the eastern Mediterranean at the precise time of Joshua's conquest. The Hittites pressed into Syria, but were unwilling to press farther south because of the growing threat of Assyria to the east and, of course, because of Egypt.

Egypt played an important role in Canaan during the time of the conquest, but the disinterest in Canaan shown by the pharaohs of this period was significant. Amenhotep II (1450–1425 BC), the pharaoh of the exodus, displayed no interest in Canaan. His son, Thutmoses IV (1425–1417 BC) conducted one military campaign in Canaan, but this was while Israel was wandering in the wilderness. Amenhotep III (1417–1379 BC) was busy defending Egypt's southern border with the Nubians. Amenhotep IV, who changed his name to Akhenaton, was consumed by his attempt to reform Egyptian worship into quasi-monotheism (the worship of Aton). He showed virtually no interest in Canaan.

Thus, as Eugene Merrill concludes, all of these eastern Mediterranean events during the fifteenth and early fourteenth centuries BC were providential for Israel, "for … the Mitannians, Hittites, and (later) the Assyrians were for the most part at loggerheads, unable to fill the vacuum that Egypt's disinterest in Canaan had produced. Only the Canaanites, themselves totally disorganized, stood in the way."[46]

Who Were the Canaanites?

The Bible speaks collectively of the Canaanites, but also mentions the many tribal groups that settled in Canaan. The name *Canaan* derives from Canaan, the son of Ham, whose descendants included those who occupied the entire Levant region (see Genesis 10:20). As many passages in Numbers, Joshua, and even Judges document, the descendants of Canaan settled along the coastline, in the valleys, and on the plains (including the Jordan valley) of the entire region later called Syria-Palestine. The Amorites generally settled in the hill country. According to Genesis 10:15–20, the Hittites, Jebusites, Amorites, Hivites, and Girgashites settled in a wider area extending from Sidon (Phoenicia) to Gaza along the coast, inland to the Dead Sea areas that included Sodom and Gomorrah.

All of these different tribes and clans spoke a cluster of Semitic languages, some of which resembled biblical Hebrew (e.g., Ugaritic). Most historians are certain of a Canaanite presence in the Syria-Palestine area by 2000 BC, about the time of Abraham. Throughout the second millennium BC, this entire region was divided among a variety of Canaanite/Amorite city states. During the period of the exodus and the conquest (1500–1380 BC), the northern Canaanite city-states were under Hittite control, while the southern city-states were nominally Egyptian. By the twelfth century BC, with the destruction of the Hittite Empire, the conquest of Canaan under Joshua, and the resurgence of Egypt, the only remaining Canaanites settlements were in Phoenicia, with Tyre and Sidon being the most important cities.[47]

Most Canaanites city-states were monarchies, which were rather absolute in their power. The kings controlled the military and had the sole power of conscription and taxation. Generally, the king controlled the military, religious, and economic affairs of the city-state. Most of these city-states were well fortified, as the book of Joshua attests.

Religiously, the Canaanites had an extensive pantheon of gods, including El, the chief god, with Baal, a fertility lord, the other prominent deity. Other gods included Hadad, the storm god, and Dagon. The goddesses Asherah, Ashtaroth, and Anath were associated with fertility, sex, and war. Canaanite temples have been found at Megiddo, Lachish, Shechem, and Hazor. Animal sacrifices were common, as was apparently cult or temple prostitution. There is also limited evidence of human sacrifice.[48] It is now clear why God wanted the Canaanites destroyed: Israel could not coexist with them (see Numbers 33:51–56; Deuteronomy 7:1–5).

Were the Hebrews of the Conquest the 'Apiru?

As early as the third millennium BC, the term 'apiru (Hapiru) has been attested in many parts of the Ancient Near Eastern world, but was most prevalent in Egyptian, Akkadian, and Hittite writings between 1800 and 1100 BC. The use of 'apiru is also quite pervasive in the Canaanite letters sent from the kings of Canaan to Egyptian pharaohs Amenhotep III (1417–1379 BC) and Akhenaton (1372–1353 BC), who had relocated the capital to Amarna (Akhetaten) north of Thebes.

There are sixteen references in the Amarna letters from Canaanite kings that mention 'apiru. Kings from Shechem, Gezer, and Megiddo are mentioned in these letters, describing the disruptive and terrifying presence of the 'apiru. Since the term 'apiru is somewhat similar to 'ibri (Hebrew), were the 'apiru the Hebrews of Joshua's conquest? Most scholars do not think so; rather, 'apiru refers not to a nationality but to a group of wandering mercenaries who sold their services to rival kings and rulers.[49]

The actions of the 'apiru described in the Amarna letters also do not correspond with the behavior of the Israelites under Joshua. However, these letters do summarize and confirm the utter chaos that obtained in Canaan in the fourteenth century BC, the period during which the conquest was occurring. But the 'apiru and the Hebrews are altogether different peoples. Merrill comments on the distinction: "The 'apiru appear to have been in Canaan prior to the Amarna age and to have frequently taken sides with opposing Canaanite kings. The Israelites entered Canaan en bloc at one time and were consistently hostile to the Canaanites. How the 'apiru and Israelites related to each other during and following the conquest cannot be known today."[50]

Was Joshua's Conquest a Holy War?

Ever since the publication of Gerhard von Rad's masterful *Holy War in Ancient Israel*, it has been common to view the conquest of Canaan as a holy war[51]. The Bible presents the complete destruction of the Canaanites as God's divine judgment on them, with Israel as the agent of that judgment. Their iniquity and horrific sin were the basis for God's judgment. (See Genesis 15:13–16; Deuteronomy 9:5). Scripture also makes clear that if unrepentant Canaanites remained in the land, their presence would drag Israel down into idolatry, injustice, and evil (see Deuteronomy 7:4; 12:29–31; 20:18). For that reason, Canaanite idols were burned and Israel was commanded to detest, not covet, the precious metals covering those idols.

However, as with all things of God, there was grace—witness Rahab and her family (Joshua 2:9) and even the duplicitous Gibeonites (9:1–27). The basis of God's command to "devote everything to destruction"[52] was His holy character, His justice, and His role as the Sovereign Lord. This applied only the cities of Canaan and nowhere else. This command for "holy war" against Canaan is never to be used as a justification for ethnic cleansing or genocide.[53]

Jericho

The biblical text presents Joshua as a brilliant strategist and commander. But the text also attributes the amazing victories of Israel to Yahweh, the Divine Warrior who fights for His people. Joshua's strategy was to divide Canaan into two parts and then conquer each separately. Therefore, crossing the Jordan River north of the Dead Sea was the best route into central Canaan—and that meant Jericho would need to be conquered first. Joshua sent spies into the Jericho area, where they were hidden by Rahab.

Joshua chapter 3 details the people of Israel crossing the Jordan, and the symbolism of the crossing is powerful. Waltke captures the symbolic power: "The Warrior, of whom no image is possible, is represented by his throne, an ark of gold (4 x2 x 2 ft.). The representative throne, carried by the Warrior's priest, leads Israel into the swollen Jordan, dries it up, and protects the holy nation as they step into the Sworn Land."[54]

Two powerful lessons are taught here: (1) The Canaanite god, Baal, was the chief god of the Canaanites because he had triumphed over the sea and or river god. But Yahweh now demonstrated that He is the true Lord over the waters, and "the triumph of I AM and of his people in the river crossing prove their claim to the Land. No wonder the Canaanite kings are fearful."[55] (2) "As the crossing of the Jordan symbolizes the transformation of all the tribes from an unsettled and arid wilderness to a settled and arable land with walled cities, wells and watered plains, so the ark symbolizes the crossing that occurs with Israel's Savior and with his priests who mediate the transformation."[56]

Before the campaign against Jericho, Joshua met "the commander of the LORD's army" (Joshua 5:15), who, because Joshua bowed and worshipped, is a theophany: worship and devotion to Yahweh preceded the battle! The commander, the Divine Warrior Himself, then gives Joshua the strategic plan for the conquest of Jericho.

The royal march around Jericho was a widespread practice in the Ancient Near Eastern world—Israel was "laying claim to territory by tracing out its bounds." Waltke furthers comments, "Seven priests marching seven times on the seventh day—the number seven is repeated three times in Joshua 6:15—signified divine perfection and so the sacredness of the event. Blowing on rams' horns signaled the presence of the King ... and the start of holy war."[57] The city's walls collapsed and the city was totally destroyed, including all people and all animals, for all were under the "ban" (*harem*) of God (Joshua 6:18).

Despite Achan's sin, Ai was eventually captured (chapters 7 and 8), and, despite Gibeon's duplicity, Joshua's treaty with the Gibeonites (chapter 9) completed the conquest of central Canaan. Since they were now in the Promised Land, it was necessary for this new generation of Israelites to renew its covenant relationship with Yahweh. Half of the tribes of Israel gathered on Mount Ebal and the other half gathered on Mount Gerizim. Joshua read the Law, and the people responded with the summary blessings and curses (Joshua 8:30–35). Canaan had now been divided, and the southern campaign began.

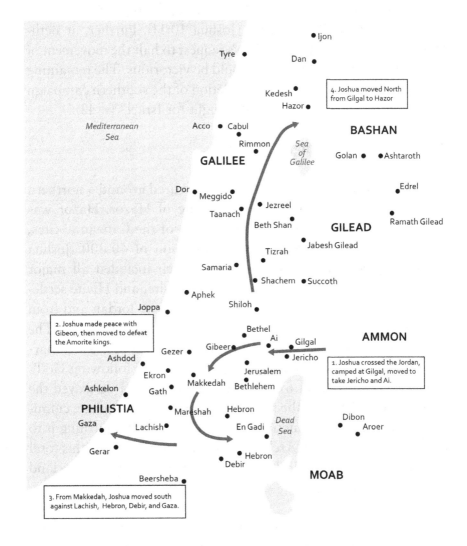

The Conquest of Canaan

The Southern Campaign

Now that Israel controlled the central hill country, Canaan was severed. A coalition of Amorite kings (from Hebron, Lachish, Eglon, and Jarmuth) led by the king of Jerusalem (Adoni-Zedek, a Jebusite) decided to punish Gibeon for its treaty with Israel. Joshua defeated this coalition at Gibeon and pursued them south. As they fled to the security of the foothills, Yahweh, the Warrior King, sent a deadly barrage of hailstones (Joshua 10:11). Further, at Beth-Horon pass He adhered to Joshua's request to halt the movement of the sun and moon so that Israel could be victorious. The remaining parts of chapter 10 detail the completion of the southern campaign "because the LORD God of Israel fought for Israel" (v. 42).

The Northern Campaign

The final phase of the conquest was structured around a northern defensive alliance formed by Jabin, king of Hazor. Hazor was probably the largest and most formidable of the Canaanite cites, covering about 110 acres with a population of 40,000. Joshua 11 details the size of this coalition, which included all major Canaanite, Amorite, Hittite, Perizzite, Jebusite, and Hivite settlements in the Jezreel Valley, on both sides of the Jordan and from Mount Hermon in the north to hill country south of Galilee. The Canaanite advantage was their lightweight, horse-drawn chariot. But the biblical text says that Joshua's army, following God's instructions (Joshua 11:6), crippled the horses and destroyed the chariots. The defeat of the northern alliance was complete, culminating in Joshua's destruction of the mighty Hazor, burning it to the ground (vv. 12–13). Archeological evidence confirms this total destruction of Hazor.[58] Joshua 11:23 concludes with "and the land had rest from war."

Waltke offers several important theological observations about the conquest: (1) "The united people of God dispossess the illegitimate rulers and thereby inherit the Promised Land. His kingdom rightfully replaces the unjust kingdoms of this world that have usurped His rule over the earth."[59] (2) God hardened the hearts of the Canaanites (11:20), so that "His longsuffering and patience, which had restrained his moral indignation and righteous anger, now bursts, and he unleashes his righteous judgment on the wicked nations who worshiped fertility deities instead of the sublime God."[60] The wicked cannot stand against Him and His holy army. (3) God keeps His promises, though centuries may intervene between the promise made and the promise fulfilled.

The Division of the Land

The second half of Joshua reflects significant literary tension. Joshua is old (Joshua 13:1), but there is much land still to possess. In other words, Israel has not yet completely defeated the Canaanites and driven them from the land (13:2–6). The implication of the text is that Joshua will not lead this final phase of the dispossession of the Canaanites—God will do it (v. 6). Therefore it is time for Israel to divide the land, the first step in completing the final conquest of Canaan.

Reuben, Gad, and half of Manasseh received the land granted to them by Moses (Numbers 32:33–42), east of the Jordan River. The land inheritance of the remaining tribes west of the Jordan is detailed in Joshua 14 through 19, interspersed with important historical vignettes of heroes such as Caleb (14:6–16) and Makir (17:1–3). Simply put, the allotments west of the Jordan were distributed in this way:

Galilee in the north—Asher, Issachar, Naphtali, Zebulun

The Central Mountains—Ephraim and West Manasseh, the two sons of Joseph

The Southern region—Benjamin, Judah, Simeon, Dan (which eventually migrated to the very northern part, see Judges 17–18).

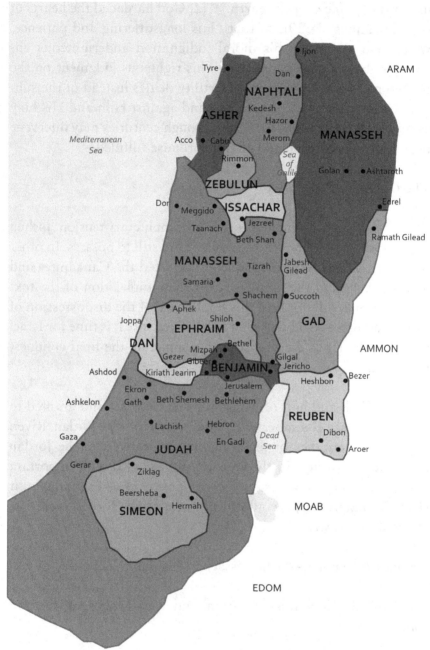

The 12 Tribes of Ancient Israel

The tribal allotments are generally described in the text according to boundary descriptions and markers and lists of key cities. Thomas Brisco has a helpful description of the nature of Israel's twelve tribes: "Each tribe was composed of clans and families united by kinship and other social ties. The clan was the basic subunit of a tribe and consisted of several families sharing a recognizable lineage. Joshua allotted the land 'according to their clans' (Josh. 15:1)."[61] At least initially, each tribe occupied its allotted land and exercised a significant amount of individual political and military autonomy.

The Lord God instructed Joshua to separate several clusters of cities for His specific purposes—the Levitical cities and the cities of refuge. Joshua 21 itemizes forty-eight cities as an inheritance for the Levites, divided among the Levitical clans—the Kohathites, Gershonites, and Merarites. Many of these cities became the religious and administrative centers of Israel. Six of the Levitical cities were considered cities of refuge (see Numbers 35:6–34), locations where someone who had unintentionally committed a homicide could flee. There that person could find asylum from family members who sought to avenge the slain relative. The cities were easily accessible throughout the land, with three on the west side of the Jordan and three on the east. Such cities evidenced God's commitment to both justice and mercy.

The Theocratic Institutions of Early Israel

As mentioned above, Israel was a theocracy; there was no king, central government, or ruling council. As the twelve tribes began to settle and administer their land grants, Israel was highly decentralized. Yahweh was in effect their king, with His rule administered and mediated through the priesthood. As was typical in the ancient world, elders in each city administered local issues, usually at the gatehouse in each city. Such elders would settle property disputes, arbitrate disagreements, and mediate marriage controversies between families. There was a system of due process involving the regulation of witnesses, the nature of evidence presented, and the types of punishment meted out to the guilty.

Since Israel was a theocracy, the place of the tabernacle was quite important. According to Joshua 18:1, Shiloh, in Ephraim's land grant north of Bethel, was the location of the sanctuary from the early days of the conquest and remained the principal location of the tabernacle through the period of the judges. By the time of Eli and then Samuel, Shiloh had become a well-established structure for centralized worship. The tribe of Levi was the primary tribe devoted to facilitating worship. Among the Levites, the descendants of Aaron were the priests who performed the sacrifices. The primary function of the Levites was to teach the Law to the people.[62]

The sacrifices and feast days associated with the tabernacle at Shiloh (and later with the temple in Jerusalem) were the vital center of the theocracy. They determined how God atoned for sin but also established the format for how the individual Israelite walked with God. The detailed legislation for this system is of course found in Leviticus. As Allen P. Ross summarizes, these sacrifices were divided into two groups—those with a sweet aroma and those without. "The sweet-aroma offerings were made *in* communion and *in celebration* of communion: burnt offering (Lev. 1), meal offering (Lev. 2), and peace offering (Lev. 3). The non-sweet-aroma sacrifices are made *for* communion: purification offering (Lev. 5) and reparation offering (Lev. 5)."[63]

1. Those sacrifices "made in communion" were "gifts or tributes presented to the LORD as acts of devotion or consecration."[64] They were part of giving praise to God for some benefit received or making a request of God (e.g., part of worship, paying a tithe, firstfruits, dedication or simply a freewill offering).
2. Sacrifices made in celebration of communion, especially the peace offering, involved "a holy communal meal eaten in the sanctuary."[65]

3. Those sacrifices made for communion, as purification for example, were presented to God for any "defilement or violation against God or humans, as long as it was not pre-meditated."[66] Reparation offerings were made for violations for which restitution could be made. As Ross comments, "The purpose of both offerings was to make atonement for sins and defilements so that union with God could be restored. In the case of sinful acts, this involved confession and forgiveness as well."[67]

In ancient Israel, there was also a series of scheduled sacrifices established as a means of expressing gratitude and devotion to the Lord, who had blessed them with life, the land, and His presence. Each offering was a reminder that God was holy and righteous and that He was setting them apart. What follows is a brief summary of the scheduled sacrifices, with the scriptural notation where each is described:

1. Daily sacrifices (Numbers 28:3–10).
2. New moon sacrifices (Numbers 28:11–15).
3. Sacrifices at the Feast of Unleavened Bread (Numbers 28:16–25).
4. Sacrifices at the Feast of Weeks (Leviticus 23:16–20; Numbers 28:26–31).
5. Sacrifices at the Feast of Trumpets (Numbers 29:1–6).
6. Sacrifices for the Day of Atonement (Leviticus 16; Numbers 29:7–11).
7. Sacrifices at the Feast of Tabernacles (Numbers 29:12–38).[68]

The theocracy of Israel was now established, with their divine King, His Law, and the covenant land, theirs by His decree and His providence. The tribal allotments had been completed, and, at least to some degree, the Canaanites had been dispossessed. Would Israel now be the blessing to all nations that was so central to the Abrahamic covenant?

Chapter 4

Anarchy in Israel: The Judges

The book of Judges records the apostasy of Israel as it accommodated worship of Canaanite gods with the worship of Yahweh, which resulted in His discipline. This apostasy seriously threatened Israel's existence in the land promised by covenant to Abraham, Isaac, and Jacob.

Despite this apostasy, God remained remarkably faithful to His people. Plainly, the contrast between Israel's apostasy and God's faithfulness is a major theme of this period. The book also establishes Israel's need for a shepherd-king who would embolden them to keep the covenant. The period of the judges explains the transition from God's mediatorial acts through Moses and Joshua to His mediatorial acts through Israel's king.

The book of Judges also affixes significant blame on the inept Levites, who were to teach the Law and mediate God's theocratic rule through the sacrificial system. Their failure to do so was lethal for Israel.

The books of Judges and Ruth also laid the groundwork for the emergence of the royal line of David, who was from Bethlehem and of the tribe of Judah. Indeed, Judges ends with, "In those days there was no king in Israel. Everyone did what was right in his own eyes" (21:25).

The Term *Judge*

Judge does not suggest a judicial function, as we normally assign it in English. Rather, the term signifies a military leader or a protector. In the book of Judges, the term is best understood as a governor or general given the task of delivering part of Israel from oppression. Waltke suggests the translation "warlord," who in foreign affairs was a deliverer; in internal affairs, an "administrator of justice" (Judges 4:5); and in religious affairs, Yahweh's "covenant keeper" (Judges 2:17, 19). But these "warlords" were not above reproach. They were, in Waltke's words, "spiritually crippled charismatic warlords."[69]

The Chronology of the Judges

As with the exodus and the conquest under Joshua, there are chronological difficulties with the period of the judges. The issues involved are complex but solvable. The chronological timeline has two markers: the beginning point, the death of Joshua, and the ending point, the coronation of Saul as king. Since most scholars date Saul's coronation to 1051 BC, the significant debate is over the date of Joshua's death.

Eugene Merrill makes a strong case for 1350 BC as the date for the beginning of the judges. The challenge is that if we add up the years for each judge, which would include the years of oppression and the intervening periods of rest, the total is 410 years, too long for a 1350 to 1051 BC period for the judges. However, as numerous scholars have concluded, several of the judges overlapped, and "there is no reason why several of the periods of judgeships should not have been contemporaneous."[70] The various judgeships of Israel between 1350 and 1051 BC, as recorded in the book of Judges, are therefore not necessarily consecutive.

The Connection between Joshua And Judges

From the early verses of Judges chapter 1, a rather distinct contrast is established between Joshua and the leaders of his generation versus the generations of the judges, a contrast between Joshua's intense devotion and obedience to God and the utter spiritual and political bankruptcy of the judges. Joshua and his generation experienced the fullness of God's covenant blessings, while the generation of the judges experienced the fullness of God's covenant curses. Joshua and his generation exclusively worshiped and obeyed Yahweh, while many during the judges period experimented with a deadly syncretism that mixed worship of Yahweh with worship of Baal.[71]

During the period of the judges, the only meaningful unity among the twelve tribes was a spiritual unity. But their obedience to Yahweh was at best sporadic. With varying degrees of success regarding God's command concerning the Canaanites, they governed their own tribal allotments. In chapter 1, there is a clear discernible pattern: in Judges 1:22–26, Israel permitted the Canaanites to live "at a distance"; in 1:27–30, with the failure to drive them out, the Canaanites lived "among the Israelites"; in 1:31–33, the "Israelites live among the Canaanites."

The point is that God's command to extinguish the Canaanites from the land had been disobeyed. In the book of Judges, God made a strong connection between the spiritual failure of Israel and its political/military failure. The responsibility of the Levites was critical in such a situation. As defined by God, they were to instruct the people in the Law and in their covenant obligations, and to facilitate the sacrificial and feast-day festivals. But from the book of Judges, we observe the failure of the Levites to fulfill that role. In fact, the author of Judges has little good to say about the Levites; they must bear much of the responsibility for the failure of the people of Israel. (See the two epilogues of the book on an idolatrous Levite, 17:1–18:31, and the violent Levite, 19:1–21:25).[72]

Yet despite Israel's spiritual failure, God still viewed them as a united people. Indeed, as Waltke observes, "Because of the common physical and spiritual bonds of the people, the writer refers to them as 'Israel' and identifies tribal names only as an 'address.'

In fact, the name Israel occurs more often in this book than in any other book of the Hebrew Bible."[73]

The Spiritual Cycle of the Judges

The spiritual apostasy of Israel is the prominent theme of Judges. In fact, in the theological overview (2:6–3:6), the author discerns a cycle: Israel sins by serving the Canaanite Baals; Yahweh responds with covenant curses via surrounding enemies; Israel cries out to God, who answers in His grace; God sends a deliverer in the form of a judge; and then the judge dies (2:19). After a period of "rest," the cycle begins all over again. This deathly cycle permeates the book of the Judges. Judges 2:20–22 declares that "the anger of the LORD was kindled against Israel, and he said, 'Because this people has transgressed my covenant with their fathers and has not obeyed my voice, I will no longer drive out before them any of the nations that Joshua left when he died, in order to test Israel by them" (ESV).

The Cycle in Judges

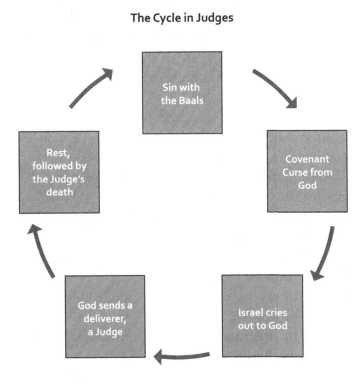

Who were the oppressors whom God used to discipline His people? There were three distinct groups that God used between 1350 and 1051 BC: (1) native Canaanite peoples whom Israel had refused to destroy; (2) settled peoples in the region of Canaan—the Philistines, the Moabites and the Ammonites; and (3) seminomadic tribal peoples who lived on the desert fringes of Canaan—the Midianites and the Amalekites.[74] Generally, these oppressing people attacked the Israelite tribal groups nearest them; rarely did they attack all of Israel.

The Twelve Judges

As stated, one of the purposes of the judges was to demonstrate to Israel their need for a righteous shepherd-king. The twelve judges of Israel are presented throughout the book to "prompt [the author's] audience to theological reflection on the kind of leader Israel needs."[75] The following chart lists the judges and Israel's oppressors. There are six major judges, marked by an asterisk, and six minor ones. As they are presented in Judges 3–16, the author moves from south to north, according to the tribe from which the judge came.

1. *Othniel (forty years as judge, from Judah), 3:7–11—against the Arameans
2. *Ehud (eighty years as judge, from Benjamin), 3:12–20—against the Moabites
3. Shamgar (?), 3:31—against the Philistines
4. *Deborah (forty years as judge, from Ephraim), 4 and 5—against the Canaanites
5. *Gideon (forty years as judge, from Manasseh), 6–8—against the Midianites
6. Tola (twenty-three years as judge, from Issachar), 10:1–2—against?
7. Jair (twenty-two years as judge, from Gilead), 10:3–5—against?
8. *Jephthah (six years as judge, from Gilead), 10:6–12:7—against the Ammonites

9. Ibzan (seven years as judge, from Judah), 12:8–10—against?
10. Elon (ten years as judge, from Zebulun), 12:11–12—against?
11. Abdon (eight years as judge, from Ephraim?), 12:13–15—against?
12. *Samson (twenty years as judge, from Dan), 13–16—against the Philistines

The Major Judges

1. **Othniel.** The son-in-law of Caleb (1:13), Othniel was the first judge and during the time of his leadership, Israel began to practice the deadly syncretism of mixing worship of Yahweh with that of the "Baals and the Asheroth" (Judges 3:7). Baal was the popular fertility god of the Canaanites, and Asherah was the female consort of El, the chief god of the Canaanites. They are referred to in the plural because apparently each local area in Israel had its own images of Baal and Asherah. Despite such defiance of God's command about singular worship of Him, in His grace, the Spirit of the Lord came upon Othniel, and he delivered Israel from apparently an early Aramean ruler (Cushan-Rishathaim). Othniel ruled for forty years (1350–1310 BC)[76]—and "the land had rest" (3:11). Othniel died and the spiritual cycle of decline resumed.

2. **Ehud.** Eglon, the Moabite king, joined with the Ammonites and the Amalekites and oppressed the east-central part of Israel for eighteen years, including the "City of Palms," Jericho. God raised up Ehud, the Benjamite, who assassinated Eglon in a gruesome manner. Ehud summoned the militia of Benjamin, which blocked the retreat of the Moabites and slew them. The land "rested" for eighty years (3:30).

3. **Deborah.** The tribes of the north and their apostasy are the focus of Deborah's judgeship. In the Jezreel Valley, Jabin, king of Hazor, and his general, Sisera, oppressed these tribes for twenty years. The text argues that Jabin's

success was because Sisera's army was one that used iron chariots (4:3). Since iron did not come into use in Canaan until 1200 BC, Merrill dates Jabin's rule in the north to about 1240–1220 BC.[77] Deborah of Ephraim summoned Barak of Naphtali to organize a coalition of the tribes of Naphtali, Zebulun, Ephraim, Manasseh, Benjamin, and Issachar (see 5:14–15) to defeat the Canaanites under Jabin and Sisera at Mount Tabor. The mighty iron chariots of Sisera were mired in mud due to the flooding Kishon River; Israel won a great victory there. General Sisera fled the battle but met a grisly death at the hands of Jael, wife of Heber the Kenite. As Waltke comments, "The contrast between Deborah and Barak suggests God raised up a woman to lead Israel because the Israelite men were cowards and declined leadership. Barak, though a gifted warrior, is tainted by his lack of faith and shamed for it."[78] In fact, the real heroine of the narrative is Jael. With her hospitality toward Sisera being a ploy, she breaks all cultural standards. "She takes the place of the male warrior, depriving him of glory, and winning glory by thrusting a tent peg through his temple ... This relative of Moses puts I AM before cultural conventions."[79] Deborah and Barak's great victory song of praise to God is recorded in Judges 5. It celebrates God's providence in dealing with Israel's enemies. But it also celebrates the contributions of Ephraim, Benjamin, Makir, Zebulun, Issachar, and Naphtali, while protesting the absence of Reuben, Gilead, Dan, and Asher. "The people of God are to offer themselves to serve all the people of God, not to behave selfishly."[80] Under Deborah, the land rested for forty years (5:31).

4. **Gideon**. Israel's continued apostasy resulted in God using the Midianites to discipline His people. Together with the Amalekites, the Midianites rode camels and raided Israel (largely the Jezreel Valley and the Galilee region) during the harvest. For seven years between 1190 and 1180 BC,[81] like locusts, they attacked quickly, devoured everything,

and raced east back into the desert (6:1–10). So bad was this oppression that Israel was driven into dens and caves to live (6:2). God therefore raised up Gideon of the tribe of Manasseh as judge; he was from the Manasseh town of Ophrah. God confirmed His presence with Gideon via a theophany and an affirmation via the fleece (6:36–40). Gideon successfully summoned other clans of Manasseh and the tribes of Asher, Zebulun, and Naphtali to meet the Midianites and the Amalekites in the Jezreel Valley near the Hill of Moreh. After God's order at the Spring of Harod to select an army of only three hundred, Gideon and his men attacked the Midianites near Endor with "lighted torches and blowing trumpets" (7:15-23). Terrified, the Midianites fled east toward the desert, and some of their leaders were captured. Gideon and his army pursued them deep into the desert.

An important note in this narrative is the growing fragmentation and disloyalty of the various Transjordan tribes. Specifically, the people of Succoth and Peniel (Gadite towns) refused to help Gideon. Gideon punished the Gadites—torturing Succoth's elders and killing the men of Peniel (8:16–17)—and murdered the Midianite kings (8:19). Returning to Ophrah, his people pleaded with him to be their king. Gideon refused, affirming the theocracy of God (8:22–23). Gideon was judge for forty years (1180–1140 BC)[82] as "the land again rested." However, near the end of his life, Gideon led his people into inappropriate worship rituals and idolatry (8:24–28). In Judges, Gideon is presented as a man of blemished character; he vacillated between faith and fear. God used him despite his lack of character. His son Abimelech killed his brothers, and the people of Shechem then made him their "king." An apostate king, his monarchy was rejected by God, and Abimelech met a violent end (9:56–57). In many ways Abimelech is a type of Saul.[83] As Waltke concludes, Gideon and his son Abimelech demonstrate "that charismatic warlords of Gideon's sort cannot lead the covenant people to permanent rest in the Land."[84]

5. **Jephthah.** Israel's apostasy deepened, not only worshiping the Baals and Asheroths, but also worshipping the gods of Aram, Sidon, Moab, Ammon, and Philistia (10:6). Thus God sent the Ammonites and the Philistines to crush Israel (10:7–8). Jephthah dealt with the Ammonites, Samson the Philistines. For eighteen years, the Ammonites continued to contest Gad's claim to the Ammonite region (i.e., Gilead). In addition, they crossed the Jordan and harassed the territories of Judah, Benjamin, and Ephraim (10:8–9). At Mizpah, the elders of Gilead chose Jephthah, a renegade member of the clan, to be their leader to free them from the Ammonites. He tried a diplomatic approach (11:12–28), but the Ammonites rejected his plea. Jephthah then dealt with the Ammonites militarily. The Spirit of the Lord was upon Jephthah (11:29), but he made an incredibly stupid vow, which caused him to offer his daughter as a sacrifice to God (11:29–40). Even though we might even question whether God approved of Jephthah as a judge (the people chose him, not God), he ruled as judge from 1106–1100 BC.[85] He was a leader with a curious mixture of faith and recklessness. Again, the book of Judges points to Israel's profound need—a righteous shepherd-king who would rule Israel.

6. **Samson.** Where Jephthah dealt with the Ammonites, Samson dealt with the Philistines. The Philistines had moved into Canaan between 1175 and 1150 BC. Originally from Crete, the Philistines were part of the great Sea Peoples migration that had occurred in the twelfth century BC, threatening much of the eastern Mediterranean. The Philistines settled in key coastal highway cites (Gaza, Ashkelon, and Ashdod) and spread inland, settling in Gath and Ekron. These five cities were the core of Philistia. They quickly assimilated the Canaanite worldview, worshiping Dagon, Baal, and

Ashtoreth. For forty years (1124–1084 BC)[86] the Philistines were an oppressive force against Judah and Dan, and to some extent Benjamin and Ephraim.[87] It was a struggle over who controlled the Shepelah. God thus sent Samson, a Danite, who was hardly a man of integrity. Indeed, Merrill comments that Samson is "an eloquent testimony to the nature of judgeship. It was not an office for which one was qualified by natural gifts, personal integrity, or inheritance, but only by the sovereign disposition of Yahweh ... [H]is success on Israel's behalf was due not to his own character but to his God."[88] Samson loved Philistine women but never their gods. Samson's marriage to the Philistine Timnah led to a series of incidents in which Samson killed thousands of Philistines. Due to the deceit and duplicity of Delilah, Samson lost his sight, his hair, and his stamina. But in Gaza at the temple of Dagon where he was a prisoner, God restored his strength and he destroyed the temple and himself, killing more Philistines in death than he had in life.

How should we think about Samson? That his character was flawed is a given. Yet God's Spirit came upon Samson four times (13:25; 14:6, 19; 15:14), more than any other judge. As Waltke astutely observes, Samson was an archetype of Israel: "In terms of the whole way it functions in the book of Judges, the story of Samson is the story of Israel recapitulated and focused for us in the life of a single man."[89] He did what was right in his own eyes, "disdaining his parents, his vows, and God; he cooperates and copulates with the uncircumcised; he is a spiteful manslayer and a self-satisfying whoremonger."[90] He wantonly broke his Nazrite vow by touching a carcass (14:5–9; 15:15), drinking wine (14:10), and cutting his hair (16:19). Indeed he mixed his faith "with the lust of the eyes (motif of seeing), lust of the flesh (motif of sex), and pride of life (motif of revenge), not with the love of God and Israel."[91] Samson's measured success did not end the Philistine threat. So serious was the Philistine threat that the tribe of Dan abandoned their original land grant and moved north to the area surrounding the ancient city of Laish, which they renamed Dan. (See Judges 17–18.) In fact, Philistine military power extended their presence as far east as Beth-shan. The first book of Samuel chapter 4 also details the Philistine conquest of Aphek in 1050 BC, a strategic city along the coastal highway, threatening Shiloh, where the ark of the covenant was located. The Philistines humiliated Israel at Ebenezer, captured the ark, and took it to Dagon's temple and then to Gaza. The plague and disgrace of Dagon caused them to return the ark to Israel. The first book of Samuel 13:19–22 also indicates that the Philistines had a monopoly on the production of iron used in making swords, spears, and all agricultural implements (plows, axes, sickles, etc.). They would remain an oppressive power against Israel until King David.

Samuel

Samson is called a judge (1 Samuel 7:15–17), but he was also a prophet (1 Samuel 3:20) and functioned as a priest (1 Samuel 9:12–13; 13:8–13). God used him to call the nation back to faith and covenant loyalty to Yahweh, to establish a semblance of unity among the people of Israel, and to inaugurate the monarchy in Israel.

The contrast between Eli, the high priest at Shiloh, and Samuel is marked. Although Eli was apparently not personally apostate, his sons had transformed Shiloh into a Canaanite shrine dedicated to Baal (1 Samuel 2:12–17, 22–25). Therefore, God used the Philistines as His instrument of discipline.

The connection of Samuel and the Philistines and Samson and the Philistines leads to the logical conclusion that Samson and Samuel overlap. Twenty years after the disaster at Aphek (1 Samuel 4), the defeat at Ebenezer, and the capture of the ark by the Philistines in 1104 BC, Samuel filled the huge vacuum in Israel's leadership by dealing with the Philistines. Loss of the ark illustrated the depth of God's discipline on His people. Samuel therefore gathered the people at Mizpah, offered sacrifices to God, and encouraged them to do battle with the Philistines. After a mighty victory, "the Philistines were subdued and did not enter the territory of Israel again" (1 Samuel 7:13 ESV). Israel regained territory lost to the Philistines, and there was peace during the entire period of Samuel's judgeship (1 Samuel 7:12–17).

As judge, Samuel rode a small circuit and transferred some authority to his sons, Joel and Abiah, whose perversions of justice partially contributed to the demand of the people for a king. Regarding this request as a personal affront, Samuel presented the case against a monarchy (1 Samuel 8). God assured Samuel they were not rejecting him; they were rejecting the theocracy Yahweh had established. Samuel would anoint Saul as king.

Ruth

The events in the book of Ruth occurred during the period of the judges (see Ruth 1:1), and Elimelech and Naomi were from Bethlehem. Because of famine, they resettled in Moab. As Merrill demonstrates, the book of Ruth redeems Bethlehem from the horrors of the idolatrous Levite and the violent Levite of judges, both of whom were associated with Bethlehem.[92] Not only does the story of Ruth redeem Bethlehem, but it establishes the royal line that produced King David and the greater King Jesus. In the presumably dismal and final days of the judges, there was the light of Ruth, for her story provides the bridge to the Davidic monarchy.

Ruth provides three key patriarchal links:

1. The elders and the people at the gatehouse of Bethlehem blessed Ruth as one "who will be like Rachel and Leah" (4:11). They also prayed that her house would be like the

house of "Perez, whom Tamar bore to Judah" (4:12). The incestuous relationship between Judah and Tamar (Genesis 38:14–30) was the result of Tamar seducing her father-in-law, Judah. Tamar, likely a Canaanite, was a foreigner to the covenant, yet she bore a son, like Ruth, in the Davidic line. Her son to Judah, Perez, came out of the womb first, asserting his ambition. The book of Ruth connects Ruth and Boaz to the royal line flowing from Perez of Tamar and Judah. Both Tamar and Ruth are profound examples of God's grace. Indeed, in the genealogy of Jesus, there are four women: Tamar and Rahab, Canaanites; Ruth, a Moabite; and Bathsheba, presumably a Hittite.

2. Ruth establishes the genealogical link between the patriarchs and the monarchy. The Davidic dynasty that would come through Ruth did not result from the Mosaic covenant but from the promise central to the Abrahamic covenant (Genesis 12:3).

3. As Merrill comments, "A descendant of the wayward and schismatic Lot [Moab], the pure and noble Ruth, effected a reunification with the Abrahamic clan from which he had separated. She was, then, not only a vital link in the messianic chain from Abraham to David (and eventually to Christ), but also an instrument to bridge the chasm between Judah and Moab ... a reconciliation which will fulfill the patriarchal blessing."[93]

The story of Ruth especially spotlights the character of God. In the midst of one of the darkest periods of Israel's history, there was God, sovereignly orchestrating events to accomplish His purpose—to establish, in Bethlehem and from the tribe of Judah, the royal line of David and His Son, Jesus Christ. In fact, Waltke discerns five significant characteristics of God in the narrative of Ruth:

1. God is sovereign in His providence. What appears to be accidental or random from the human perspective (e.g., Elimelech and Naomi sojourning in Moab, the meeting

of Ruth and Boaz) is actually the amazing superintending work of God in human affairs. Each step in the narrative is clearly under God's control.

2. God is the giver of life. God restored fertility to the land, and He provided fertility for Ruth, resulting in an unimaginable blessing for Naomi (4:13).

3. God is the Redeemer. The Hebrew term *go'el* occurs twenty times in the narrative. Boaz was the kinsman-redeemer of Ruth, but God was the true redeemer for Naomi and for Ruth—from famine, from hurt and pain, and ultimately from death. Boaz as Ruth's *go'el* prefigures the astonishing work of Christ as Redeemer.

4. God is compassionate. In the Ruth narrative, He provided bounty for the alien, the poor, the widow, and the fatherless. The theme of compassion is central to Ruth—and central to God's saving grace in Christ.

5. God manifests *hesed*. God's abounding, unfailing, covenant love for Israel is prominent in the book of Ruth. Through Ruth and her great-grandson David (and ultimately through Jesus Christ), God restored sinful Israel and gave them a future with hope when all seemed lost. "He blesses them with life and prosperity and memorializes them with enduring fame."[94]

A focus on Ruth is the appropriate way to end the tragic period of the judges. Despair and anarchy—both political and spiritual— were replaced with a sense of order, purpose, and hope. When things seemed at their worst, God broke through with a reminder of His sovereignty and that His plan to fulfill the Abrahamic covenant—"in you all the nations will be blessed"—was on track.

Chapter 5

The Covenant-Making God and the United Kingdom

From Deuteronomy 17:14–20, we learn that it was God's intent for Israel to have a king: one "whom the LORD your God will choose" and one who was to govern according to the principles of the Law. The shift from the theocracy established at the time of the exodus to the monarchy centers on Saul, David, and Solomon. It was a tectonic shift, for it involved the shift from Shiloh to Jerusalem, from charismatic judges to an eternal kingship, and from twelve tribes to a unified nation.[95] The monarchy began with Saul, a "king like all the other nations" (1 Samuel 8:5), who was replaced by David, a "man after God's own heart" (Acts 13:22), who was succeeded by his son, Solomon, who at first sought wisdom but ended in debauchery and idolatry.

The monarchy of Israel demonstrated once again Israel's need for a righteous shepherd-king who would lead them in covenant obedience to God. Saul, David, and Solomon all had special gifts, but they all ultimately failed as king. From the perspective of Scripture, only King Jesus meets perfectly the need for a righteous shepherd-king.

Saul the Benjamite: A Dynasty and a King Rejected

Saul seemingly met all the qualifications for kingship: he was regal, came from a good family, and was physically strong. He even exhibited a degree of humility (1 Samuel 9–10). When Samuel anointed Saul as king, the situation in Israel was dire. Samuel was old and his two sons were corrupt. Israel was also vulnerable, for

60

the Arameans were a growing threat to the north, as were the Ammonites to the east. Further, there was the perpetual threat of the Philistines to the west. Samuel had warned the people that if they sought a king "like all the other nations," they would be unified, but he would tax them and conscript their sons into his army (1 Samuel 8:11–18). As the people persisted in their demand for a king, God acquiesced and commanded Samuel to choose a king (1 Samuel 8:19–22).

The first book of Samuel chapter 9 demonstrates completely God's sovereignty—and thereby His choice—of Saul as king. Ostensibly about lost donkeys, the focus of the text is really about God super-intending events to make Saul king. But Saul seemed oblivious to all this and found incredible the idea that he was to be king. In fact, Saul's lack of faith in God is important in understanding his flawed character. Waltke comments, "[A] person of faith would see the hand of Providence in all this. Saul does not. Providence is backed up by Samuel's amazing prophecies, leaving Saul without excuse for his unbelief. Unbelieving Israel is about to crown the kind of king they deserve."[96] After the three confirming signs prophesied by Samuel—two men at Rachel's tomb, three men going to Bethel, and a procession of prophets (10:1–13)—the Spirit of God came upon Saul. Samuel proclaimed him king and coronated him at Mizpah (10:17–24).

After his coronation at Mizpah, Saul's reign as king (1051–1011 BC)[97] began. He located his capital at Gibeah, a Benjamite town north of Jerusalem. But as 1 Samuel 10:27 makes clear, Saul needed to prove himself to many of the Israelites. That opportunity came when the Ammonite king Nahash attacked Jabesh Gilead, a town east of the Jordan River. Nahash laid siege to the town, demanding the right eye of every male to break the siege. The Spirit of God came upon Saul (11:6–7), and he assembled the army and scored a significant victory in rescuing Jabesh Gilead from the Ammonites. Samuel then took this victory as an occasion to have the people confirm Saul as king at Gilgal, north of Gibeah.

The downfall of Saul occurred in two stages. Stage one centered on the Philistines. In a sense, Saul's major mandate was to free Israel from the tyranny of the Philistines. He won important victories against Moab, Edom, the Aramean kingdom of Zobah, and the Amalekites (1 Samuel 14:47–48), but Saul never was successful against the Philistines (see 1 Samuel 14:52). The Philistines moved their forces into Israel toward Michmash, raiding east, west, and north. This strategic initiative was augmented by the Philistine monopoly of the iron trade (13:19–22). Saul's son, Jonathan, a paradigm of faith in this narrative, defeated a Philistine garrison at Geba, south of Michmash. As the Philistines ruthlessly responded with chariots and horsemen, Israel was terrified, hiding in caves, holes, and cisterns (13:6). Saul retreated to Gilgal.

Apparently personally frightened, Saul violated Samuel's clear instruction to wait for him at the sacred site of Gilgal. Probably as a test of Saul's faith, Samuel delayed coming, and Saul offered a burnt offering to God in preparation for battle. Upon his arrival, Samuel severely rebuked Saul, stating that because of his actions God had now rejected his dynasty—"your kingdom shall not continue" (1 Samuel 13:14).

Why did God reject Saul's dynasty? Merrill argues that "Saul's failure, then, lay in his appropriating to himself priestly prerogatives which may have been associated with pagan kingship but which, without specific divine sanction, were inappropriate to him or to any king of Israel."[98] Out of fear, Saul attempted to manipulate God. Samuel thus declared that God now sought a "man after his own heart" (13:14), a man who had surrendered his will to God's, obviously something Saul had not done. The king needed to trust in God, not his own resources or his own manipulative strategies. As Waltke observes, the king was to be one who "relies on God's true strength (i.e., sees the situation from faith's perspective of the transcendental situation). Saul lacks the faith that radically alters the perception and judgment of reality."[99]

Stage two was God's rejection of Saul as king, which is one of the great tragedies of Scripture. In Deuteronomy 25:19, God had declared that He would totally destroy the Amalekites, one of the archenemies of Israel. According to 1 Samuel 15:1–3, Saul was intended to be the agent to carry out this divine decree of judgment; no human or animal was to be spared. But Saul and his army spared the best animals—and king Agag (15:4-9). Amazingly, Saul even had a monument built to himself, presumably in honor of his defeat of the Amalekites (15:12).

When Samuel arrived on the scene, he twice charged Saul with defiant disobedience; each time Saul blamed his army. Even Saul's "confession" was not genuine, for he only sought to avoid humiliation before his people. That day God rejected Saul as king, regretting "that He had made Saul king over Israel" (15:35). Saul was a king of significant human strength, but he was not a man of faith. As Waltke declares, "He is not the stuff that brings about God's will on earth as it is in heaven."[100] Therefore, "the Spirit of the LORD departed from Saul" (16:14).

The Spirit then came upon David (16:13). Such an anointing from God came after Samuel, instructed by God, traveled to Bethlehem and anointed David with oil as Israel's next king, about 1029 BC. Amazingly, Saul then chose David to serve in his court. David played music for Saul and became his armor–bearer, for Saul "loved him greatly" (16:21). David's great victory over Goliath the Philistine (1 Samuel 17), caused the people to champion David as a mighty warrior, far greater than Saul. David's holy zeal against Goliath evidenced the faith of a "warrior-king who joined his God in battle against all who would challenge his sovereignty."[101]

The jealousy and bitter hatred of Saul for David frames the narrative of 1 Samuel 19–30. There are several aspects of this narrative that are important in revealing the character of David:

1. *His relationship with Jonathan.* Jonathan, Saul's son, pledged his loyalty to David as God's anointed. The contrast between Jonathan and his father is marked. Jonathan

recognized God's sovereignty in the choice of David and deferred to it. Unlike his father, Jonathan was a man of extraordinary faith. The bond between him and David was sealed by a covenant (1 Samuel 18:1–5). He clothed David in his royal attire and pledged allegiance to David, even to his dynasty (20:16).

2. *His relationship with Saul.* Saul's hatred of David grew so intense that he pursued David, even to the remote desert regions of Ziph, Maon, and En-gedi. While in En-gedi, David had an opportunity to kill Saul (1 Samuel 24; also see chapter 26), but, despite the pleadings of his men, he believed he "could not touch the LORD's anointed" (1 Samuel 24: 6). David would not murder the king, even though Saul sought David's life. David left Saul's destiny to God. This is in contrast to the growing obsession of Saul with David. Saul had had eighty-five defenseless priests slaughtered because he perceived them to be disloyal (1 Samuel 22:6–19). He had the entire community of Nob annihilated, including women and children, because David had taken refuge there (22:6–23). By contrast, after Saul was killed by the Philistines on Mount Gilboa (1 Samuel 31), David's lament and mourning for Saul and Jonathan bore evidence of genuine grief and sorrow.

3. *His relationship with God.* After he killed Goliath, David was a war hero, exalted and praised. But when Saul sought his life, he became a fugitive. Why did God permit this? If He had rejected Saul, why not have David become king immediately? David was not ready to be king. God needed to develop his skills to govern Israel, especially his leadership skills, and he needed to develop his faith. In 1 Samuel 24, as David responded to his men's demands that he kill Saul, he evidenced a growing ability to lead. His conviction about God and his understanding of God's sovereignty informed his decisions, not the impulse of the moment. He would need this perspective because Israel's enemies were formidable, and under Saul, Israel's security had actually

become worse. Israel was on the verge of being destroyed or absorbed by one its enemies, especially the Philistines. Further, David took a band of four hundred distressed, bitter, and debt-ridden vagabonds and made them into the core of an army that would be loyal to him for the rest of his life (1 Samuel 22:1–2). David had learned a dependence upon God, even in the midst of some foolish decisions on his part (see chapter 27). David was indeed a "man after God's own heart" (Acts 13:22). He deferred to God's rule and sovereignty, and he trusted Him. Unlike Saul, David was a man of faith.

David: The Covenant King of Israel

The rise of David as king marked the beginning of Israel's golden age. Together with his son, Solomon, David made Israel a wealthy, formidable power in the eastern Mediterranean. Over a nearly eighty-year period, David and Solomon established a kingdom that stretched from the Sinai to the Euphrates River. In addition, the twelve tribes of Israel were truly unified around the king and the temple in Jerusalem. Finally, God established an unconditional covenant with David—an eternal throne, kingdom, and dynasty—which would be fulfilled by David's greater son, the Lord Jesus Christ.

The historic context of David's rise to power is important. As Merrill makes clear, the division between Judah and the rest of the tribes of Israel had characterized Saul's reign. In fact, 1 Samuel presents Israel and Judah as virtually two separate identities within Israel pursuing two separate destinies.[102] For this reason, a civil war ensued shortly after Saul's death.

The leaders of Judah logically and sensibly declared David king in 1011 BC,[103] and he ruled from Hebron in Judah. Not only was David of the tribe of Judah, but, when he sought refuge from Saul among the Philistines, he attacked the enemies of Judah persistently, thereby further winning the favor of the Judahites (see 1 Samuel 27:8–12).

Saul had a surviving son, Ish-bosheth, whom the northern tribes supported. Ish-bosheth established his capital at Mahanaim along the Jabbok River, east of the Jordan River. Abner, Saul's cousin, was his military commander; Joab, David's cousin, was his commander. The civil war lasted for two years, with one major recorded battle near the pool of Gibeon (2 Samuel 2:12–32). When Abner attempted to forge an agreement with David, Joab killed him, avenging Asahel, his brother, who died at the battle of Gibeon. Ish-bosheth's men then murdered Joab, and the northern tribes declared their loyalty to David. He ruled a united Israel from Hebron for seven years (2 Samuel 5:1–5).

Since Hebron was in Judah's land grant, David understood that he needed to establish a new capital. He could not show favoritism toward Judah. He chose Jerusalem, a Jebusite city. No tribe controlled this city, so Joab, following David's orders, took the city by entering via the "water shaft" (a vertical shaft to a water source outside the city's wall; see 2 Samuel 5:8). In 1004 BC, Jerusalem became the Israel's capital, and David built his palace there, receiving the cedarwood and materials from Hiram, king of Tyre, a major trading city of the eastern Mediterranean.

Wisely then, David had the ark of the covenant moved from Keriath-jearim to Jerusalem, building a tent shrine to house it. As Brisco argues, "In one stroke David united both the political and religious loyalties of the tribes and paved the way for a royal theology centered on Jerusalem, David and his descendants."[104] David ruled from Jerusalem for thirty-three years.

David's military campaigns vanquished Israel's enemies and established Israel as a formidable power in the eastern Mediterranean. David's army had at its center an elite core of extremely loyal men. (See 2 Samuel 23:8–38.) In addition, he employed a professional army composed of mercenaries, which included Hittites, Philistines, and Ammonites as well as Israelites.[105] David's military strategy had three major components:

1. He neutralized the power of the Philistines. As the Philistines challenged his rule over Jerusalem (2 Samuel 5:17–25), David's defeat of them resulted in Israel controlling the entire Shepelah. The Philistines would never again threaten Israel.
2. David established control of the Transjordan region, defeating the Edomites, the Moabites, and the Ammonites. (See 2 Samuel 8.)
3. David defeated Hadadezer, king of Zobah, an Aramean kingdom. His defeat of the Aramean army meant that David controlled virtually the entire territory north of Israel. Hence, he constructed a major garrison at Damascus. His kingdom now stretched from the border of Egypt in the south to Syria in the north. Brisco summarizes his accomplishments: "The Jezreel Valley, the Shepelah, all of Galilee, as well as the Transjordan with its vital trade routes were part of David's kingdom. Ammon, Moab, Edom and certain Aramean kingdoms paid homage by sending tribute to the court in Jerusalem."[106]

The movement of the ark to Jerusalem triggered David's desire to build a temple to house the ark and as a place of worship. (See 2 Samuel 7.) Through His prophet Nathan, the Lord rejected this plan. David was a warrior-king who had shed blood. The temple must symbolize "peace without bloodshed,"[107] which is the essence of Solomon's name—shalom. Waltke notes that in this chapter, the Lord calls David "my servant," an accolade bestowed on Moses and Joshua, which connotes responsible obedience, faithful dependence, personal intimacy, and humility.[108] Even though David would not build the temple, the Lord made a covenant with him: He promised David that his kingdom, his throne, and his dynasty would be eternal (2 Samuel 7:16). This covenant is technically a royal grant "by which a sovereign graciously bestowed a blessing,"[109] which in David's case was the blessing of eternal kingship. (Jesus Christ, the "son of David" per Matthew 1:1, fulfilled completely the promise of eternal kingship, with an eternal kingdom on an eternal throne).

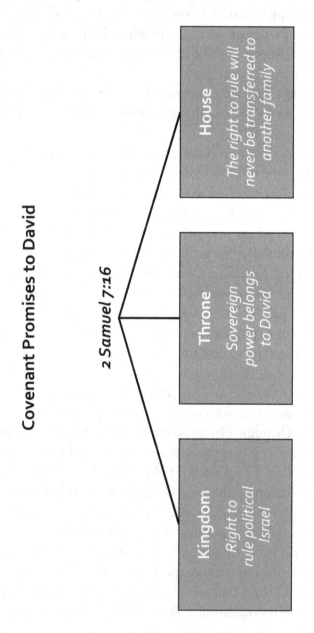

Covenant Promises to David

2 Samuel 7:16

House
The right to rule will never be transferred to another family

Throne
Sovereign power belongs to David

Kingdom
Right to rule political Israel

With the marvelous covenant promise of eternal kingship in his mind, David began to make preparations for building the temple. From Araunah the Jebusite, David purchased the threshing floor north of Jerusalem as the location for the temple (1 Chronicles 21:18–22:1). He then began to make elaborate preparations for its building. He chose stonecutters from resident aliens to prepare building blocks according to the specific measurements he had received from the Lord (see 1 Chronicles 28:12–19). Most probably from the booty of war, he prepared iron, bronze, and cedarwood for the temple. He charged Solomon with the task of building the temple (1 Chronicles 22:6–13) and commanded that Israel's leaders support all Solomon did (22:17). David pledged that the finances to pay for the temple would come from the royal treasury, from his own resources, and from the freewill offerings of Israel's leaders, which resulted in over 190 tons of gold, 375 tons of silver, 675 tons of bronze, and 3,750 tons of iron (1 Chronicles 29:6–9).[110]

David centralized the administration of the kingdom of Israel in several ways. He placed supervisors over each one of the tribes (1 Chronicles 27:16–22) and appointed administrators over treasuries, storehouses, vineyards and olive trees, herds of animals, the olive-oil industry, and all the workers involved (1 Chronicles 27:25–31). Such regulatory control implies royal ownership of much of the industry and agriculture of Israel.

Gad and especially Nathan played significant prophetic roles during David's kingdom, advising and rebuking him when he sinned (e.g., 2 Samuel 7:2–17 and 12:1–15). David also reorganized the Levitical priesthood, dividing it into twenty-four units to serve and lead in corporate worship (2 Chronicles 24:1–19). He also recognized two high priests, Zadok and Abiathar.[111] In short, David established an administrative structure upon which his son Solomon could build.

David was a man after God's heart, but he was also a man of sin. The tragic fall of David is recorded in 2 Samuel 9–20. His adultery with Bathsheba (ca. 992 BC) is the vital center of his fall. The second book of Samuel chapters 10–12 place this sin in the context of war. Joab and the army were battling the Ammonites at Rabbah, while David was in Jerusalem. Bathsheba was bathing, and from the royal palace David easily saw her.

Important to the narrative is that Bathsheba was the daughter of Eliam, son of Ahithophel of Gilo, one of David's elite warriors (2 Samuel 23:34), and the wife of Uriah, a Hittite member of David's elite warriors (2 Samuel 23:39). By his adultery, David betrayed God and two of his elite warriors!

Bathsheba became pregnant, and the cover-up began. When Uriah, summoned by David ostensibly for some respite from battle, refused to sleep with his wife, David ordered Commander Joab to place him in the front of the battle. Uriah was thereby killed.

What a contrast: Uriah, loyal and faithful to the covenant; King David, immoral, duplicitous, and disloyal to the covenant. After months of cover-up, Nathan the prophet confronted David with his sin, and David repented. The penitential Psalm 51 indicates the depths and genuineness of his repentance. David was granted God's forgiveness and experienced His grace and mercy. But the consequences of his sin were dire indeed!

In the years following his sin, David was a different ruler. Where he had been decisive and forthright, he now evidenced the opposite qualities. Waltke captures this change: "David is blind and inactive with regard to his sons ... David is self-absorbed with his own flesh and blood. Imperceptive, indecisive and incredibly self-absorbed, he stumbles into one tragedy after another and finally plunges the nation into two wars: a revolutionary war and a civil war."[112] The sequence of this downward spiral was as follows:

1. *Amnon's Rape of Tamar (2 Samuel 13:1–38, ca. 987 BC)*. David's oldest son lusted for and eventually raped his

half-sister Tamar. The duplicity and horror of this incestuous rape are detailed in the text, but the inaction of David is the main point. Amnon's lust turned to hatred, and Tamar was left "desolate" (v. 20), meaning she was dehumanized and ruined for life.[113] Amnon refused to marry Tamar and refused to repent. Because of his sin with Bathsheba, David lacked the moral courage to hold Amnon accountable. Filled with rage and a desire for revenge, Absalom, Tamar's brother, therefore took the matter into his hands. Through equal duplicity, Absalom had Amnon murdered (13:23–38) and then fled to Geshur (the Golan Heights region). The parallel with David's sin is obvious: sexual violation followed by murder.

2. *Absalom's Revolt against King David (14:25–16:14, ca. 976 BC).* At first, David refused to reconcile with Absalom. Absalom, popular, handsome, with an attractive family and political demeanor, gained influence in the kingdom. Through manipulation, he forced Joab to effect reconciliation with the king. There was no repentance, no justice, but there was superficial reconciliation with his father David. Absalom, still emotionally distant from David, plotted a revolt. From Hebron, where his father was first crowned king, Absalom initiated the revolt and, at the sound of trumpets, had himself declared king (2 Samuel 15:10). To preserve Jerusalem from a destructive siege, David fled the city with his loyal bodyguards and close allies (15:13–37). God's providence was evident as He thwarted the wise council of Ahithophel to immediately attack David. Absalom and the war council accept Hushai's counsel to delay the attack. David and his forces thereby had time to regroup and prepare for civil war (2 Samuel 17).

3. *The Civil War (17:24–19:1).* The primary battle was in the Transjordan area between Mahanaim (David's forces) and Gilead (Absalom's forces). Because of his long hair, Absalom became entangled in a tree, where Joab, contrary

to David's orders, killed him. David's response to all this was astounding. Whereas his previous priority had been the good of his kingdom, now he turned inward. Waltke captures the essence of the change: "From here on David is off-balance and out of step with his true supporters and the kingdom of God."[114] His lament over his "spoiled and incorrigible son" (18:31–33) manifested his unreasonable focus on himself and not the kingdom of Israel.

4. *The North-South Conflict (19:40–20:23)*. The persistent rivalry between Judah and the northern tribes surfaced again around the rebellion of Sheba, a Benjamite. Sheba led a secession movement and revolt against David and Judah (20:1–2). This evidenced the continued tension between David's seeming preference for Judah at the expense of the northern tribes. (See 19:41–43.) Such a sentiment continued into Solomon's reign and eventually produced the divided monarchy. Sheba and his forces fled north to Abel, near Dan, where Joab and the army laid siege to the city. The people of the city killed Sheba and cut off his head, giving it to Joab, who then returned to King David.

At the end of David's reign, Israel was in disarray and the old decentralizing tendencies were evident once again. The kingdom's future was muddled. Would the covenant promises of God be honored? Would the nation remain united and endure?

Despite King David's failures at the end of his reign, 2 Samuel 22–24 serve as a "reminder of David's greatness and of [the] hope in the house of David in spite of the king's escalating failures at the end of his reign."[115] David's prayers and acts of propitiatory justice in dealing with the Gibeonites (21:1–14) are followed by the listing of David's mighty men of valor (21:15–22; 23:8–39). Similar to both Hannah's song (1 Samuel 2) and Psalm 18, David's Song (22:1–51) celebrated God's sovereignty and His faithfulness, grace, mercy, and covenant loyalty (*hesed*). More than anything else, it demonstrated why David was a man after God's heart. David's last words (23:1–7) summarized God's covenant promises and were an offer of praise to God for choosing him and his dynasty to rule Israel (2 Samuel 7:16).

The mysterious census of David (chapter 24, ca. 975 BC) resulted in God's judgment but also provided the context for David purchasing the threshing floor from Araunah the Jebusite. There he prayed and offered sacrifices to the Lord, the same place "where in the past Abraham offered up Isaac and where in the future priests would offer sacrifices on the temple altar."[116] God thereby halted the judgment.

Quoting Raymond Dillard, Waltke comments, "At the place where Abraham once held a knife over his son (Gen. 22:1–19) ... [t]he temple is established there as the place where Israel was perpetually reminded that without the shedding of blood there is no remission for sin (Heb. 9:22). Death for Isaac and for David's Jerusalem was averted because the sword of divine justice would ultimately find its mark in the Son of God (John 19:33)."[117] The book of Samuel ends with a picture of the future King whose death would bring salvation and restoration to the kingdom.

Solomon: Covenant Failure, the King with a Divided Heart

Solomon's reign was indisputably the golden age of Israel. But his ascension to the throne was not without incident. Adonijah, his brother and the eldest serving son of David, challenged Solomon. Adonijah was aided by Joab, David's commander, and by Abiathar the priest, both of whom apparently feared significant loss of influence should Solomon be the king.

But Bathsheba, together with Nathan the prophet and Zadok the priest, thwarted Adonijah's plan. David then anointed Solomon king and gave him a charge that focused on the covenant God made with him and the instructions on kingship in Deuteronomy

17. David "slept with his fathers" (1 Kings 2:10), ending his forty years as king (1011–971 BC).

As he began his rule, Solomon's divided heart was evident. He married Pharaoh's daughter (something that violated the spirit of Deuteronomy 17:16), and yet he exhibited a sense of inadequacy in ruling Israel (1 Kings 3:1–15). Solomon demonstrated the need for a "wise and discerning heart ... to know what is right and just and fair in matters too fine to be caught in the mesh of the Law."[118] God granted Solomon wisdom, and his judicial wisdom was evident in settling the dispute between the two prostitutes (1 Kings 3:16–28). This God-given wisdom was also evident in the administration of his growing empire (4:1–19) and managing his complex economic relationships in the eastern Mediterranean (4:20–28).

Solomon's financial and economic expertise produced vast wealth for Israel, which in turn enabled him to embark on a vast building program that included the temple. Because of the land acquired through David's wars, Solomon controlled the two major international highways: the International Coastal Highway (the Via Maris) and the King's Highway. The maritime and overland routes, which strategically intersected in Israel, were now under Solomon's control. As merchandise entered and exited Israel, Solomon levied customs taxes, adding significant wealth to the royal treasury.[119] Through these maritime and overland connections, Solomon accessed all the major trading networks of this part of the world.

Perhaps most important was his commercial relationship with King Hiram of Tyre, the key city of the Phoenician Empire. The Phoenicians had trading colonies that stretched throughout the Mediterranean, as far west as Spain. An aspect of his relationship with Hiram was the joint venture of constructing the port city of Ezion-geber on the Gulf of Aqabah (1 Kings 9:26). Hiram provided the craftsmen and sailors to construct and maintain the fleet needed by Solomon. Through this port, Solomon's ships linked with parts of Africa, Arabia, and the Red Sea (perhaps even India) to bring gold, sandalwood, precious stones, ivory, apes, and ba-boons into his kingdom (1 Kings 9:26–28; 10:11–12; 22).[120] In fact, the Queen of Sheba's (modern Yemen) visit illustrated the growing importance of Israel. Although she came to Jerusalem to inquire of Solomon's wisdom, the visit may have also been for commercial trade purposes. (See 2 Chronicles 9:1, 9.) His naval activities may have posed a challenge to her domination of the Red Sea and east African trade.[121]

Administratively, Solomon restructured and centralized Israel, a nation of tribes and clans. According to 1 Kings 4:7–19, he di-vided the nation into twelve administrative districts, following the twelve tribes and the twelve months of the year. Each district was administered by a governor, who reported to a supervisor. Each district provided food allotments to the central government for an entire month each year. Conscription from each district for both military and civil service needs was common. According to 1 Kings 9:15–22, Solomon also employed non-Israelite slave labor, presum-ably remnants of the Canaanites. Remarkably, Solomon treated Judah and Jerusalem as some form of federal district, exempting them from taxation, conscription, and other burdens.[122] This fact no doubt was a contributing factor to the division of the kingdom into north and south after Solomon's death.

Solomon's empire was extensive and important. Indeed, along with Assyria and Egypt, Israel was one of the three great powers of the tenth century BC. Of course, the administrative center of Israel comprised the land grants made to the twelve tribes. Solomon never incorporated additional territory into these land grants. However, Solomon did incorporate into his kingdom several different terri-tories. Merrill provides a helpful way to organize these domains.[123]

Aleppo

Tiphsah

HAMATH

Hamath

Qatha

Arvad

Kadesh

Tadmor

Mediterranean Sea

Gebal

PHOENICIA

Sidon

Damascus

Tyre

ARAM

Kedesh

Hazor

Acco

Meglado

Edrel

Shechem

AMMON

Joppa

Rabbah

PHILISTIA

Gibeah

Ashdod

Madeba

Jersusalem

Gaza

Beersheba

MOAB

Tarmar

Kadesh

EDOM

SINAI

Kingdom of David and Solomon

Saul's Kingdom

David and Solomon's Kingdom

Territory Under Solomon's Control

1. *The Provinces.* Inherited from his father David was a complex of provinces that consisted of kingdoms immediately
   contiguous to Israel: Damascus, Ammon, Moab, and Edom.
   Each was ruled directly by Israelite governors and was subject
   to taxation and conscription. All had obligations to defend
   Israel militarily. Israel promised to provide them security.
2. *The Vassal States.* Areas that were brought under Israel's
   control but maintained a degree of autonomy (e.g., their
   own rulers and fiscal policy) included Zobah, Hamath,
   Arabia, and perhaps Philistia. Each recognized Israel's
   suzerainty by paying annual tributes to the king and maintaining loyalty to Israel in wartime. In exchange, Israel
   promised protection and security.
3. *The Allied States.* Solomon negotiated a series of treaties
   and alliances with surrounding nations, including Hiram
   of Tyre and Egypt (1 Kings 9:10–29; 11:40).

Solomon's immense wealth made his extensive building program possible. Both the Bible and recent archeological excavations confirm the extent of this program. In terms of architecture, Brisco suggests that Solomon "drew freely upon foreign architectural traditions, especially Phoenician and Aramean, and may have employed a royal architect to execute his plans."[124] Important to his building program was defense. Solomon constructed three strategic chariot cities—Hazor, Megiddo, and Gezer—along the International Coastal Highway (1 Kings 9:15). Refortified sites included Baalah and Beth-horon, which guarded passes from the coast into the heart to Judah. Ramat Matred, Baalath-beer, Arad, and Beersheba were fortified to protect and guard the caravan routes and the southern boundary of his kingdom. He also fortified Jerusalem by building a circumferential wall which enclosed the original Jebusite town (Ophel), the City of David, the temple, and the public buildings of the city.[125]

North of the old City of David was Solomon's royal palace complex, which resembled the plan of a neo-Hittite palace, like ones found in northern Syria. It took thirteen years to build (1 Kings 9:10), and consisted of an entrance hall (the Hall of Pillars, 1 Kings 7:6), the House of the Forest of Lebanon (7:2–5), the porch, or Hall of the Throne (Solomon's place of judgment, 7:6) and either wings or semidetached structures that included Solomon's private quarters. As a part of the complex, he built a house for his wife, Pharaoh's daughter (7:8). Another indication of his divided heart was that Solomon spent more time building his own palace complex than he did the temple of Yahweh.[126]

His most significant building project was the temple in Jerusalem. Thomas Brisco describes the way Jerusalem is located on a series of ridges that run from north to south, with deep valleys on all sides. "The Kidron Valley separates the eastern ridge from the higher elevations of Mount Scopus and the Mount of Olives (2,684 feet). The Hinnom Valley descends alongside the western ridge, encircling the two ridges to the south before joining the Kidron Valley. A central valley ... divides the two ridges."[127] Canaanite and Jebusite Jerusalem centered on the southern tip because the principal water source—the Gihon Spring—was there. This is what David conquered around 1004 BC. David bought the threshing floor from Araunah on Mount Moriah to the north, along the eastern ridge, where Solomon built the temple.

The temple of Yahweh was one of the most noteworthy and beautiful structures of the ancient world. As mentioned above, King David cleared the site on Mount Moriah and prepared much of the material needed to begin construction. According to 1 Kings 5:13–18, Solomon conscripted 30,000 Canaanites as lumbermen to work in Lebanon with Hiram's workers. He also conscripted 70,000 carriers of the lumber and 80,000 stonecutters in the quarries near Megiddo and Samaria. Supervision of these conscripted workers was done by 3,300 foremen overseen by Adoniram, who presumably was responsible to Solomon. The temple builders were a combination of Solomon's skilled workers, skilled craftsman from Hiram, and the "men of Gebal" (1 Kings 5:18, i.e., men of Byblos, a Phoenician city north of Tyre).[128]

Nothing of Solomon's temple survives, for it was destroyed by Nebuchadnezzar's armies in 586 BC. So, although it somewhat resembled the tabernacle in its basic outline, it is impossible to capture the beauty and grandeur of this magnificent structure. From the details in Scripture, the temple contained "both cosmological and royal symbols that teach I AM's absolute sovereignty over the whole creation and his special headship over Israel."[129]

It was a rectangular structure of three main parts (ninety feet long, thirty feet wide, and forty-five feet high). You entered the temple from the east through a porch flanked by two bronze pillars, called Boaz and Jachin. In the porch area were the great bronze altar (fifteen feet high and thirty feet in length and width) and the great bronze laver or basin (7.5 feet high and fifteen feet in diameter).

The primary portion of the temple was the Holy Place, which contained three pieces of furniture—the golden lampstand (a menorah), the altar of incense, and the table of shewbread. At the western end of the temple was the Holy of Holies, which contained the ark of the covenant, over which there were two gilded olive-wood cherubim. The outer walls of the temple consisted of white limestone, while the interior walls were made of cedar. The floor coverings, doors, door frames, and furnishings were made of cypress and olive wood. Interior walls contained gold, ornate carvings, and precious stones.[130]

Led by King Solomon, the dedication of the temple marked the apex of Israel's walk with Yahweh. The dedication occurred during the fall festival and involved Israel's leaders, the elders and priests, as they transferred the ark of the covenant from its place in the tabernacle in the City of David on Mount Zion to its new resting place, the temple on Mount Moriah (1 Kings 8:1–11). As God had instructed, the ark was placed in the Holy of Holies behind the veil; the temple was filled with Yahweh's presence (the *shekinah* glory).

Solomon addressed the people, summarizing how the temple fulfilled God's promise made to his father, David, that his son would sit on the throne of Israel. Solomon affirmed the sovereignty and omnipresence of God, and stressed that the temple and the unique manifestation of His glory in the temple evidenced His providential care for Israel, His people. In a glorious dedicatory prayer, Solomon reviewed the relationship between God and His people (1 Kings 8:22–53). But he warned that if they sinned, they would experience the covenant curses (e.g., defeat, drought, disease, and even captivity). With repentance, the people must look to God, who would forgive and restore them. Israel is His and, as He redeemed them from Egypt, He would do so again. Following the prayer, Solomon offered an astonishing sacrifice to Yahweh, involving thousands of animals, after which he proclaimed a fourteen-day festival (8:62-64).

Solomon's apostasy is one of the great tragedies of Scripture. 1 Kings 10 and 11 tie together Solomon's accumulation of gold and horses with his apostasy. (See 10:14–29.) Both clearly violated God's instruction in Deuteronomy 17:16–17.

Solomon's divided heart constitutes a major theme of Scripture. His devotion to Yahweh was mixed with a bizarre penchant for syncretism that involved the worship of his wives' gods. It began with his marriage to Naamah, Pharaoh's daughter, who bore him Rehoboam. He also took wives from Moab, Edom, Sidon, and the Hittites. His multiple wives motivated him to worship Ashtoreth, Molech, and Chemosh, as well as Yahweh. He built places of worship and high places for his wives, violating every premise of godly kingship laid down in Deuteronomy 17:14–17. The first book of Kings 11:9 concludes that the Lord was angry with Solomon because "his heart turned away from the LORD, the God of Israel."

God's judgment of Solomon therefore began. He raised up Hadad of Edom (1 Kings 11:14–22) and Rezon of Damascus (11:23–25) to destabilize Solomon's kingdom. But unquestionably Solomon's greatest threat was Jeroboam, a superintendent of Solomon's work force (11:26–40). Ahijah the prophet promised Jeroboam that he would rule over the northern ten tribes of Israel after Solomon's death. Somehow, Solomon learned of this and sought to kill Jeroboam, who fled to the protection of Egypt. He remained there until Solomon's death.

If Solomon wrote the book of Ecclesiastes near the end of his life, as many believe, there is evidence that Solomon returned to the Lord. He declared that without God at the center of life, "all is vanity" (Ecclesiastes 1:2ff). All manifestations of self-indulgence fail. (See chapters 2–5.) At the end of his forty-year reign, he learned that the most important focus of life was to fear God and obey Him (12:13). Nothing else satisfies or brings purpose to life.

Solomon was restored to his relationship with God, but when Jeroboam led the rebellion against Rehoboam after Solomon's death, the nation suffered the consequences of his apostasy. The unity of Israel was destroyed and the divided monarchy followed.

Chapter 6

The Divided Kingdom: Israel

Because of Solomon's covenant infidelity, God declared that He would "tear the kingdom" from him and that it would be divided (1 Kings 11:11–13). In tearing his garment into twelve pieces and giving ten garment pieces to Jeroboam, Ahijah the prophet, one of Solomon's trusted overseers in Ephraim (1 Kings 11:26–40), symbolically reinforced God's judgment on Solomon. For that reason, Solomon sought to kill Jeroboam, who fled to Egypt for protection.

At the death of Solomon, the ten tribes of the north, led by Jeroboam, revolted against the tribes of Judah and Benjamin, splitting the united kingdom into two distinct kingdoms—Israel and Judah. The period of the divided kingdom (931 to 586 BC) provides the context for much of the Old Testament. Much of 1 and 2 Kings and 2 Chronicles documents the kings of the divided kingdom, and most of the prophets, major and minor, did their work during this period.

The Rebellion of Jeroboam and the Kingdom of Israel

Rehoboam was Solomon's son and, as his firstborn, was clearly his heir apparent (1 Kings 14:21). The tribal divisions and jealousies that had persisted during the united kingdom surfaced after Solomon's death in 931 BC.[131] The preference for Judah and Jerusalem that had characterized David and Solomon's rule constituted the backdrop for the discussion between Rehoboam and the elders of the various tribes at Shechem (see 1 Kings 12). Probably in deference to the northern tribes, Rehoboam traveled to Shechem for his coronation.

Jeroboam, recently returned from exile in Egypt, apparently was the leader and perhaps chief negotiator for the ten tribes. Because of the heavy taxation and conscription of labor that had characterized Solomon's reign, the northern tribes sought relief from Rehoboam as a condition of loyalty to him. He refused. In fact, he threatened even more oppressive measures for these tribes. The tribal leaders, apparently led by Jeroboam, consequently rejected the Davidic monarchy and seceded from the kingdom, forming their own nation, Israel, sometimes called Ephraim (1 Kings 12:16). The new kingdom consisted of the ten northern tribes: Reuben, Simeon, Dan, Naphtali, Gad, Asher, Ephraim, Manasseh, Issachar, and Zebulun.

Israel then declared Jeroboam to be their new king.

A capable leader, Jeroboam immediately consolidated his rule. He made Shechem his new capital, eventually moving it to Tirzah, six miles northeast of Shechem. Although God had promised Jeroboam an unending dynasty if he remained faithful, his early actions as king betrayed an apostasy that would characterize the entire northern kingdom.

Fearing that the people of Israel would still seek to worship in Jerusalem, Jeroboam established two cult centers, one at Bethel in the south, just across the border with Judah, and one at Dan in the north. Apparently, he chose two worship centers instead of one for pragmatic reasons. Bethel was associated with Jacob and the birthplace of "Israel" (see Genesis 28:10–22; 32), and Dan had been associated with the tribe of Dan, which had relocated to the north and established their own cultic center with their own priesthood (see Judges 18). Indeed, Moses' grandson, Jonathan, was the Danite priest associated with this cult center at Dan (see

Judges 18:30). Worshipers from the north, therefore, could easily go to either site.

But who or what would they worship? Jeroboam ordered that golden calves be built at each site, describing them as the gods who had delivered Israel from Egypt (I Kings 12:28). He also established a non-Levitical priesthood and alternative feast days as well. The worship of bulls as gods was associated with the exodus and Aaron's apostasy, but was also associated with the fertility gods of Canaan, especially Baal. As Waltke argues, "Jeroboam tries to establish a syncretistic religion that satisfies the worshipers of I AM by worshiping the name of I AM, and at the same time satisfies worshipers who crave fertility, not justice, by a symbolism that represents their lusts."[132]

After twenty-two years as king, Jeroboam died, but his apostasy established a pattern of 210 years of disastrous rule by ungodly kings from nine separate dynasties, each of whom ruled over a false, non-Davidic kingdom. In contrast, the southern kingdom of Judah had one dynasty—the Davidic—and a series of righteous kings. The standard for Israel was Jeroboam (see I Kings 13:34; 14:16; 15:26, 30; 16:2; 2 Kings 3:3; 10:29; 13:2), while the standard for Judah was King David.

The chart below[133] organizes the kings of Israel around the nine dynasties of the north and shows chronological connections with the kings of Judah. The northern kingdom of Israel went out of existence in 722 BC, when it was destroyed by the Assyrian Empire. The southern kingdom of Judah endured for several more generations, going out of existence in 586 BC, when it was destroyed by the Babylonian Empire. The political instability of the northern dynasties was illustrated by several assassinations of kings, marked on the chart by an asterisk (*).

A Covenant People

The Kings

Kings of Israel		Kings of Judah	
10 tribes *9 dynasties, all evil* *Cultic centers, Dan and Bethel* *Widespread syncretism*		*2 tribes* *1 Davidic dynasty, 8 good and 12 evil kings* *Temple in Jerusalem* *Relative conservatism*	
DYNASTY #1			
Jeroboam I	*931-910*	Rehoboam	*931-913*
*Nadab	*910-909*	Abijam	*913-911*
		Asa	*911-870*
DYNASTY #2			
Baasha	*909-886*		
*Elah	*886-885*		
DYNASTY #3			
Zimri	*885*		
DYNASTY #4 - THE OMRIDES			
Omri	*885-874*		
Ahab	*874-853*	Jehoshaphat	*873-848*
Ahaziah	*853-852*		
*Jehoram	*852-841*	Jehoram	*848-841*
DYNASTY #5 - JEHU			
Jehu	*841-814*	Ahaziah	*841*
		Athaliah	*841-835*
Jehoahaz	*814-798*	Joash	*835-796*
Jehoash (Joash)	*798-782*	Amaziah	*796-767*
Jeroboam II	*793-753*	Uzziah	*885-874*
*Zechariah	*753*		
DYNASTY #6			
*Shallum	*752*		
DYNASTY #7			
Menahem	*752-742*	Jotham	*750-731*
*Pekahiah	*742-740*		
DYNASTY #8			
*Pekah	*752-742*	Ahaz	*735-715*
DYNASTY #9			
Hoshea	*732-722*	Hezekiah	*729-686*
Fall of Israel in 722 BC		Manasseh	*696-642*
		Amon	*642-640*
		Josiah	*640-609*
		Jehoahaz	*609*
		Jehoiakim	*609-598*
		Jehoiachin	*598-597*
		Zedekiah	*597-586*
* Assassinated		*Fall of Judah in 586 BC*	

The idolatry and syncretistic apostasy of the north was comple-mented by a changing geopolitical situation in which the divided kingdom made both Israel and Judah more vulnerable. As the Mesopotamian valley saw the rise of Assyria and then Babylon to superpower status in the ancient world, a resurgent Egypt challenged this rising power and influence. The rivalry between Mesopotamia and Egypt often found Israel and Judah caught in the middle. The kings of Israel and Judah sought political and mil-itary alliances with these two great powers, ignoring the counsel of the prophets to trust in God, not military might.

The rest of this chapter is the story of the kingdom of Israel and its collapse. The next chapter focuses on the kingdom of Judah and its demise. Both kingdoms are stories of apostasy and disobedience. In Judah, a series of good kings, who strove to reform the kingdom and bring the people back to God, caused God to postpone His discipline for several generations.

The Differences between Israel and Judah

To understand the development of each kingdom during this period, the economic and geographical differences between Israel and Judah are significant. The northern kingdom of Israel was far wealthier than the southern kingdom of Judah. Part of this was due to its size. Israel included all of Galilee north to Dan, Samaria, and much of the Transjordan, including Gilead and northern portions of Moab. In addition, important parts of the two international highways (the King's Highway and the Coastal Highway) cut through Israel, providing revenue and access to the wealth of the ancient world.

Brisco summarizes the important connection with Phoenician cities to the north: "[These cities] provided powerful commercial allies to boost the economy. Israel's geographical openness to other cultures fostered cosmopolitanism in her cities and villages, not only in material culture and social customs, but even in religion."[134] For example, Baalism from Phoenicia deepened during the reign of

King Ahab. Although Shechem and later Tirzah were capitals of Israel, it was Samaria, built by King Omri, that became the center of Israel's political culture.

In contrast, Judah was poorer and far more isolated than Israel. Its only port was Ezion-geber, and this was only an advantage when Judah was strong militarily. No international highways crossed Judah, and the more rugged territory of Judah enhanced its isolation.

Because of the temple, Jerusalem was unquestionably the heart of Judah. This was the City of David and was both the political and religious center of the kingdom.

Because it was small and isolated, Judah was continually attacked, especially by Edom from the south. However, Judah's great advantage was its relative political stability. From 931 to 586 BC, there was but one dynasty—David's. As Brisco observes, "Judah possessed an innate stability based on her tribal traditions and loyalties, which permitted her to survive more than 130 years longer than her powerful northern rival."[135]

Geopolitical Changes

Changes in Egypt were most threatening during the period of the divided kingdom. Partially due to the strength of David and Solomon, as well as internal weaknesses, Egypt had played no threatening role during the united kingdom. But in 918 BC, Pharaoh Shishak I invaded Judah under Rehoboam and then plundered Israel under Jeroboam. (See 1 Kings 14.) Although Shishak withdrew his forces, over the next 250 years, Egypt played an increasingly important role in both Israel and Judah.

As David and Solomon had brought Moab, Ammon, and Edom into the kingdom as vassal states, after Jeroboam's revolt, Israel lost control of all three. Depending on the relative strength of Judah's kings, even Judah was exposed to threats from Moab and especially Edom, which constantly ravaged Judah. (See the book of Obadiah.)

The Aramean states to Israel's north had special arrangements with King Solomon, but these arrangements lapsed during the divided kingdom. The Arameans spoke a West Semitic dialect rather similar to Hebrew. By 1000 BC, the Arameans formed tribal kingdoms in northern Syria and northern Mesopotamia.

The Old Testament mentions several of these Aramean tribal kingdoms—Aram-Zobah, Geshur, Beth-rehob—but most important was Aram-Damascus. Damascus was the city where the King's Highway and the Coastal Highway intersected. For that reason, Aram-Damascus and Israel were rivals, each seeking special control over these highways.

Between 850 and 800 BC, Aram-Damascus was the most powerful state in the region, constantly threatening Israel. Aramean kings Ben-hadad I and Ben-hadad II played important roles during the Omri dynasty of Israel. When the Assyrian Empire began to move into the region in 750 BC, Aram-Damascus receded as a regional power.[136]

Between 1200 and 900 BC, no major superpower was active in the eastern Mediterranean. Through alliances and sometimes through war, the Aramean states, the Phoenicians, and Israel dominated the region during this period, and David and Solomon's kingdoms thrived as a result. However, by 900 BC, things began to change. The empire of Assyria from the Mesopotamian valley to the east sought increasing influence in the Levant region. The Aramean kingdoms bore the brunt of these initial attacks, but eventually Israel was threatened as well. First under Ashurnasirpal II (883–859 BC) and his son Shalmeneser III (859–824 BC) and then under Tiglath Pileser III (745–727 BC), Assyria became the dominant power in the eastern Mediterranean.[137] This increasing dominance had a significant impact on Israel and to some extent Judah. Indeed, the Assyrian Empire would destroy Israel in 722 BC.

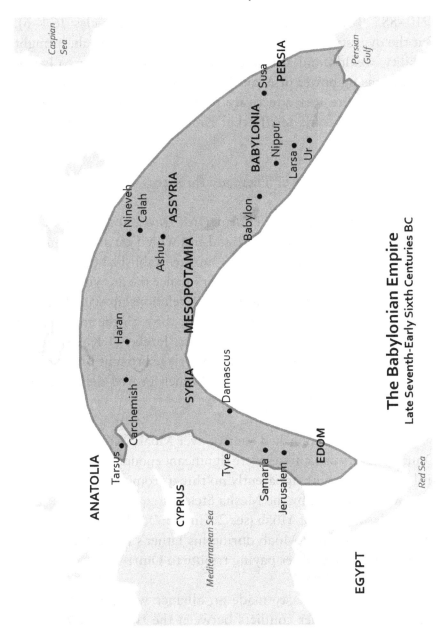

The Babylonian Empire
Late Seventh-Early Sixth Centuries BC

The Omri Dynasty of Israel, 885–841 BC

After Jeroboam's death, Israel experienced a period of relatively weak, yet apostate rulers—Nadab, Baasha, Elah, and Zimri

(910–885 BC; see 1 Kings 15:25–16:22; 2 Chronicles 16:1–6). But the dynasty of Omri, especially under his son Ahab, brought stability, wealth, and a degree of international prestige to Israel. The increasing power of Aram-Damascus and the growing threat of Assyria were met effectively by Omri. In fact, extrabiblical sources from Assyria testify that Israel was known as the "land of Omri."[138]

Why was he so effective? There are three reasons.

First, Omri reengaged the Phoenicians. David and Solomon had had strong trading and commercial ties with Tyre and Sidon, key Phoenician cities north of Israel. Omri reestablished those ties for economic reasons but also to counterbalance the growing threat of Aram-Damascus. Omri solidified this relationship with Ethbaal, king of Tyre and Sidon (887–856 BC), through the marriage of his son Ahab to the Ethbaal's daughter, Jezebel (1 Kings 16:31). Although politically expedient, the marriage brought Baalism into Israel as a state-sponsored religion, which proved disastrous for Israel and later for Judah.

Second, Omri reestablished control over Moab. We can infer that Omri's military capabilities were significant enough to exercise control over Moab, with apparently no threat from Aram-Damascus. This was confirmed by the Mesha Stele, discovered in 1898, written by Mesha, king of Moab (see 2 Kings 3:4), which declared that Omri had conquered Moab during his father's reign. But, Mesha boasts, he was no longer paying tribute to Omri.[139]

Third, the Omri dynasty made an alliance with Judah. For numerous years, border conflicts between the two kingdoms were routine. Ahab arranged a marriage between his daughter Athaliah and Jehoram, Jehoshaphat's son, the king of Judah. This alliance had military and commercial dimensions, for Judah's use of the port of Ezion-geber benefited both Judah and Israel. Obviously, in reestablishing the importance of this port, the goal of both kingdoms was to restore the sources of Solomon's wealth—trade with Arabia, eastern Africa, even India. For Jehoshaphat, king of Judah, however, an unintended result of this alliance was that Athaliah brought Baalism into the court of Jerusalem, which would later be disastrous for Judah.[140]

King Omri relocated Israel's capital from Tirzah to Samaria. About 880 BC,[141] Omri bought Samaria, a commanding hill 1,400 feet above sea level and six miles northwest of Shechem, from Shemer (I Kings 16:23–24). There, Omri built the new capital, Samaria, into an almost invincible fortress city. He and his son Ahab also built the royal acropolis, with architecture that exhibited the influence of Phoenicia. Brisco summarizes the splendor of this royal acropolis: "The stonecutting and craftsmanship at Samaria were exceptional. Walls were set in rock-cut trenches, with each stone dressed at the site to ensure a precise fit ... A hoard of ivories recovered from the citadel ... display Phoenician, Syrian and Egyptian motifs and demonstrate both the cosmopolitan society and luxury of the royal court."[142] (See Amos 3:15; 6:4.)

Although Omri was obviously an effective ruler economically and militarily, the Bible dismisses him with a mere eight verses (1 Kings 16:21–28). His apostasy in bringing Baalism into the kingdom was no doubt the reason.

***

Excursus: The Prophetic Roles of Elijah and Elisha

Despite the apostasy of the Omri dynasty, Yahweh's voice was not silent. The powerful and mysterious voices of Elijah and his successor Elisha resounded through Israel. Elijah the Tishbite came from Gilead (1 Kings 17:1) and wore a garment of sheep or goat-skin (2 Kings 1:8). The tone of 1 Kings 17 is that suddenly Elijah appeared to King Ahab and declared that drought would plague Israel because, since Ahab and the nation were following the Baals, they had violated covenant loyalty to Yahweh. The ravens fed Elijah (1 Kings 17:2–7), and Elijah, the widow of Zarephath, and her son were miraculously sustained by flour and oil (17:8–16). The message was clear: life comes from Yahweh, not Baal. Elijah was thereby confirmed as Yahweh's prophet—his words were Yahweh's words.

Three years later, Elijah challenged Ahab and the nation on Mt. Carmel, the site of a significant Baal shrine (I Kings 18). There Elijah proved Yahweh's sovereignty and supremacy, humiliating Jezebel and the Baal cult. The utter impotence of Baal was now obvious to Ahab, to Jezebel, and most importantly, to the nation. John Bright captures the essence of Elijah's prophetic role: "[He] regarded Ahab and Jezebel as the ultimate anathema. His was the God of Sinai, who brooked no rival and would exact blood vengeance for crimes against covenant law such as Ahab had committed. Elijah therefore declared Holy War on the pagan state and its pagan god."[143]

After the victory on Mt. Carmel in 857 BC, out of both fear and exhaustion, Elijah fled to Mt. Horeb (Mt. Sinai), where he learned that the "God of Mt. Carmel was the God of Mt. Horeb."[144] At the same point where God had spoken to Moses, where He had outlined the Mosaic covenant, and where He had manifested Himself to His people, He spoke to Elijah in a whisper. Hazael of Syria would judge Israel because of its worship of Baal; Jehu would root out Baal worship; and Elisha would continue the prophetic resistance to the Baal cult. Baal worship would not triumph.

As Schreiner observes, "Elijah is virtually a new Moses in the story, reaffirming Israel's covenant with Yahweh at Sinai."[145] So powerful was Elijah in the history of redemption that he foreshadowed the ministry of John the Baptist in the New Testament. (See Malachi 4:5–6; Luke 1:17; Matthew 11:14; Mark 9:13.) He appeared with Moses attending to Jesus on the Mount of Transfiguration (Matthew 17:3–13).

Anointed by Elijah in 855 BC, Elisha continued the prophetic work of his master, receiving, as he requested, a "'double portion' of Elijah's spirit" (2 Kings 2:9). Elisha was a part of a "school" of prophets apparently centered in Bethel and Jericho, standing in direct opposition to the corrupt Omri monarchy. These prophets shared living quarters in some form of monastic community (2 Kings 6:1–2). But the miracles of Elisha (2 Kings 4–8) were most important. They not only confirmed the inherent power of the prophetic word, they also confirmed that "life and sustenance come from the Lord, not Baal, and herald the coming of a new creation, a new heaven and new earth, where there is life, fullness and joy."[146] In many ways, Elisha's miracles anticipated the miracles of Jesus.

***

Omri's son Ahab effectively ruled Israel (874–853 BC), building on his father's commercial and military success. Ahab also successfully protected Israel from the Aramean threat, twice defeating Ben-Hadad II's forces (1 Kings 20:1–34). Shrewdly, Ahab also joined with Ben-Hadad II in halting the advance of the Assyrian army under Shalmaneser III at Qarqar on the Orontes River (853 BC), one of the more significant battles of the ancient world. (Ahab contributed two thousand chariots and ten thousand soldiers). Finally, Ahab continued his father's peaceful alliance with Judah under Jehoshaphat.[147]

But the Bible portrays Ahab as one of the worst of all kings (1 Kings 16:30). His wife Jezebel of Tyre brought the worship of Baal Merqart and Asherah into Israel, with the goal of making Baal worship the state religion of Israel. She therefore slaughtered the prophets of Yahweh and oversaw the building of a temple to Baal Merqart in Samaria (1 Kings 16:32). The result was that both the royal court and the ruling class were thoroughly paganized, driving all supporters of Yahweh underground.

The demise of Ahab and Jezebel was wrapped around events associated with Ahab's wars with the Aramean kingdom and with King Jehu. For reasons that are not clear, Ben-Hadad II laid siege to Samaria (1 Kings 20:1–43). Seemingly hopeless, Ahab turned to God, who graciously intervened and miraculously routed Ben-Hadad's forces (1 Kings 20:13–21). A second victorious battle with Ben-Hadad at Aphek, east of the Sea of Galilee, equally demonstrated Yahweh's sovereign power to both Ahab and the Arameans.

Finally, in 853 BC, despite the favorable treaty with Ben-Hadad II after his defeat at Aphek, Ahab sought (in an alliance with

Jehoshaphat of Judah) to recover Ramoth-Gilead, a strategic city and district capital under Solomon. In spite his efforts to disguise himself, Ahab was killed during the battle. His body was returned to Samaria, where dogs licked up his blood, as Elijah had predicted. (See 1 Kings 21:19; 22:38.) His sons Ahaziah (853–852) and later Joram (Jehoram; 852–841) succeeded him as kings of Israel.

In 841 BC, to fulfill God's prophecy to Elijah (1 Kings 19:16), Elisha sent an unnamed prophet to Ramoth-Gilead to anoint Jehu, one of Joram's commanders. Once he was anointed and acclaimed by his army as king, Jehu raced at high speed on his chariot to Jezreel, an administrative center of Ahab's kingdom, close to the vineyard Ahab seized from Naboth (1 Kings 21). There he killed King Joram, and his warriors mortally wounded Ahaziah, king of Judah, who eventually died at Megiddo.

Jehu then entered the city of Jezreel, had Jezebel thrown from her window, killed the seventy sons of Ahab, and slaughtered numerous worshipers of Baal. (See 2 Kings 9:30–10:31.) Jehu then traveled to Samaria, where he slaughtered the forty-two relatives of Judah's king, Ahaziah, and, with duplicity, lured the prophets and priests of Baal into the temple in Samaria. His soldiers massacred them all and razed the temple to the ground, turning it into a public latrine. The two principal cities of Israel were now his. With almost unimaginable brutality, Jehu brought to an end both the house of Omri and state-sponsored Baal worship in Israel. (See 2 Kings 10:18–28).

The Dynasty Of Jehu, 841–753 BC

Jehu, the son of Judah's king, Jehoshaphat, ruled from 841 to 814 BC, but his rule was a veritable disaster for Israel. Although he purged the land of Baalism and destroyed the Omri dynasty, he perpetuated apostate worship at Dan and Bethel, previously established by Jeroboam, as 2 Kings 10:28 and 13:6 make clear. Further, his brutal seizure of power placed the entire Davidic line in jeopardy. He killed Judah's king, Ahaziah. To eliminate all potential rivals and thereby retain her power as the queen mother, Athaliah, Ahaziah's mother and Ahab's daughter, then instituted a thoroughgoing purge of the Judean royal family. But, in God's sovereignty, the infant son of Ahaziah, Joash, was protected from Athaliah's purge.

Jehu's reign weakened the political and military stability of Israel. As a result of Jehu's purge, the various alliances that had provided the relative stability of the Omri dynasty were destroyed. His slaughter of Jezebel and the prophets and priests of Baal ended all favorable relationships with the Phoenicians. Further, the murder of King Ahaziah and much his family ended the alliance with Judah. Thus, the structure of Israel's economic prosperity and the foundation of her military alliances were gone.[148] Israel was more vulnerable than ever, and both Damascus and Assyria exploited that vulnerability.

In 1 Kings 19:15–17, God commanded Elijah to anoint Hazael king of Arameans. That command was fulfilled by Elijah's successor, Elisha, who traveled to Damascus to anoint Hazael king immediately before he anointed Jehu king of Israel. (See 2 Kings 8:7–15, 28.) Hazael had murdered King Ben-Hadad II and become king sometime between 845 and 841 BC. Elisha wept over this anointing, presumably because he understood that Hazael would not be good for Israel.

In fact, Hazael seized virtually the entire Transjordan area south to the Moabite frontier on the Arnon River. So thorough was Hazael's control over Israel that Jehu's son, Jehoahaz, was permitted by Hazael only a bodyguard of ten chariots and fifty horsemen, plus a police force of ten thousand (2 Kings 13:7). Hazael moved into the coastal plain of Philistia, and only when Jehoash, king of Judah, paid him an enormous tribute was he deterred from invading Judah. As Bright correctly argues, "With all her territory in Transjordan, in Esdraelon, and along the sea—and presumably also in Galilee—in Aramean control, [Israel] had been reduced to the status of a dependency on Damascus."[149]

Under Jehu, Israel also experienced humiliation and significant financial loss to Assyria. Although the coalition of Israel and Aram-Damascus had stopped Assyrian emperor Shalmaneser III at Qarqar in 853 BC, Shalmaneser invaded the region again in 841 BC, devastating but not completely conquering Damascus, and then moving along the Phoenician coast and into Israel. During the first year of his reign, Jehu was willing to pay an enormous tribute to Shalmaneser as the price to halt a major invasion of Israel. Indeed, in the British Museum is the famous Black Obelisk, which depicts King Jehu in bas-relief bowing and paying his tribute to Shalmaneser III.[150] Shalmaneser III did not remain in the Levant for long. He withdrew his armies, thereby permitting King Hazael of Damascus the leeway to wreak his havoc on Israel.

After the rather ineffectual rule of Jehu's son, Jehoahaz (814–798 BC; 2 Kings 13:1–9), his son, Jehoash (Joash), became king (798–782). Under Jehoash, Israel began to experience resurgence. He sought the counsel of the aging Elisha in 796 BC (2 Kings 13:14–19). Elisha encouraged him to attack the Arameans, against whom Jehoash achieved three decisive victories. He thus recovered the "cities of Israel" lost to the Arameans (2 Kings 13:25). This apparently means the cities west of the Jordan River, but could mean the Transjordan area as well.[151] Assyria's relentless pressure on Damascus weakened the Arameans.

Furthermore, Jehoash successfully defeated Judah at the battle of Beth Shemesh in 783 or 782 BC, under King Amaziah, who had foolishly attacked Israel.[152] Jehoash took Amaziah prisoner and moved on Jerusalem, destroying some of its wall and looting it before he returned to Samaria.

Jehoash was succeeded by his son Jeroboam II (793–753 BC), who had served as coregent with his father Jehoash for over ten years. Under Jeroboam II, Israel experienced significant prosperity, and Jeroboam's campaigns restored the borders to those of Solomon's time (see 2 Kings 14:25–28), including Damascus, which had no independent ruler but was incorporated directly into Jeroboam's sovereign rule.[153] In restoring these boundaries, Israel was now the most important nation in the eastern Mediterranean.

How did Jeroboam II achieve this surprising feat? It was not because he was righteous, for he did evil in the eyes of the Lord (2 Kings 14:23). Rather, God's mercy explains Jeroboam II. In fact, Jonah the prophet declared that, in blessing Jeroboam II, Yahweh had shown mercy on His people and had recalled His pledge not to destroy them. (See 2 Kings 14:25–27.)

The weakness of Assyria at this time was also a dimension of God's mercy. In a period of decline and because of a series of weak rulers from 783 to 746 BC, Assyria was wracked by internal strife and significant military defeats at the hands of the Urartu peoples. It posed no threat to Jeroboam II.

In addition, the capable Uzziah, who ruled Judah during Jeroboam II's reign, established a peaceful alliance with Israel and undertook offensive operations against Edom and the Arabian tribes. With control of the two major international highways—the Coastal Highway and the King's Highway—now established, the rebuilding of the port at Ezion-geber (2 Kings 14:22), and more than likely a reestablishment of a treaty with the Phoenicians, prosperity and economic renewal followed for both kingdoms.[154]

The Eighth-Century Prophets and the State of Israel

The prosperity and military stability of Israel was a facade; beneath the surface was a foul, decaying society. As they called kings and the people to covenant obedience, the eighth-century prophets exposed the corruption and rot of Israel.

By the eighth century, the role of the prophet had changed. From 1000 to about 750 BC, there had been a series of nonwriting prophets (e.g., Samuel, Elijah, and Elisha, as well as numerous

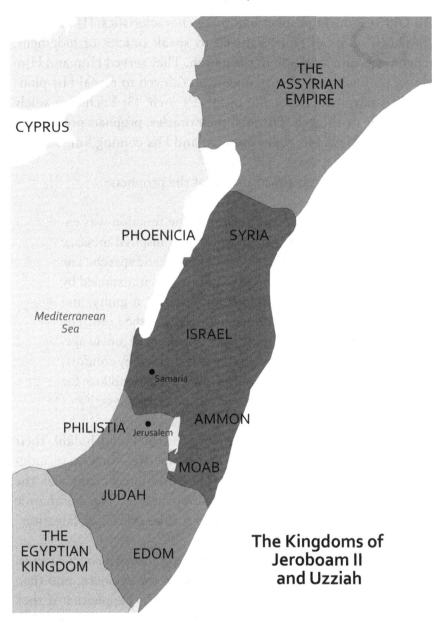

The Kingdoms of Jeroboam II and Uzziah

unnamed ones). But by about 750 BC, the writing prophets came on the prophetic scene. They were not in the center of the religion or politics of their day; rather, they stood outside the circles of influence as counselors.

An Old Testament prophet had three characteristics: (1) Each was conscious of a call from Yahweh to speak oracles of judgment, repentance, and salvation to the nation. They served Him and Him alone. (2) Each was an instrument of Yahweh to reveal His plans and His purposes, never the prophet's own. (3) Each was solely responsible to Yahweh. Through their oracles, prophets proclaimed God's moral law, His righteousness, and His coming kingdom.[155]

Van Gemeren captures the mission of the prophets:

> By the eighth century the prophetic function was enlarged to that of a *preacher*, whose inspired message was cast into distinct forms of prophetic speech. The prophet was a *covenant prosecutor*, commissioned by the Lord to indict [the nation], declare it guilty, and forewarn it of the coming judgments of the Lord. The prophet was also a *visionary*, speaking of a new age. This message of another day was marked by comfort, hope, and a call for an individual response to love for the Lord, with whom is mercy and forgiveness.[156]

As the prophets declared God's Word to Israel (and Judah), their oracles were both proclamatory and predictive—oracles of judgment, repentance, and salvation. The Mosaic covenant was the basis for the oracles of judgment and repentance. The Abrahamic and Davidic covenants were the basis for the oracles of salvation.

Typically, the judgment oracles had the structure of a court case: an address, an accusation, the presentation of the evidence, and then the judicial sentence. God had declared to His people that if they walked with Him in obedience to the Torah, they would experience blessing. If they did not, they would experience His discipline. (See Deuteronomy 28.) That discipline could involve exile from the land, which is the prophetic explanation for the exile by Assyria after 722 BC and the exile to Babylonia after 586 BC. In short, God always disciplined His people on the basis of the Mosaic covenant.

The oracles of salvation were always based on the Abrahamic and Davidic covenants. When the prophet declared an oracle of judgment, including exile, there was always the promise of restoration—the promise of return to the land, of abundant blessing in the land, and of a king who would rule forever. They were God's people, and He would never give them up. He would fulfill His unconditional promises made to Abraham (land, seed and blessing) and to David (an eternal dynasty, throne, and kingdom.)[157]

As a part of the predictive element of their oracles, the Old Testament prophets often mixed near fulfillment of their promises (e.g., return from exile) with distant fulfillment of God's promises that applied to the first advent and the second advent of Christ. The New Testament Gospels and Epistles, therefore, enable us to have a deeper understanding of the prophetic promises that apply to Christ's second coming.

The Structure of Israel's Theocracy Under the Monarchy

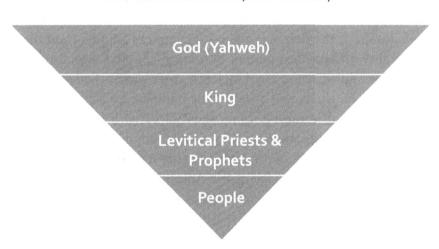

Three prophets of the eighth century are relevant for our study.

Jonah. The second book of Kings 14:25 indicates that Jonah served as a prophet during Jeroboam's reign. His familiar story focuses on Nineveh, the key Assyrian city. The weakness of Assyria, described above, best fits this period. Assyria was in decline, there was widespread suffering, and there was a total eclipse of the sun on 15 June 763 BC; Assyria was therefore ripe for spiritual awakening. Jonah's prophetic ministry in Nineveh corresponded with the reign of Assur-dan III (772–755 BC),[158] when revolt, plague and famine characterized Assyria. As Jonah preached his message of repentance, the people and the ruler of Nineveh repented, and God spared them. In citing Jonah's time in the great fish as an analogy of his three days in the grave (Matthew 12:40) and of Nineveh as a paradigm for repentance (Luke 11:32), Jesus attested to the historicity of Jonah.

Amos. Amos, a herdsman of Tekoa, was an independent prophet in the court of Jeroboam II. His prophetic oracles (see Amos 1–2) applied to specific and identifiable historic events in the kingdoms of Damascus, Philistia, Tyre, Edom, Ammon, and Moab. But Judah and especially Israel were the primary focus of his oracles . His message of covenant curses for Israel was a devastating attack on the social evils of the kingdom, especially the oppression and exploitation of the rich over the poor (chapters 5 and 7) and their immorality and baseless pursuit of luxury (chapters 4 and 6). The prosperity and wealth created by Jeroboam's success had produced corruption, injustice, and cruelty. The pampered wealthy sleeping on their beds of luxury, gorging themselves with luscious foods and wine, were all candidates for God's judgment, His "day of the Lord" (Amos 5:18, with details in chapters 6–9). Yet in Amos 9:11–15, using the language of the Abrahamic and Davidic covenants, God promised future restoration and blessing to His people.

Hosea. Hosea of Israel also prophesied during Jeroboam II's reign (Hosea 1:1). Using his own marriage and the unfaithfulness of his wife Gomer as a paradigm, Hosea charged Israel with covenant infidelity against Yahweh, who loved them. Israel was engaged in "spiritual adultery," superficially worshiping Yahweh, yet passionately pursuing the Baal cult, with all the moral failure and decadence that followed. Both Israel and Judah were, in effect, no longer His people (1:9) and thus under the covenant curses. Because they were unrepentant, He would judge them. But He envisioned a day when He would restore them to their land and once again "betroth" Israel to Himself (14:1–7).

As John Bright asserts, "The state of Israel, externally strong, prosperous, and confident of the future, was inwardly rotten and sick past curing."[159] That was the message of the prophets. Israel had in effect begun to die—and the remaining kings would see Israel finished off as a nation.

The End of Israel, 753–722 BC

Zechariah, Jeroboam II's son, came to the throne in 753 BC but was assassinated by his successor, Shallum, the founder of the sixth dynasty of Israel, who was killed within a month (2 Kings 15:8–15), thereby plunging Israel into a time of anarchy and horrific atrocity (7:16). Menahem replaced him, establishing Israel's seventh dynasty, and would rule from 752–742 BC.

During Menahem's reign, Assyria reasserted its role in the eastern Mediterranean. Tiglath- Pileser III (called "Pul" in Scripture), who ruled Assyria from 745 to 727 BC, consolidated his rule by neutralizing the threat of the Urartu people. He established control of southern Mesopotamia and restored order in the area of Babylonia. His primary goal, however, was to reestablish a formidable presence in the Levant. In 743 BC, he moved into Syria, and by 738 BC virtually all of the eastern Mediterranean was under Assyrian control.

Unlike previous Assyrian rulers, Tiglath-Pileser forced the lands he conquered to become Assyrian provinces. He deported native rulers and people who might threaten revolt—a policy later Assyrian leaders emulated. His 743 BC campaign reached Israel, and he forced Menahem to pay a sizable tribute, which Menahem raised by a head tax on the wealthy of Israel. Israel was now a vassal state of Assyria.[160] (See 2 Kings 15:19–20.)

Menahem was succeeded by his son, Pekahiah, who ruled a mere two years (742–740 BC). One of his military commanders, Pekah, in conjunction with an anti-Assyrian group from Gilead, assassinated him in the Samarian palace. Pekah was declared the king, and he immediately broke the treaty Menahem had made with Assyria (2 Kings 15:23–25). The anti-Assyrian sentiment from Gilead was no doubt due to the heavy taxation Menahem had instituted to pay the Assyrian tribute money. Pekah joined with Rezin, king of Damascus, and the Philistines in a coalition to resist Assyrian domination.

Pekah and Rezin of Damascus understandably sought to include Judah in this coalition against Assyria. But Judah's kings, Jotham and his son Ahaz, refused to join the coalition. Thus, Pekah and Rezin invaded Judah, threatening Jerusalem. In addition, the Philistines, apparently joined by the Edomites, raided the Negeb and the Shepelah, even gaining control of Elath (Ezion-geber, the port city).

Ahaz, terrified by all of this and unwilling to trust in Yahweh's care, appealed to Tiglath-Pileser III of Assyria for aid (2 Kings 16:5–9). He willingly and ruthlessly complied with this request, invading the entire region with a formidable army between 734 and 732 BC. In 734 BC, he captured key Philistine cities, grabbing all territory to the boundary of Egypt, thereby preventing any possible coalition support from Egypt. He then struck Israel again, conquering Galilee and the Transjordan, destroying Megiddo and Hazor (key military cities), and deporting significant portions of Israel's population.

Tiglath-Pileser divided the territory of Israel into three provinces: Gilead, Megiddo (Galilee), and Dor (the coastal plain). In 732 BC, King Pekah was murdered by Hoshea, who surrendered and agreed to pay tribute to Assyria. Israel was again a vassal state of Assyria and Hoshea a puppet king of the ninth and final dynasty of Israel.

Finally, Tiglath-Pileser conquered Damascus, killed King Rezin, and deported many of its citizens. Assyrian domination of the entire eastern Mediterranean was now complete.[161]

Tiglath-Pileser had incorporated much of the northern kingdom into his empire, basically leaving Hoshea with only the land grants of Ephraim and West Manasseh to rule. When Tiglath-Pileser III was succeeded by his son Shalmeneser V (727–722 BC), Hoshea perceived a weakness and sought a way out of Assyrian dominance. He made an alliance with weak, divided Egypt (2 Kings 17:4) and stopped tribute payments to Assyria. Hence, in 724 BC, Shalmeneser marched on Israel (2 Kings 17:2–6). Hoshea attempted to placate Assyria by belatedly and personally giving his tribute to Shalmaneser, who refused and instead took Hoshea captive. Shalmeneser then laid siege to the capital city, Samaria, which lasted from 724–722 BC.

In the fall of 722 BC, Samaria fell. (Although Sargon II, Shalmaneser V's successor, claimed to have conquered Samaria, the account in 2 Kings 17 is correct in assigning that achievement to Shalmeneser.) With the fall of Samaria, the kingdom of Israel ceased to exist. A deportation of thousands of Israel's citizens (Assyrian records claim 27,290) to Upper Mesopotamia and Media followed.[162] The second book of Kings 17:7 declares that the fall of Samaria and the deportation occurred because Israel had sinned against their God. Israel's covenant loyalty was compromised by their worship of other gods, despite frequent warnings from the prophets (2 Kings 17:15–17).

Sargon II (721–705 BC) had organized the deportation of Israelites, but he also organized the resettlement of non-Jewish people into Samaria. (See 2 Kings 17:24–41.) The biblical text identifies these people as coming from the region of Mesopotamia around Babylon and from place names associated with the region of Syria.[163] Obviously, these new settlers represented people of different languages and religious practices, and greater cultural diversity. Since they did not worship Yahweh, He sent judgment upon them in the form of lions (v. 26). Sargon II therefore sent Israeli priests from Babylon to teach the new settlers about Yahweh (vv. 27–28). The result was a religious system that mixed worship of Yahweh with the worship of many other Ancient Near Eastern gods (vv. 29–34).

As the area of Samaria continued to develop, this chaotic situation resulted in Israelites intermarrying with these settlers, which was the origin of the Samaritans, who would play an important part in the New Testament era.

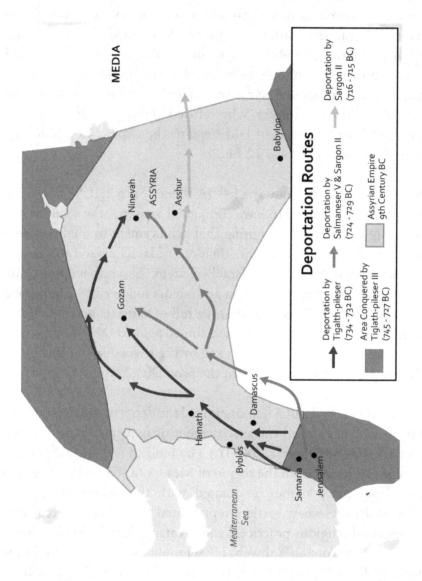

The southern kingdom of Judah survived the Assyrian onslaught—and would endure for nearly another 140 years. The story of Judah is the subject of the next chapter.

Chapter 7

The Divided Kingdom: Judah

When the second generation of Israel was about to enter the Promised Land, Moses wrote the book of Deuteronomy. It reviewed and summarized the covenant loyalty and devotion expected of God's people. Deuteronomy also reviewed kingship and what expectations God had for the coming king of Israel (17:14–20). The king was not to trust in the normal things that brought kings power, prestige, and wealth: horses from Egypt, many wives, and vast amounts of gold and silver. Instead, the king was to devote himself to Yahweh, immerse himself in His Law, fear the Lord, and keep His commandments.

In short, the king was to rule as a shepherd, guiding, modeling, and forcefully keeping Israel's focus on the one true God.

In a very real sense, only one king came close to meeting these covenant stipulations—David. He is the key to understanding the kingdom of Judah. Willem Van Gemern summarizes what he calls the "Davidic ideal":

> The Davidic ideal clearly takes on special significance for Judah because its kings were in David's family line. He was not just the pattern for Judean kings; he was their *father*. David's style of kingship was the goal that the kings ought to attain; he was the standard to which they are compared. The king's heart was to be loyal to Yahweh … The Davidic ideal pertained to covenantal

loyalty and to the benefits extended to God's people. The extent to which they fulfilled or failed that purpose determined whether a king was good or evil.[164]

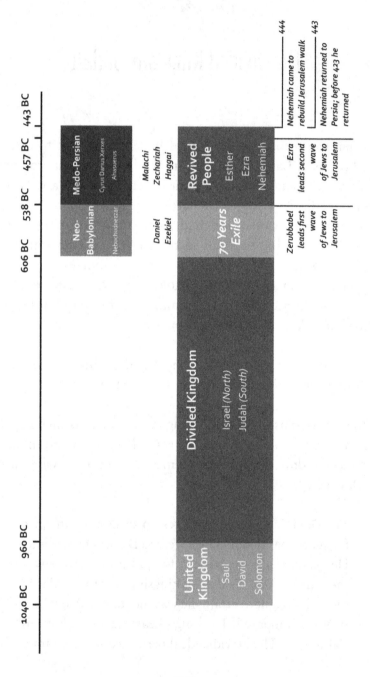

Judah's king was therefore to have a zeal for Jerusalem (2 Chronicles 26:9–15); honor the Davidic covenant (2 Chronicles 19:8–10); ensure the spiritual welfare of his people through the teaching of God's Law (2 Chronicles 13:10–12; 19:10); and be receptive to God's Word through the prophets (2 Chronicles 12:5–8).[165] A few reform kings of Judah (e.g., Hezekiah, Josiah) came close to the Davidic ideal, but, as Scripture argues so centrally, only Jesus Christ fulfills and upholds perfectly that ideal.

Rehoboam 931–913 BC

Solomon's heir apparent, Rehoboam, became king at Solomon's death and vowed to continue his father's taxation and labor conscription polices, intensifying both. When the northern tribes sought concessions from him on these matters as a condition for supporting him, he declined. Led by Jeroboam, the northern tribes seceded from the kingdom of David and formed their own kingdom—Israel.

Scripture gives no indication that Rehoboam attempted to force the ten tribes back into a union under the Davidic monarchy. His kingdom was now small and military support was questionable. But to prevent Benjamin from joining the revolt, he occupied Benjamin's territory, thereby solidifying Benjamin and Judah as the Kingdom of Judah. He also built a string of fortresses around his kingdom, placing his sons as commanders of fifteen fortified cities (2 Chronicles 11:5–23). Because of their southern and western locations, such fortifications were apparently defenses against Egypt and the Philistines.

Although shrewd in terms of defense, Rehoboam was as apostate as Jeroboam. Indeed, 1 Kings 14:23–24 details that he returned Judah to Canaanite practices—high places, idolatrous images, Asherim poles, and the participation of male prostitutes as a part of the worship ritual. As with his father, Solomon, Rehoboam promoted a lethal syncretism that mixed worship of Yahweh with Canaanite abominations. The second book of Chronicles 12:2 argues that Yahweh therefore sent Egypt to the land as a form of discipline.

In 918 BC, Shishak (945–924 BC), founder of the Twenty-First Dynasty in Egypt, invaded Judah with ruthless force. His armies devastated the entire area of Judah and pressed deep into Israel as well. Everywhere his troops went, they looted, including rich treasures from the temple. Some scholars suggest Rehoboam allowed this plunder to keep Shishak from destroying Jerusalem.

For reasons that were probably related more to the politics of Egypt, Shishak did not stay in the land; he withdrew. (The Bubastite Portal of the main temple of Amon at Karnak in Egypt details the conquests of Shishak, giving specific validation to the biblical account in 1 Kings 14:25–28.[166]) The second book of Chronicles 12:12 hints that, because of Shishak's invasion, Rehoboam was humbled and God's wrath turned away from Rehoboam—evidence of God's grace.

The remaining years of Rehoboam's rule were apparently given to a series of border wars with Jeroboam. (See 1 Kings 14:30; 2 Chronicles 12;15.) There is no evidence that these were decisive or resulted in any significant territorial gain or loss for either side.

Abijam and Asa 913–870 BC

Evidence of God's grace and of the central importance of the Davidic covenant in Judah accompanies the account of Abijam's short reign (913–911 BC). Despite Abijam's failure to walk with God, Yahweh declared that because of David, he would give Abijam a "lamp in Jerusalem," alluding to the continuation of David's dynastic line through Abijam (1 Kings 11:34–39; 15:4–5). Grace was also evident in the failure of every attempt by Jeroboam of Israel to defeat him. In fact, in 2 Chronicles 13:4–21, Abijam argued that because Judah represented the true Davidic line (vv. 5, 8), had the only valid priesthood (vv. 10–11), and evidenced vibrant faith in the Lord (vv. 13, 18), the northern tribes should return to Judah. Jeroboam mocked this appeal, but God fought for Abijam and Judah in the battle of Zemaraim, giving Judah control of Bethel as a result (2 Chronicles 13:20).

Abijam's son Asa, who ruled for forty-two years (911–870 BC),[167] was the first of eight good kings in Judah. Asa's reign turned back the idolatry and apostasy in much of Judah (1 Kings 15:9–15; 2 Chronicles 15:16). He brought an end to the use of male prostitutes in the worship rituals. He deposed the queen mother Maacah (actually his grandmother) because of her idolatry. After a decisive victory against Egypt, Asa called an assembly of the people of Judah and several tribes from the northern kingdom to renew the covenant with the Lord (see 2 Chronicles 15:8–15), offering sacrifices and praise to Yahweh.

Trouble from Egypt continued during Asa's reign. In 898 BC, Zerah the Ethiopian attacked Judah near Maresha. (Most scholars identify Zerah as a general in the service of Pharaoh Osorkon I, son of Shishak.) Asa pleaded with the Lord for help (2 Chronicles 14:11). The Lord defeated Zerah, giving opportunity for Asa and his army to plunder their enemies. Egypt would be absent from Judah for the next 150 years.[168]

In addition, trouble with Israel ensued when the new king of Israel, Baasha, sent his troops across the border to capture Ramah, about five miles from Jerusalem. With Jerusalem threatened, Asa, instead of seeking the Lord, sought the help of Ben-Hadad I of Damascus, who broke his agreement with Baasha and harassed Galilee, forcing Baasha to withdraw. As a result, Ben-Hadad now controlled access to the Mediterranean coast, dominating not only the King's Highway that crossed Damascus, but also the Coastal Highway down into Egypt.[169] For that reason, Hanani the prophet chastised Asa for drawing Ben-Hadad into the conflict with Baasha. His lack of trust in the Lord would have significant negative consequences for the future, for had he trusted in God, as he had against

Zerah, he would have won a more significant victory. Asa's pride apparently caused him to turn on Hanani, for he imprisoned and tortured him. Asa's long reign did not end well.

A New Era: Alliance with Israel, Jehoshaphat to Athaliah 873–835 BC

Jehoshaphat, son of Asa, ruled for thirty-five years (873–848 BC)[170] and was one of Judah's most righteous and capable kings. He walked with Yahweh, and his fervent spirit affected Judah spiritually, politically, and economically. As with Asa, he continued to purge Judah of idolatry (I Kings 22:43; 2 Chronicles 17:3–6), including some, but not all, of the "high places." Further, Jehoshaphat directed political officials and the Levites to travel throughout Judah and teach God's Law to the people (2 Chronicles 17:7–9). Later in his reign, some of these leaders even traveled north into Ephraim, teaching God's Law. (See 2 Chronicles 19:4.) He evidently believed that God's Word was the key to spiritual renewal. The king could not simply mandate obedience to God; the people needed to walk with God personally, and His Word was the key to that walk.

***

Excursus: A Word about the "High Places"

The phrase "high places" appears regularly throughout 1 and 2 Kings and 2 Chronicles. Although there are several positive characterizations of this phrase, as in Solomon offering sacrifices at Gibeon (2 Chronicles 1:2–6), once the temple was built, the phrase takes on negative, often idolatrous, connotations. The phrase is associated with Rehoboam bringing Canaanite idolatry into Judah (1 Kings 14:23). Beginning with Asa, king of Judah, there is a repeated reference to the king either not removing or removing the "high places" in Judah. The phrase "high places" also apparently referred to former Canaanite places of worship that the Israelites took over for the worship of Yahweh. But once the temple was built, their existence was no longer necessary, and their continued use could potentially lure the people of Israel or Judah into Canaanite apostasy. It was King Hezekiah of Judah who removed all the high places (2 Kings 18:4, 22).[171]

***

Jehoshaphat's focus on spiritual renewal transformed Judah in many ways. Indeed, Jehoshaphat demonstrated the function of the Mosaic covenant: walk closely and obediently with Yahweh, and He will bring blessing, peace and stability to the land. As the king walked with God, God would shepherd His people in worship and obedience. (See Deuteronomy 17:14–20.) Yahweh would then walk with His people in blessing.

Jehoshaphat brought prosperity and fiscal reform to Judah. He regularized the fiscal affairs of the nation by reorganizing its administrative districts.[172] Because of these reforms, Judah gained position economically in the region, such that its neighbors (e.g., the Philistines and the Arab tribes living south and southwest of Judah) voluntarily submitted to this domination by paying Judah tribute. (See 2 Chronicles 17:10–11.)

Jehoshaphat also reorganized the judiciary of Judah, assigning judges to the important cities of the kingdom. He established a court of appeals in Jerusalem, composed of Levites, priests, and elders, a landmark in the legal history of the nation. (See 2 Chronicles 19:5–11.) By this reform, Jehoshaphat obviously sought to normalize judicial procedures, eliminate injustice, and provide a system of appeal for disputed cases.[173]

The relationship between Judah and Israel, which had been hostile since the days of Jeroboam and Rehoboam, changed during Jehoshaphat's reign. For example, he sealed a political and, presumably, economic alliance with King Ahab of Israel by the marriage of Ahab's daughter, Athaliah, to his son, Jehoram (1 Kings 22:44). The futures of both the house of Omri and the house of David were now inextricably linked. This marriage made political sense, but it was a calamity for Judah, for it brought Baal worship into the court of Judah.

In 853 BC, King Ahab of Israel persuaded Jehoshaphat to join with him to take Ramoth Gilead from the Arameans (1 Kings 22:1–4). It was a catastrophe, for Ahab was killed, and it had the unintended consequence of further unfortunate wars for Judah. A coalition of Moab, Edom, and Ammon, sensing a vulnerable Judah, attacked Jehoshaphat (2 Kings 3:4–27; 2 Chronicles 20:1). King Jehoshaphat appealed to God, calling for a national fast and time of national prayer. Yahweh answered these petitions and threw their enemies into confusion, resulting in a significant triumph for Judah and its king.

In addition, Jehoshaphat was linked with Ahab's son, Ahaziah, in shipbuilding at Ezion-geber, but every vessel, as the prophet Eliezer had prophesied, was destroyed (1 Kings 22:48–49; 2 Chronicles 20:35–37). The alliance with Israel made political and perhaps economic sense for Judah, but it led to a tragic level of apostasy and the near extinction of the Davidic line.

Jehoram, Jehoshaphat's son, was coregent with his father for four years, and ruled from 848–841 BC. He was an unrighteous and evil king. There is absolutely no evidence that Jehoram learned anything spiritually from his father; in fact, the text characterizes him as walking in the "way of the kings of Israel," as Ahab had done. The comparison is not to David, but to Ahab. Yet God did not destroy Judah, for He remembered His covenant with David (2 Kings 8:18–19).

The most significant influence on Jehoram's life was his wicked wife, Athaliah, who introduced the Baal cult into the royal court. Perhaps due to her influence (see 2 Chronicles 22:10–12), Jehoram executed all six of his brothers and their supporters, despite the favor Jehoshaphat had shown to each one (2 Chronicles 21:3–4). No potential rivals would threaten his rule.

His short reign quickly began to unravel. First, Edom, at one time a loyal vassal state of Judah (see 2 Kings 3:4–27; 2 Chronicles 20:1–29), revolted and set up its own ruler. Although Jehoram attempted to squelch the revolt, Edom remained independent (2 Kings 8:20–22; 2 Chronicles 21:8–9). Libnah, an important priestly city in the Shepalah, also successfully revolted against Jehoram, presumably because of his idolatry.

The perceived weakness of Judah under Jehoram produced an 848 BC invasion from the Philistines and Arabs, who had been paying tribute to Jehoshaphat (2 Chronicles 17:11). The royal palace was plundered, and Jehoram's entire family, except his youngest son Ahaziah, was killed (2 Chronicles 21:16–17). This destruction had been prophesied by Elijah in a letter to Jehoram (2 Chronicles 21:12–15), the only surviving writing of this noble prophet. Jehoram, as prophesied by Elijah, died a horrible death from a gruesome intestinal disease.[174]

Jehoram's son **Ahaziah** ruled for one year, 841 BC. He was the only surviving family member from the Philistine and Arab raid in 848 BC. As had been the case with his father, Athaliah had the strongest influence on Ahaziah's life. (See 2 Chronicles 22:3.) He even followed the counsel of those who advised Ahab's court in Israel (22:4–5). Ahaziah was killed in 841 BC by Jehu during his purge of the Omri dynasty.

Athaliah (841–835 BC) was a usurper to the Davidic throne and manifested the heartless, harsh, and vindictive character of her mother Jezebel. Her singular goal was to establish the Baal cult in Judah as her mother had done in Israel. (See 2 Kings 8:18, 27; 11:18.) With Ahaziah dead, she saw an opportunity to seize the throne, and therefore ordered the murder of her sons and grandsons, all potential rivals. She thereby brought the Davidic line to point of near extinction.

But God intervened. The narrative's heroine is Jehoshabeath, Jehoram's daughter and the wife of Jehoiada, the chief priest (2 Chronicles 22:11), who rescued Joash, the infant heir, and hid him in the temple for six years. In a well-orchestrated coup, Jehoiada, along with other military and religious leaders, brought Joash into the temple, placed the Davidic crown on his head, and read from the Mosaic law—the "royal protocol" (presumably Deuteronomy 17:18–20). The Davidic line was restored to the throne, and those assembled cried out. "Long live the king" (2 Kings 11:9–12).[175]

Hearing all this, Athaliah rushed into the temple, crying, "Treason, treason." She fled but was caught by Jehoiada's men and executed. Jehoiada then led the people in a ceremony of covenant renewal, pledging loyalty to the new king and to Yahweh. The people demolished the temple of Baal and all the altars and pagan idols associated with Baalism, and executed the resident priest of Baal, Mattan (2 Kings 11:17–19). Finally, Jehoiada restored worship of Yahweh in the temple. In the early years of Joash's reign, Jehoiada advised the young king, no doubt instructing him in the Law and in his duties as a shepherd king (2 Kings 12:2).

A Century of God-Honoring Kings, 835–731 BC

As stated earlier in this chapter, there were eight relatively good kings of Judah. During the century 835 to 731 BC, four of these eight kings ruled. In each case during this century, the king's reign can be divided into two periods: a period of relative obedience and blessing, followed by a period of apostasy and judgment. The reference point was always David.

Joash, 835–796 BC, was a godly king for most of his reign, largely due to the influence of the high priest, Jehoiada, who even chose Joash's wives (2 Chronicles 24:3). Under the apostasy of Jehoram and Athaliah, the temple had fallen into disrepair, and appropriate services were neglected. Regular funds were to be collected, but the priests had been slow in doing so and the repairs were not done. So, in 814 BC, Joash, in his twenty-third year, took over the repair project.

In addition to the assessment on male citizens and the offerings that were a part of the temple, Joash embarked upon a fund-raising project that centered on the freewill offerings of the people, who placed their offerings in a special container near the altar. The response was overwhelming. With the necessary repairs completed, the surplus was dedicated to making the gold and silver temple vessels and implements (2 Chronicles 24:13–14).

The influence of Jehoiada, the high priest, on King Joash was profound. When Jehoiada died, that influence was gone. Joash then began to adhere to the counsel of ungodly advisors, especially those of the deposed Baal cult (2 Chronicles 24:17–18). When Zechariah, Jehoiada's son, rebuked Joash, Joash had him killed (2 Chronicles 24:20–22). As discipline on King Joash, the Lord sent the Arameans under King Hazael. They invaded Judah, attacked Jerusalem, killed many of Judah's leaders, and wounded King Joash (2 Chronicles 24:23–25). Because of Joash's murder of Zechariah, the leaders of Judah and many of Joash's servants conspired together and assassinated Joash as he was recovering from his wounds. As was a pattern during this period in Judah's history, a king who began his rule righteously ended in dishonor.

Because his father was assassinated, **Amaziah** (796–767 BC) needed to consolidate his power as king of Judah. Mosaic law demanded that his father's assassins be brought to justice, which he did, but he did not kill their children because of Deuteronomy 24:16. Early on, following God's Law was important to Amaziah.

As a defensive measure, Amaziah reorganized and rebuilt Judah's military, which included hiring 100,000 mercenaries from Israel (2 Chronicles 25:5-6). A prophet ("a man of God," 2 Chronicles 25:7) challenged this decision, arguing that Amaziah should trust the Lord, not Israel, for God was not with Israel. Obediently, Amaziah dismissed the mercenaries and sent them home. Infuriated, these mercenaries looted and pillaged towns in Judah on their way home.

Meanwhile, Amaziah attacked Edom, which had been lost due to a revolt during Jehoram's reign fifty years earlier. Edom's control of the King's Highway and southern trade routes no doubt played an important role in this decision. His victory against Edom was brutal and decisive, and included the capture of the capital city of Sela (2 Chronicles 25:11–12). Edom was once again Judah's vassal state.

Incredibly, Amaziah then brought Edom's idols into Jerusalem and worshipped them. Such rank idolatry provoked God's anger, but a prophet He sent did not turn Amaziah's heart from Edom's gods. Indeed, Amaziah killed that prophet (2 Chronicles 25:14–17).

When he returned from his Edomite victory, Amaziah learned of the mercenaries who had looted Judean towns. Believing that this massacre had been tolerated, if not encouraged, by the king of Israel, Amaziah then challenged Jehoash. Both rulers were arrogantly confident, for Amaziah had just defeated Edom and Jehoash had just defeated the forces of Ben-Hadad. By relating an allegory about a cedar tree (Israel) and a thistle (Judah), Jehoash mocked Amaziah (2 Chronicles 25:18–19).

At Beth Shemesh, west of Jerusalem, in 792 BC,[176] the two armies met. Amaziah's loss to Jehoash was total: the Judean army was routed and Amaziah was captured. Jehoash forced Amaziah to watch Jehoash's seizure of Jerusalem. He broke down some of its walls, pillaged the temple of its treasures, including the sacred vessels, and looted Amaziah's palace. Jehoash took Amaziah back to Samaria as his prisoner.

Amaziah's son, Uzziah (also called Azariah), was coregent with his father after 792 BC, the date of his father's capture by Jehoash.

After Amaziah was released from Samaria upon Jehoash's death, Amaziah lived in Jerusalem for nearly fifteen years. But he got word of a conspiracy (of priests and military officials?) against him and fled to Lachish, the most important fortified city after Jerusalem.

In 767 BC, Amaziah was assassinated and Uzziah became king. There is a real possibility that Uzziah was one of the conspirators. Amaziah's apostasy in desecrating the temple with Edomite gods was the reason for the assassination(2 Chronicles 25:27).[177] When Amaziah obeyed God, he was blessed; when he did not, he was disciplined.

Uzziah (792–740 BC) was one of the longest-reigning kings in either Judah or Israel. At the beginning of his reign, he was coregent with his father, Amaziah, and for the last sixteen years he was coregent with his son, Jotham.[178] He was made king by "all the people of Judah" (see 2 Chronicles 26:1), an unusual and quite abnormal way to describe his ascension as king. Amaziah's idolatry was no doubt the reason. Presumably during the early years of his reign, Zechariah (not Jehoiada's son) mentored him in the Law and in his walk with the Lord.

Uzziah is considered one of Judah's strongest kings, for during his reign, Judah, cooperating with Israel under Jeroboam II, was in resurgence. Together, Uzziah and Jeroboam II basically restored the boundaries of David and Solomon's empire, making the kingdom once again a power in the eastern Mediterranean (see previous chapter on Jeroboam II).

King Uzziah's accomplishments were significant:

1. Uzziah repaired the walls and defenses of Jerusalem, destroyed by Jehoash's invasion during Amaziah's disastrous conflict with Israel. Uzziah reorganized and retooled Judah's army into a fighting force of over 300,000. He

also introduced new siege technology, such that slingers and bowmen could be more effective in their attacks on walled cities.[179]

2. Uzziah used this rebuilt army to restore lost territory to Judah. (See 2 Chronicles 26:6–15.) He consolidated control over Edom, which his father had defeated. He built port facilities on the Gulf of Aqaba to enhance Judah's trading enterprises. He attacked the ancient enemy Philistia, conquering Gath, Jabneh, and Ashdod. For defensive purposes, he then built cites in the middle of Philistine territory. Next, he neutralized the various Arab tribes between Beersheba and Arad, forcing them to pay tribute. He subjugated the nomadic Meunites, who lived near the Dead Sea. Finally, he conquered the Ammonites, forcing them to once again pay tribute to Judah. Judah now had access to and significant control over the trading ports, the King's Highway, and other trading routes of the southern regions. Increased wealth, prestige, and influence resulted.[180]

3. Uzziah "loved the soil" (2 Chronicles 26:10), enthusiastically expanding farming and agricultural settlements in the Negev, the wilderness of Judah, in the foothills of the Shepelah, west of Jerusalem, and along the coastal plain. He built a string of forts to protect these settlements and the caravan routes in the Negev region particularly. Uzziah's engineering and agricultural technology provided a model for "later generations including the Nabateans and even the Israelis of [today]."[181]

Uzziah's accomplishments were momentous, but "he grew proud" (2 Chronicles 26:16). His arrogance caused him to enter the temple and offer incense to Yahweh, a role singularly given to the priests. The second book of Chronicles 26:16 describes Uzziah as "unfaithful." In offering incense, Uzziah trespassed, thereby impugning God's holiness.[182] (See Exodus 30:1–10; Numbers 16:40). He arrogantly refused to acknowledge the rebuke of Azariah the priest. God struck him with leprosy, thereby contaminating the temple and rendering Uzziah ceremonially unclean. For the rest of his life, he lived in an isolated community, handing over the government to his son, Jotham (2 Chronicles 26:21). In death, he was buried in a field next to the tombs of the kings, for he "was a leper" (26:23).

Uzziah's reign served as a poignant reminder of how the Mosaic law was to function under the monarchy. Harmony among king, priests, and temple secured God's blessings (see 2 Chronicles 13:12); disharmony His discipline. As VanGemeren argues, "Care of the temple and priestly and Levitical system was rewarded by evidences of God's blessedness: victory, prosperity, and peace. Lack of loyalty to the temple became associated with assassination, disease, war, and adversity, which eventually culminated in the Exile."[183]

The tragedy of Uzziah was that he demonstrated no loyalty to the temple, the priesthood, or Yahweh. One would not place "success" as an epitaph on his tombstone!

The final king in this series of God-honoring kings is **Jotham** (750–731 BC). As stated above, Jotham served as coregent with Uzziah until Jotham died in 731 BC. Jotham's son, Ahaz, also served as coregent with Jotham from about 735 BC. In other words, for about four years, Judah had Uzziah as the chief ruler, Jotham as his coregent and Ahaz as Jotham's coregent.[184] A righteous king, Jotham walked with the Lord and continued the formidable defense policies of his father. He added to the fortifications in Jerusalem, building an important temple gate (the "upper gate," 2 Chronicles 27:3) and the walls to the south of the temple. He also built fortifications around various cities and defensive positions throughout Judah. Finally, he won a meaningful victory against the Ammonites, who paid Jotham a sizable tribute for three years (27:5).

Even though Jotham was evidently righteous, the people of Judah continued to worship pagan deities in the "high places" (2 Chronicles 27:2). For that reason, God raised up the prophet

Isaiah, who began his ministry during Jotham's reign. Isaiah warned the people continuously of the consequences of idolatry. God's discipline would be at the hands of the Assyrians, who by the end of Jotham's reign were reasserting themselves in the Levant under Tiglath-pileser III.

Judah Alone: The Threat of Assyria 735–640 BC

The collapse of the northern kingdom of Israel in 722 BC occurred during the final days of King Ahaz in Judah. By the end of his reign, Judah was a vassal state of Assyria, and blasphemous practices of idolatry permeated the kingdom. Ahaz was an apostate king, whose actions forced Judah to pay a heavy price. With Israel's downfall, Judah, the Davidic kingdom, was alone. Two reform kings, Hezekiah and Josiah, offered hope to the faithful of Judah, but the apostasy was growing—and that would eventually lead to the doom of Judah at the hands of Babylon.

Ahaz (735–715 BC) was a wicked, apostate king who constructed idolatrous images of Baal, engaged in horrific Canaanite rituals (sacrificing his own children to the god Molech), fostered Canaanite worship in the high places, practiced divination, and even closed the temple sanctuary (2 Kings 14:3,5, 10–16; 2 Chronicles 28:2–4, 23–25). The second book of Chronicles 28:4 therefore declares that God sent judgment upon Ahaz—from the north.

As discussed in the previous chapter, kings Pekah of Israel and Rezin of Damascus pressured Judah to join in an alliance to defy the Assyrian Empire. When Ahaz refused, they invaded Judah separately, each inflicting heavy casualties. Many were taken prisoner, perhaps with the thought of enslaving these Judean captives (2 Chronicles 27:10). Only the intervention of the prophet Oded secured their release (2 Chronicles 27:9–11).

Although Ahaz was an apostate, he was a shrewd diplomat: he saw the inevitability of Assyrian domination of the eastern

Mediterranean. Because Judah was weakened by the Syro-Ephramite coalition, Edom and the Philistines began to raid Ahaz's territory. With nowhere else to turn—for he refused to turn to God—Ahaz turned to Tiglath-pileser for help. (Isaiah warned Ahaz to trust in the Lord in Isaiah 7:1–12, but to no avail.)

Thus, in 733 BC, King Ahaz made Judah a vassal state serving the Assyrian Empire. Ahaz even traveled to Damascus to meet with his new lord, Tiglath-pileser III (2 Kings 16:10). As was the practice in the Ancient Near East, political subservience also involved homage to your lord's gods, which Ahaz paid at the bronze altar to Assyria's gods in Damascus. Ahaz then had a copy of this bronze altar made for Jerusalem's temple.[185]

Ahaz survived as Judah's king, but at an overwhelming price. He had to rob the temple to pay the protection money demanded by Tiglath-pileser, after which he desecrated and closed down the temple. As a Davidic king, he ordered the blasphemous construction and worship of pagan gods throughout Judah. This was certainly one of the lowest points in the history of Judah. Ahaz had no loyalty to the priesthood, the temple, or the Mosaic law. He had one interest—self-preservation—and Judah paid heavily for his apostasy.

Hezekiah, Ahaz's son, was a reform king, seeking to undo the damage of his father. He ruled from 729–686 BC, for the first thirteen years as coregent with his father, thereby seeing the fall of Samaria in 722 BC. He became the sole king upon his father's death in 715.

***

Excursus: The Prophets Micah and Isaiah

The eighth century BC witnessed two prophets who were especially important for Judah—Micah and Isaiah. Isaiah, addressing Israel and Judah at first, argued forcefully that both had violated the covenant and that Yahweh's disciplinary judgment was imminent. The blessings of the Mosaic covenant would be revoked, and both would go into captivity—Israel to Assyria and Judah to Babylon. Although Isaiah also delivered oracles of judgment against the nations that oppressed and seduced Judah (chapters 13–23), he promised that a remnant would return to the land (chapter 27).

Since Judah was the center of the Davidic monarchy, Isaiah delivered several of the most important messianic prophecies of the Old Testament. He spoke of God's presence in Immanuel (7:10–17) and of the coming messianic kingdom of righteousness and peace (9:1–17; 11:1–11). The Servant Songs throughout chapters 40–55 stress the messianic Servant who would die for His people and restore God's sovereign rule through His kingdom, which would culminate in a new heaven and new earth (chapters 65–66).

Micah, a contemporary of Isaiah, gave special focus to the sinful leadership of Judah's rulers, priests, and prophets (chapters 2–3). But Micah also underscored the revitalization of Davidic kingship in the Messiah and the coming kingdom of Yahweh (chapter 5). Both the Abrahamic and Davidic covenants informed the oracles of Micah and are the center of Yahweh's renewal, which He would bring to His people.

What was the importance of these two prophets for Judah? Although these prophets provide important details for both the first and second advents of the Messiah, in the eighth century BC, Micah and Isaiah gave clarity to what had happened to Israel in 722 BC, and why Judah had fallen under Assyrian domination as a vassal state. Yahweh was displeased, and only covenant renewal by His people would bring the restoration of blessing.

The polices of Ahaz were diametrically opposed to everything Micah and Isaiah were declaring. His cowardly act in submitting to Assyria and his blasphemous idolatry were shameful and in total disregard of the covenant. Those loyal to the covenant were ready to rally round someone who would bring Judah back to its position of covenant loyalty to Yahweh. Hezekiah would do just that.[186]

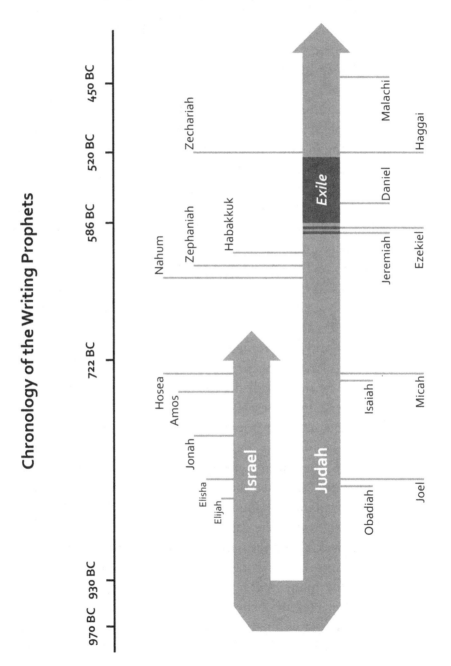

Chronology of the Writing Prophets

***

Hezekiah generated a significant reformation in the spiritual life of Judah, which politically produced a significant realignment of Judah in the eastern Mediterranean world. The second book of Chronicles links these two developments. First, his reforms brought spiritual vitality to Judah, still reeling from the apostasy of Ahaz:

1. At the beginning of his reign in 715 BC, Hezekiah reopened the temple. He began by repairing it and then cleansing it of the pagan cult objects that had been installed there (2 Chronicles 29:3–19). This included destroying the Mosaic bronze serpent, which had become an object of pagan worship (2 Kings 18:4). Those objects were burned in the Kidron Valley (2 Chronicles 29:16). Because of Ahaz's apostasy, all objects and sections of the temple were ceremonially unclean, so the priests and the Levites needed to cleanse the building before it could be reopened for worship. This ritualistic purification took sixteen days. When it was completed, Hezekiah called an assembly. The priests made burnt offerings and sin offerings on behalf of the people of Judah. As these sacrifices occurred, the temple choir and orchestra engaged in an unbridled expression of worship and praise to God (2 Chronicles 29:25–30). With the consecration of the temple and the priests and Levites complete, individual thanks offerings and sacrifices followed (2 Chronicles 29:31–36). Beginning with King Hezekiah, then the priests and Levites, and then the entire nation, this was a renewal of the covenant with God. Spiritual renewal in Judah began with a renewal of the covenant.

2. King Hezekiah led the nation in the celebration of Passover (2 Chronicles 30). Evidently, Passover had not been celebrated for many years, certainly not during the reign of Ahaz. But Hezekiah soon discovered that he could not restore Passover as a national celebration due to a shortage of priests (vv. 1–9). Therefore, he postponed it for one month.

In an extraordinary gesture of unity, Hezekiah sent written invitations throughout Judah and all of Israel to come to Jerusalem for the Passover celebration. These letters (vv. 6–9) were actually a call to national repentance and covenant renewal, as well as a call to the Passover. Thus, Hezekiah was actually calling for religious unification around Jerusalem, the temple, and covenant renewal. Although many from Israel mocked and scorned Hezekiah's appeal (vv. 10–11), others did come to Jerusalem for the ceremony. Graciously, God was pleased with this celebration and "healed" (i.e., forgave and spiritually renewed) the people (v. 20). Hezekiah extended the celebration for an additional week. The second book of Chronicles 30:26 observes that there had not been such a time of joy and celebration since the days of Solomon.

3. King Hezekiah reorganized the priesthood (2 Chronicles 31). As a prelude, throughout all of Judah and into "Ephraim and Manasseh" (v. 1), all remnants of past pagan idolatry, including the high places and altars, were dismantled and destroyed. Hezekiah then reorganized the priests and Levites for the offerings of sacrifice and praise (v. 2) and reinstated the collection of tithes and offerings to support the temple and the priests (vv. 4–19). The people responded with astonishing generosity, such that additional storage facilities had to be built. Hezekiah also appointed special stewards to oversee the storage facilities and the fair distribution of the contents to the priests and Levites in Jerusalem and other cities.

4. Because Micah and Isaiah were close to Hezekiah personally, it is fair to assume that Hezekiah oversaw administrative and judicial reforms in his kingdom. Justice was important to these prophets. More than a thousand jar handles dating from Hezekiah's reign have been found, each with a royal stamp (*lmlk*). These certainly involved some form of fiscal or administrative reform introducing a standard measure for the collection of taxes or tithes, thereby curbing dishonesty in such duties.[187]

The result of all these reforms was prosperity in the land (2 Chronicles 31:21). King Hezekiah exemplified the vision of kingship in Deuteronomy 17: he set his heart to follow the Lord, kept His Law, and shepherded his people. Therefore, God blessed him and his people.

Since repudiation of the Assyrian gods, which Hezekiah's reformation had done, was an act of rebellion in the ancient near eastern world, Hezekiah was clearly plotting rebellion against Assyria.[188] He needed to prepare for the consequences of this revolt. When Sargon II, King of Assyria, died in 705 BC and was succeeded by Sennacherib (705–681 BC), Hezekiah made his move. He ended Judah's tribute payment (2 Kings 18:7). He took the lead in the anti-Assyrian revolt, which included Phoenician cites, Philistine cities, Moab, Edom, and Ammon. His polite reception of the envoys sent by Assyria's mortal enemy, Merodach-baladan (2 Kings 20:12ff), further evidenced his desire to be free of Assyria's yoke.

Hezekiah instituted a policy of fortifying his nation's defenses. He built up the defenses of Jerusalem, including enclosing the western hill of Jerusalem (the Broad Wall), and safeguarded its water supply by constructing the Siloam tunnel (Hezekiah's tunnel), which connected the Gihon Spring with the Pool of Siloam.

To defeat this anti-Assyrian coalition, Sennacherib struck in 701 BC. He crushed Tyre and replaced her king with his own; the other Phoenician cities capitulated. Moab, Edom, and Ammon followed, restoring their tribute payments. Sennacherib attacked and subjugated the Philistine cities. Then he moved on the cities of Judah, destroying forty-six of Judah's fortified cities and deporting some of their populations. He laid siege to Jerusalem. Indeed, a famous stele of Sennacherib states that he had Hezekiah trapped "like a bird in a cage."[189]

In answer to Hezekiah's prayer (2 Kings 19:19) and in fulfillment of Isaiah's prophecy (2 Kings 19:20–28), God supernaturally intervened (2 Kings 19:35–36), causing the loss of 185,000 Assyrian soldiers and the end of the siege. In humiliation, Sennacherib returned to Nineveh. In 681 BC, Sennacherib was assassinated by his sons, with Esarhaddon succeeding him as king.[190]

Hezekiah's last years are perplexing. The chronology of these years is difficult, but it appears that his fatal illness (recorded in 2 Kings 20:1–19; 2 Chronicles 32:24–26; Isaiah 38–39) preceded Sennacherib's invasion of 701 BC by a few months. Isaiah 38 presents Hezekiah's prayer for God to spare his life as a selfish prayer, which God nonetheless graciously answered, granting him another fifteen years of life.

In addition, Merodach-baladan of Babylon, who was leading rebellion against Sennacherib, which began in 703 BC, sent envoys to Hezekiah to seek his support for the rebellion. Out of pride, Hezekiah showed these envoys his wealth and that of his treasury (2 Chronicles 32:25). The prophet Isaiah admonished him for doing so, prophesying that one day the Babylonians would return and destroy the city and Hezekiah's descendants would be taken to Babylon in captivity (Isaiah 39:5–7). Hezekiah selfishly brushed off this prophecy because his remaining days would be filled with peace and security; the catastrophe would be for his descendants to bear (39:8). Hezekiah died in 686 BC, succeeded by his son Manasseh.

Manasseh (696–642 BC), Hezekiah's son, ruled for fifty-five years, serving as coregent with his father for ten years (696–686); he was Judah's longest-reigning king. The power of Assyria reached its peak during his reign, causing fear and terror in Judah. Therefore, Manasseh remained a loyal vassal of Assyria. In fact, the name "Manasseh, king of Judah," appears on both the Prism of Esarhaddon and the Prism of Ashurbanipal as one of the twenty-two vassal states of the Assyrian Empire.

In distinct contrast to his father, Manasseh's long rule was horrific, marked especially by the astonishing religious syncretism he fostered as king. His new national religion involved a revival of Baalism, a cult of Astarte at the "high places," astral worship, spiritism, and divination in all its forms throughout the land. He placed a carved image of the Canaanite goddess Asherah in the temple, presumably as a consort to Yahweh. For Manasseh, Yahweh was merely one god among many,

Manasseh offered his sons as a sacrifice in the valley of Hinnom (2 Kings 21:1–17; 2 Chronicles 33:1–21). He even named one son Amon after a major Egyptian god. Those who protested the syncretistic apostasy of Manasseh were killed, including, according to tradition, the prophet Isaiah.

According to 2 Chronicles 33:10, the Lord spoke to Manasseh and the people of Judah through the prophets. Their stubborn refusal to heed God's word resulted in the king of Assyria (more than likely Ashurbanipal, 668–627 BC) capturing Manasseh and, with hooks and chains, bringing him to Babylon. Because Ashurbanipal had invaded this entire region, including Egypt, to suppress a larger rebellion in which Manasseh apparently participated the year of Manasseh's captivity was 648 BC.[191]

It is unclear how long Manasseh was in Babylon, but he repented of his flagrant sin, and the Lord graciously restored Manasseh to his throne. Manasseh removed many of the vestiges of paganism that he had erected earlier in Jerusalem, and led the nation in worship of the one true Lord God. Manasseh also refortified Jerusalem, no doubt as a gesture to Assyria, which desired that Judah be a buffer state against Egypt. Thus, apparently Judah remained a vassal state of Assyria.[192] Merrill comments, "The chronicler's inclusion of Manasseh's sin, deportation, repentance, and restoration is most instructive, for it serves as a foreshadowing in microcosm of the Judean captivity itself."[193]

Amon, Manasseh's son, ruled for only two years (642–640 BC). He restored the religious apostasy of his father and was assassinated, evidently by a party of "anti-Assyrians" (2 Kings 21:24; 2

Chronicles 33:25), who in turn were killed by a group of counterrevolutionaries who made Amon's eight-year-old son, Josiah, king.[194]

Josiah: Judah's Last Chance at Spiritual Renewal, 640–609 BC

King Josiah (640–609 BC) was the greatest reform king of Judah, exceeding even Hezekiah. Scripture gives singular focus to his religious reform of Judah, undoing the apostasy of his grandfather, Manasseh, and father, Amon. Josiah was the epitome of Deuteronomy 17:20; he followed God's Law and walked with Him faithfully (2 Chronicles 34:2). Josiah's campaign of spiritual renewal occurred in three stages:

1. In the eighth year of his reign (632 BC), Josiah turned his heart to the Lord and renounced the religious syncretism that had characterized his grandfather's and father's reigns. When the great Assyrian king Ashurbanipal died in 632 BC, Josiah, then sixteen years old, defied Assyria by refusing to honor the Assyrian gods.
2. Four years later (636 BC), Josiah extended his personal spiritual renewal by renouncing religious syncretism throughout the nation.
3. Now Josiah began to return the nation to the worship of Yahweh. The repair of the temple was the first step. In 622 BC, the eighteenth year of Josiah's reign, both 2 Kings 22:8 and 2 Chronicles 34:14–15 stress that Hilkiah, the high priest, discovered the "Book of the Law of Moses" in the temple. Shaphan the scribe then took the Law and read it to Josiah. Out of fear of God's wrath and remorse for sin, Josiah tore his clothes. Hilkiah then consulted with Huldah the prophetess, wife of a court official, who confirmed that God's judgment was indeed imminent, but that Josiah would be spared. Josiah then gathered the various leaders of Judah in Jerusalem, read them the Law's statutes, and led them in a national renewal of the covenant with the Lord (2 Chronicles 34:29–33).

Josiah's reforms were incredibly thoroughgoing, greater even than Hezekiah's. Josiah not only destroyed the "high places" in Judah and Benjamin, he also destroyed them throughout the land of Ephraim (the former northern kingdom) as far north as Naphtali in Galilee. His decrees called for the removal of every vestige of heathen worship in the land (2 Kings 23:19–20; 2 Chronicles 34:6–7). (Importantly, Josiah's reforms fulfilled the prophecy made when Jeroboam built the altars at Dan and Bethel; see 2 Kings 23:15–18). Finally, when Josiah reinstituted the Passover celebration, 2 Chronicles 35:18 declares that it was without parallel since the days of Samuel, evidently even surpassing the Passover celebration of Hezekiah.

Tragically, however, Josiah's reforms were superficial. The prophets (e.g., Jeremiah, Zephaniah, and Habakkuk) indicate that the hearts of the people were not directed to the Lord their God. When Josiah died, apostasy returned with a vengeance.

Josiah's reign occurred during a period when the entire eastern Mediterranean was undergoing significant geopolitical realignment. The Assyrian Empire was overextended, and once the capable Ashurbanipal died in 627 BC, the empire entered a period of rapid decline. The troublesome Chaldean area of southern Mesopotamia aligned itself with the kingdom of the Medes. This alliance, under the leadership of Nabopolassar, conquered Nineveh, Assyria's capital, in 612 BC, an event prophesied by the minor prophet Nahum. In addition, Egypt, a vassal state of Assyria, was in resurgence once again, challenging the domination of Mesopotamia in the eastern Mediterranean.

Josiah took advantage of this realignment. That Josiah's goal was to restore the Davidic kingdom, including its borders, is compelling. For example, as a part of his religious reforms, Josiah reestablished some semblance of authority over Samaria, Megiddo, possibly Gilead, and areas along the coastal plain. Of necessity, Josiah's reforms must have included, therefore, the reorganization of the military and the administrative machinery of his kingdom.[195] During Josiah's reign, Judah enjoyed peace, prosperity, and spiritual renewal.

When Pharaoh Neco II sought to aid the Assyrians against the approaching Babylonians at Harran, he moved into Josiah's kingdom, which Josiah regarded as a threat to his vision (2 Kings 23:29). He therefore challenged Neco and tragically was killed by Neco in 609 BC at the battle of Megiddo. All Judah mourned his death, including the prophet Jeremiah, who composed a lament for Josiah (2 Chronicles 35:24–25). Judah was now a vassal state of Egypt.

Judah's Last Four Kings, 609–586 BC

During the final years of Josiah's reign and through the collapse of Judah under Babylonia, several important prophets declared God's truth and His plan. The consistent message of the prophets to Judah was that persistent, impenitent, and flagrant covenant violations would get them expelled from the land. That is certainly what had happened to Israel in 722 BC.

Most importantly, Jeremiah severely chastised Judah and its leadership for the nation's apostasy. Despite their many opportunities to repent, they continued to reject the word of the Lord (Jeremiah 25:1–7). As the downward spiral accelerated, Jeremiah prophesied that God would send Judah into exile for seventy years, but would bring them back to the land (Jeremiah 25). As a part of the hope of restoration, Jeremiah spoke of a new covenant that Yahweh would make with His people (Jeremiah 31), which included forgiveness, placing His Law on their hearts, and walking with His people once again. Jeremiah recorded in great detail the destruction of Jerusalem under Nebuchadnezzar and the exile of his people to Babylon (Jeremiah 52).

Because it records a dialogue between God and a prophet, the book of Habakkuk is unique. Habakkuk was profoundly disturbed by the violence, apostasy, and injustice of Judah and thereby charged God with indifference (1:1–4). God's response was that He was raising up the Babylonians to judge Judah, to which Habakkuk offered a protest. God's response was to affirm His sovereignty and insist that Habakkuk trust Him (1:5–2:4). He would, after all, then judge Babylon. Habakkuk responded in the only way one could to a declaration of God's sovereignty—praise and worship (chapter 3).

Finally, the prophet Zephaniah made the use of the phrase "day of the Lord" to describe God's coming judgment on Judah. His judgment would be dreadful and inescapable. But Zephaniah also promised a time of national restoration of the Jewish people to their land. Yahweh, Zephaniah declared, is just, righteous, and pure. He also keeps His promises. He made unconditional covenant promises to the descendants of Abraham and to David, and He would keep those promises.

Each one of these prophets mixed words of destructive judgment with words of hope anchored in God's covenant promises to Israel and David. Those promises would be central to maintaining their hope and trust in Yahweh during the years of exile in Babylon.

The story of the last four kings of Judah is, at one level, one of the downward spiral of idolatry, violence, and injustice, and, at another, one of a tiny kingdom caught between two rival superpowers—Babylon and Egypt. Chosen by the "people," **Jehoahaz,** the middle son of Josiah, ruled for only three months, deposed by Pharaoh Neco in favor of Josiah's eldest son, Eliakim, whose name was changed by Neco to Jehoiakim—a sign of vassalage. Neco also demanded a severe tribute from Judah in the form of a heavy tax, which continued into the reign of Jehoiakim. As Jeremiah had predicted, Jehoahaz was taken to Egypt as a prisoner, where he died (Jeremiah 22:11–12).

Jehoiakim (609–598 BC) was an incompetent and self-centered ruler. Oppressive and selfish, Jehoiakim embarked on a building program, principally a new palace for himself built with slave labor. The return of religious apostasy was swift under his reign, and the decay was noted poignantly by both Jeremiah and Habakkuk. In addition to the resurgence of all forms of idolatry, now that he was a vassal of Pharaoh, he also introduced the worship of Egyptian gods. He murdered those who opposed him, including the prophet

Uriah. He mocked and defied Jeremiah, most graphically by burning one of his scrolls. (See Jeremiah 36:22, 26.)

In the fourth year of Jehoiakim's reign, Nebuchadnezzar, the young, gifted ruler of Babylonia, achieved an astonishing victory at Carchemish (605 BC), gaining control of the entire eastern Mediterranean to the border of Egypt. Jehoiakim was now a vassal of Nebuchadnezzar. King Nebuchadnezzar took with him back to Babylon the best and the brightest of Judah, including the esteemed Daniel (see Daniel 1:1–3), the first of three waves of exiles to Babylon.

When Babylon lost a major battle to Egypt in 601 BC, despite Jeremiah's warning to the contrary, Jehoiakim rebelled against Nebuchadnezzar, aligning Judah with Egypt. Nebuchadnezzar responded by sending Babylonian troops and those from some of his vassal states (e.g., Edom, Moab, and Aram). He then bound King Jehoiakim in chains. Jehoiakim relented in his rebellion, but Nebuchadnezzar still took many of the temple artifacts to Babylon. Until he died in 598 BC, Jehoiakim remained a loyal subject of Babylon.

Nebuchadnezzar appointed **Jehoiachin** (598–597 BC) king of Judah when his father died on 6 December 598 BC. He actually ruled for only three months and ten days (2 Chronicles 36:9). Jehoiachin continued the idolatry and oppression of his father, such that Jeremiah prophesied the end of his reign and of his dynasty (Jeremiah 22:24–26). On 16 March 597 BC, Nebuchadnezzar laid siege to Jerusalem, which then surrendered.[196] Nebuchadnezzar subsequently took Jehoiachin, his mother, and other court officials, as well as ten thousand people, to Babylon. One of those exiles was Ezekiel. (See Ezekiel 1:2–3.) Nebuchadnezzar appointed Jehoiachin's uncle, Mattaniah, renamed Zedekiah, to succeed him. In Babylon, Jehoiachin was treated as a royal prisoner. He never returned to Jerusalem. After Nebuchadnezzar died, he received a pension and was treated as an honored guest of Babylon (2 Kings 25:27–30). For most of the exiles and for the prophets Jeremiah and Ezekiel, Jehoiachin was the last legitimate king of Judah.

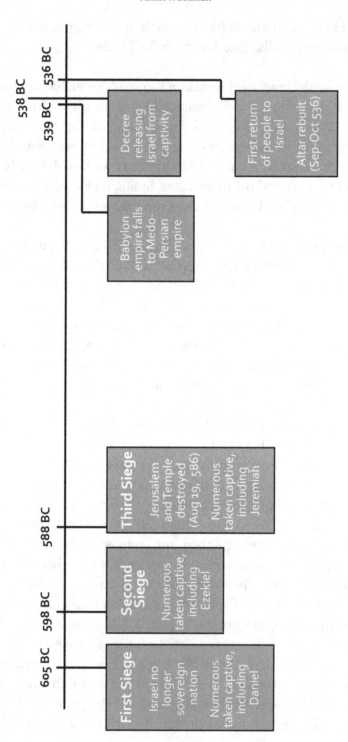

Zedekiah (597–586 BC) was the youngest son of Josiah. His brief reign was marked by growing apostasy and moral degeneracy. (See the explicit details in Ezekiel 8–11 and 22). Despite the warnings of Jeremiah (see chapter 27), Zedekiah aligned Judah with Egypt and a coalition that included Edom, Moab, Ammon, and Phoenicia. At first, Zedekiah resisted, even sending an envoy or going personally to Babylon to affirm loyalty to Nebuchadnezzar (Jeremiah 29:3). But under the influence of the pro-Egyptian party in his court, Zedekiah joined the coalition and openly rebelled against Nebuchadnezzar, breaking the oath he had sworn to Nebuchadnezzar in the name of Yahweh (see Ezekiel 17).

Nebuchadnezzar's armies then came and laid siege to Jerusalem in 588 BC. After two and a half years of a brutal siege, Jerusalem fell on 18 July 586 BC. Zedekiah escaped to Jericho, where he was captured and taken before Nebuchadnezzar. There he witnessed the execution of his sons and was blinded. In chains, he was taken to Babylon, where he died.

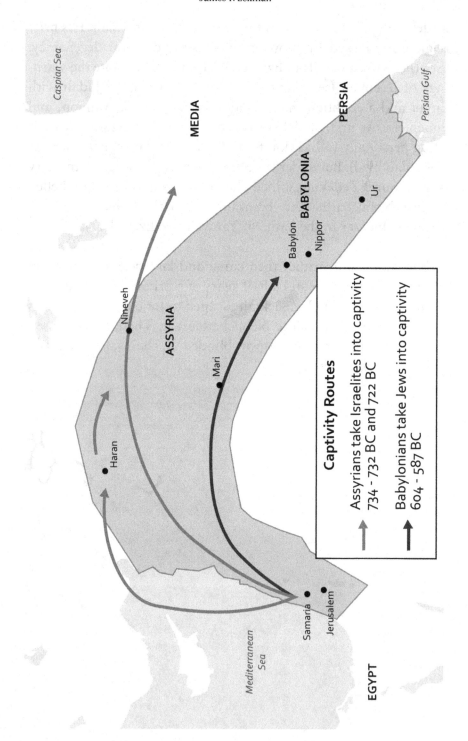

Caspian Sea

MEDIA

PERSIA

Persian Gulf

BABYLONIA

Ur

Babylon

Nippor

Nineveh

ASSYRIA

Mari

Haran

Captivity Routes

Assyrians take Israelites into captivity 734 - 732 BC and 722 BC

Babylonians take Jews into captivity 604 - 587 BC

Samaria

Jerusalem

Mediterranean Sea

EGYPT

Under the command of Nebuzaradan, Babylonian troops completely destroyed Jerusalem, burning the city and breaking down its walls. The temple was utterly destroyed, and any remaining artifacts were taken to Babylon. Nebuchadnezzar, at his camp in Riblah, executed the high priest and other religious and civil officials of Judah. Except for the very poor, most of the people of Judah were deported to Babylon, where they would live for seventy years.

Jeremiah cautioned them to live a normal life in Babylon. They were to marry, have children, and work the land in Babylon until God brought them back to Jerusalem. (See Jeremiah 29:4–6.) As Merrill observes, "The burden of covenant continuity now rested upon the exiles scattered throughout the eastern Mediterranean world from Egypt to the Persian Gulf. Yahweh would work with them to effect his immutable promise of redemption and reconciliation. And to this all the prophets of the time testified."[197]

The message of the prophets was also that a new day was about to dawn for Israel, a day centered on a new covenant that God would make with them (Jeremiah 31:31–37; Ezekiel 36:22–36; 37:15–28). This covenant would extend beyond the return from the exile; it would center on God's new King, the Messiah of Israel.

Chapter 8

Exile and Restoration to the Land

The year 586 BC was indisputably the most significant crisis in Israel's history. The nation was destroyed; there was no ruling Davidic king; all national institutions were gone; and, most importantly, the temple, the religious and theological center of the nation, was in ruins. Most of the people of the nation were uprooted, defeated, and scattered. Furthermore, the presence of God in their midst, symbolized by the *shekinah* in the Temple, was also gone, for Ezekiel in one of his visions saw the *shekinah* depart to the Mount of Olives (Ezekiel 11:23).

The exile to Babylon would forever cure the people of Israel of their penchant for idolatry. But their national identity as a people was in question. Without a Davidic king, without the temple, without the sacrificial system, who were they? Were they still God's people?

During these harsh, crucial years, Judaism was born. They would return to the land as a disciplined, chastised people, but they would not rule themselves as an independent nation, save during the brief Hasmonean period, until AD 1948.

After the exile, they were restored to their land, and that restoration played a central role in God's redemptive plan. VanGemeren captures the connection:

> The era of restoration, however, is both climactic and transitory. It is climactic because it brings upon

the twelve tribes the fullness of God's wrath and judgment. He freely dissociates himself from the people, removing his presence, grace and compassion. The curses of which Moses and the prophets had forewarned fell upon the twelve tribes: sickness, famine, starvation, fire, blood, and war. The covenant people have joined the lot of the rest of the nations that were left in darkness, anguish and alienation. The period is also transitional, though, because judgment and alienation mark the road that leads from Babylon to Bethlehem ... [T]he Lord raised up a new people from the ashes of the conflagration. They were the remnant, the heirs of the promises.[198]

The Nature of the Babylonian Captivity

The differences between the Assyrian and the Babylonian captivities are important. Both empires deported the best and brightest to their respective kingdoms. But in Babylonia, the most capable captives were taken into the Babylonian court and educated in the language and worldview of Babylonia, with the objective that these captives would serve in Babylon's bureaucracy. Daniel was a prime example of this strategy (Daniel 1). The Assyrian empire had no such practice.

Another important difference was the nature of the populations in the conquered territories. After 722 BC, Assyria repopulated Israel with foreigners, who then intermarried with the remaining Jews. Babylon did not repopulate Judah with foreigners. Judah was a province of Babylon, ruled by a governor appointed by the king. Gedaliah, from an important Jewish family, was the first such governor, who established Mizpah as the capital of this new Babylonian province. The second book of Kings 25:12 explains that he governed "the poorest people," who were left to cultivate the land of Judah. The military commander Nebuzaradan redistributed the land and provided a small contingent of troops for Gedaliah.

Life in Judah was harsh and difficult; the book of Lamentations provides evidence of this. Virtually all of the fortified towns and cities had been razed. Thousands had died in battle and from starvation and disease, while others had been executed. (See Lamentations 2:11–21; 2 Kings 25:18–27; Jeremiah 42). The entire population of Judah was probably less than 20,000 people.[199]

In 582 BC, Ishmael, a Jewish military officer, in alliance with Baalis, the Ammonite king, assassinated Gedaliah (Jeremiah 41:1–10). Another military officer, Johanan, intervened and ended the coup attempt, chasing Ishmael into Ammonite territory. Fearing Babylonian reprisal, Johanan and other Jewish leaders fled to Egypt, taking Jeremiah with them. (See Jeremiah 41:16–43:8.) Apparently, Babylon responded by taking another cohort of Jews to Babylon as punishment. (See Jeremiah 52:30.)[200] After Gedaliah's assassination, the northern part of Judah was incorporated into Samaria, and the Edomites moved into the southern part, which would become known as Idumea.[201]

The Jewish exiles in Egypt developed into a robust community. Jeremiah 43 explains that they settled in Tahpanhes in the Nile Delta, while other exile groups settled in Migdol, Memphis, and Pathros (Jeremiah 44:1). Another Jewish colony developed much farther south along the Nile at Yeb (Elephantine). This group of Jews built a temple and observed a number of rituals and festivals, albeit mixed with pagan rituals.[202]

The Babylonians settled the Jewish exiles in small, previously abandoned villages and settlements around the cities of Babylon and Nippur: Tel-abib, Tel-melah, Tel-harsha. (See Ezekiel 1:1; 3:15; Ezra 2:59.) Since Jeremiah had instructed these exiles to pursue normal lives during the seventy years in Babylon, we can infer that theirs was a life of security and well-being. Indeed, Ezekiel mentions living in his own house (Ezekiel 8:1).

Some exiles served in the Babylonian government. (See Daniel 1–5.) The exiles maintained some form of local administrative leadership, for both Jeremiah and Ezekiel mentioned "elders," as well as "prophets and priests," serving in leading and teaching roles (Jeremiah 29:1). The exiles could also write and receive letters. (See Jeremiah 29:1, 25; 28:3–4.) Yet, as in Psalm 137, the exiles longed for Jerusalem and everything it meant to them.[203]

Babylon, Persia, and the End of the Exile

Babylon

The Babylonian Empire under Nebuchadnezzar was, at that time, the most powerful empire of the ancient world. Nebuchadnezzar ruled for forty-three years (605–562 BC) and subdued Tyre, Moab, Syria, and Ammon. In 568 BC, he neutralized the power of Egypt. His building program was legendary, especially the temples (ziggurats), palaces, and canals of his capital city of Babylon, as well as its walls. The Hanging Gardens were built for his queen, who came from mountainous Media to the north.

Nebuchadnezzar's successors were weak and often incompetent, and the decline of Babylon accelerated. However, Nabonidus (556–539 BC) was an exception. He brought stability to Babylon after several disruptive rulers. His controversial decision to elevate the worship of the Babylonian moon god, Sin, at the expense of Marduk, the traditional head of the pantheon, caused him to lose favor with the political and religious elite of Babylon.

In terms of Israel's history, what was significant about his rule was that, due to his controversial religious policies, he transferred his residence to Tema, southeast of Edom in the Arabian desert, where he lived for ten years. His son, Belshazzar, ruled in his place in Babylon. According to Daniel 5, when Belshazzar was hosting a festival in Babylon, miraculous writing on the palace wall warned him of looming disaster. Daniel, the "third ruler" of the Babylonian kingdom, was summoned by Belshazzar. That very evening, Daniel revealed, Babylon would be conquered.

On 12 October 539 BC, the commander of the Persian army, Gubaru, took the city as Nabonidus, who had just returned from Tema, looked on. On 29 October, Cyrus the Great , the emperor of the Persian Empire, entered Babylon. He prohibited the destruction of the city and ordered his soldiers to respect the religious practices and beliefs of the Babylonian people. He also restored the worship of the Babylonian god, Marduk, as the head of the pantheon.[204]

Persia

One hundred and sixty years beforehand, the prophet Isaiah, writing about 700 BC, named Cyrus as the chosen one of God who would shepherd His people, return them to their land, and decree that they should rebuild their temple (44:24–45:7). Cyrus was God's instrument through whom He fulfilled His covenantal promises to the Jewish people.

This prophetic passage in Isaiah also speaks of God guiding the conquests of Cyrus as he built his empire. This is indeed what occurred. Cyrus began his rise to power in 550 BC, when he conquered the Medes northeast of Mesopotamia. By 546 BC, he had conquered Lydia (modern Turkey), including the Greek city-states of Ionia along the western coast. In 539 BC, he conquered Babylonia, thereby controlling much of the eastern Mediterranean world.[205] The Persian Empire would eventually extend from Macedonia in the west to the Hindu Kush mountains of the east. It also included much of Egypt and Libya in northern Africa.

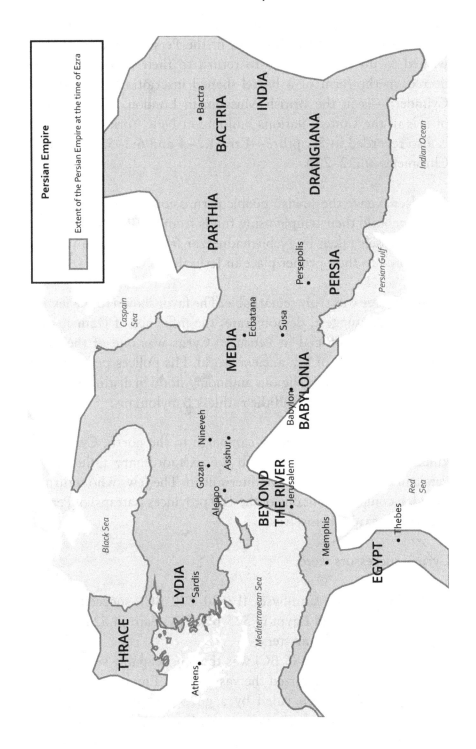

In 538 BC, Cyrus issued one of the most important decrees in all of history: all captive peoples in the Persian Empire, if they wished to do so, were free to return to their homelands. The decree, in the form of a barrel-shaped inscription—the "Cyrus Cylinder"—is in the British Museum in London, and a replica of it is in the United Nations building in New York. The decree is also recorded in Scripture—Ezra 1:2–4 and 6:3–5. (See also 2 Chronicles 36:22–23.)

The decree gave the Jewish people permission to return to Judah and to rebuild their temple using funds from the Persian treasury. All the vessels taken by Nebuchadnezzar from Jerusalem were to be restored to their proper place in Jerusalem.

Cyrus's decree was truly remarkable. The favor shown to the Jewish people, some suggest, demonstrates the influence of Daniel, who became a royal official in Persia.[206] Cyrus was one of the most enlightened rulers of the ancient world. His polices permitting a degree of cultural and religious autonomy stood in distinct contrast to the brutal Assyrians and the ruthless Babylonians.

In 530 BC, during a military campaign to the north, Cyrus was killed. His successors continued the extraordinary influence of Persia in the entire eastern Mediterranean. The Jews who returned to Judah comprised but one of the 120 provinces (satraps) of Persia; they did not rule themselves.

Cyrus's successors were:

1. Cyrus's son, Cambyses II (530–522 BC), succeeded him. He conquered Egypt in 525 BC. His death in 522 BC was surrounded in mystery.
2. Darius I (522–486 BC) was the most capable successor to Cyrus. He organized the vast Persian Empire into regions (satrapies), each ruled by a governor. He established a postal service, built a major road system, and constructed

the royal retreat at Persepolis. Darius invaded Greece in 490 BC, but was halted at the famous battle of Marathon.

3. Xerxes I (486–465 BC), the husband of Esther (known in the Hebrew Bible as Ahasuerus) also invaded Greece, but, after an initial victory at Thermopylae (480 BC), saw embarrassing defeats at the naval battle of Salamis (480 BC) and the land battle of Plataea (479 BC).

4. Artaxerxes I (465–425 BC) dealt with significant challenges from both Egypt and Athens. The various treaties and agreements he signed reflected the diminishing power and influence of Persia. Nehemiah was the cupbearer of Artaxerxes, who authorized Nehemiah's work in Jerusalem in 445 BC. Artaxerxes was no doubt the king mentioned in Ezra 7:7 (458 BC).[207]

The Restoration to Judah

The return of the Jewish exiles to Judah occurred in three waves. The first wave in 537 BC was under Sheshbazzar, a "prince of Judah" (Ezra 1:8) appointed by Cyrus as governor of the province (Ezra 5:14), who led the initial group of exiles back to Jerusalem (Ezra 1:11). According to Ezra 2:64–65, 42,360 exiles plus 7,337 slaves and 200 singers constituted this initial group. Sheshbazzar was of the royal lineage of David, one of the sons of Jehoiachin (the Shenazzar of 1 Chronicles 3:18). Cyrus also entrusted to him the job of returning the sacred vessels taken by Nebuchadnezzar (Ezra 5:13–16).

Under Sheshbazzar, the returnees began to lay the foundations of the temple (Ezra 5:16). Although this cannot be validated, more than likely Sheshbazzar died shortly after his return (he was in his sixties) and Zerubbabel, his nephew, succeeded him.[208] Joshua, the high priest, assumed responsibility for the spiritual affairs of the fledgling community.

Under the leadership of Joshua and Zerubbabel, the workers built an altar on the ruins of the original one, celebrated the Feast of Tabernacles, and offered burnt offerings to the Lord (Ezra 3:1–7).

Joshua and Zerubbabel organized the priesthood, which supervised temple construction. Building materials from Lebanon were ordered, and, with the foundation completed (536 BC), joyous praise and worship from the people followed, singing the same hymn King David had composed (1 Chronicles 16:34). But, due to the modesty of this foundation, those who remembered the glory of Solomon's temple wept (Ezra 3:12–13).

For the next sixteen years, virtually nothing further was done on the work of rebuilding the temple. Opposition from the Samaritans, descendants of the intermarriage between transplanted Assyrians and Jews from the northern kingdom, was part of the reason. At first, the Samaritans offered to aid in the project, but the Jewish leaders, fearing compromise with the syncretistic Samaritans, rejected the offer.[209] In addition, the returnees began to focus more on rebuilding their own homes and farming the land. (See Haggai 1:3–11.. The poverty of the people intersected with discouragement and lethargy. Work on the temple stopped.

The Old Testament prophets Haggai and Zechariah were central in lifting the morale of the people to finish the temple work (Ezra 5:1). Haggai, whose oracles date from 520 BC, exhorted the people to set aside work on their own homes and farms and finish the temple (Haggai 1:4–9). Truly, Yahweh would soon "shake the nations" and make Jerusalem and the temple again the center of His plans for the world (2:1–9).

The prophecies of Zechariah complemented those of Haggai. His visions affirmed that the temple, the center of Yahweh's kingly rule, must be completed, for Judah would be the center, with Jerusalem, of God regathering His people from all over the earth. Chapters 3 and 4 focus on Joshua and Zerubbabel standing with the Messiah in the future kingdom, with Joshua a prototype of the Messiah (6:9–15). Joshua, the high priest, and Zerubbabel, the ruler, together manifested the renewal of the Davidic line, for the Messiah would be both priest and king.

In about three weeks, Zerubbabel and Joshua assembled enough workers to resume the work. Finally, in 516 BC, the temple was completed, twenty years after the foundations had been laid. As Merrill correctly demonstrates, the year 516 marked the end of the "seventy years" Jeremiah had set for the exile, for with a functioning temple, Yahweh could dwell once again with His people.[210] Thus begins what is often called the Second Temple Period.

Between the first and second wave of exiles, the events recorded in the book of Esther occurred. The book begins in 483 BC, in the Persian capital of Susa, during the reign of Xerxes. When Queen Vashti humiliated Xerxes during a lavish banquet for all the officials of Persia, Xerxes deposed her and, by 479 BC, had made Esther, a Jew, his queen (Esther 1 and 2). Esther represented the Jews who chose not to return to Judah with Sheshbazzar. That Esther and her older cousin, Mordecai, were at the upper levels of the Persian government indicates how deep Jewish assimilation into Persian culture was. Their names also testify to this fact: "Mordecai" was Hebrew for the Babylonian god Marduk, and "Esther" was a form of Ishtar, the Babylonian god of love and war. Esther's Hebrew name was Hadassah.[211]

Esther's elevation coincided with Xerxes' failure to subdue the Greek city-states during the final phase of great Persian Wars in 479 BC. The conspiracy that Mordecai uncovered may have resulted from this humiliating defeat. Xerxes made the arrogant Haman his prime minister. Haman demanded that everyone pay him homage. Because of his Jewish faith, only Mordecai refused to kneel in Haman's presence. Seeking revenge, Haman convinced Xerxes to launch a genocidal campaign against all Jews in the empire. Xerxes issued the order on 25 June 474 BC. Interestingly, Haman was an "Agagite," a descendant of King Agag of the Amalekites, and Mordecai was a descendant of Kish, the father of Saul. The conflict between Mordecai and Haman mirrored the conflict between Saul and Agag five hundred years earlier.[212]

When Xerxes searched the royal archives, he found the record of Mordecai's revelation about the conspiracy years earlier. Consequently he elevated Mordecai to a high position in the government. At that time, Queen Esther revealed her Jewish identity to Xerxes and also revealed Haman's evil, genocidal plot. Xerxes ordered Haman executed on the very gallows he had been building for Mordecai. Xerxes also decreed that the Jews could resist, with violence if necessary, the implementation of Haman's pogrom. The Feast of Purim (9:26-28) celebrated this victory of the Jews over the forces loyal to Haman.[213] Even today, it is a joyous and important time of celebration.

The book of Esther profoundly teaches the sovereignty and providence of God in protecting His people, the Jews: "Yahweh is king, and the Jews are his people. No plot to annihilate them will ever succeed, for Yahweh made a covenant with Israel and will fulfill his promises to them."[214]

The second wave of exiles (about 1,500) returned under the leadership of Ezra in 458 BC. Judah was part of the satrapy called "Beyond the River" (Abar-nahara), the lands west of the Euphrates River, which included Syria, Samaria, Judah, Phoenicia, and Cyprus. King Artaxerxes of Persia, after defeating Athens and neutralizing the threat from Egypt, an ally of Athens, authorized Ezra, the "Minister of State for Jewish Affairs,"[215] to take another group of Jewish exiles to Judah. Empowering him to establish the Mosaic law in the province of "Yehud" (Judah), within the larger satrapy of Beyond the River, Artaxerxes also authorized him to appoint civil magistrates to enforce the Law, and to further adorn the temple. The book of Ezra provides a copy of Artaxerxes' decree (7:11–26), which stipulated that the king would provide gold and silver for the temple (9:25–27) and the ability to receive more if needed from the royal treasury (7:20). For political reasons, Artaxerxes no doubt saw the value of a strong Jewish province as a buffer against Egypt.[216] Ezra assembled the returnees near Babylon, and after a nearly four-month trip of nine hundred miles, they arrived in Jerusalem.

As Schreiner argues, "A fundamental theme of Ezra-Nehemiah is the danger of syncretism, for Israel suffered exile because it did not exclusively worship Yahweh but also participated in the worship of other gods."[217] Thus when Ezra arrived in Jerusalem, he saw that many within Judah had married foreign women who worshipped other gods (Ezra 9–10), something condemned in the Law (Exodus 34:16; Deuteronomy 7:3–4). This practice was especially prominent among the "officials and chief men" (Ezra 9:2). The people were again violating covenant stipulations and ignoring God's grace, the same practices that had produced the exile. When confronted by Ezra, the people repented and "put away" (i.e., excommunicated from the covenant community)[218] their foreign wives and children. (See chapter 10.)

The third return of the exiles occurred under Nehemiah in 444 BC. In Susa, Nehemiah was Artaxerxes' cupbearer, a position with high rank and easy access to the king. In December 445 BC, a delegation from Jerusalem, including his brother Hanani, informed Nehemiah of the deplorable conditions in Jerusalem. Among other things, this had resulted from the chaotic condition of the entire satrapy. Allied with Athens in Greece, Egypt had revolted against Persia in 488 and 461 BC. Rebellion and counterrebellion, along with Samaritan defiance, had no doubt contributed to the devastation in Jerusalem.

Nehemiah, therefore, approached Artaxerxes, who granted Nehemiah authority to rebuild the walls of Jerusalem using materials from the royal forests. Artaxerxes was interested in consolidating Persian authority there and reestablishing some semblance of loyalty in that distant province.[219]

When Nehemiah and the exiles who traveled with him arrived in Jerusalem, they found not only horrific conditions, but also fierce opposition to the rebuilding of Jerusalem. Their principal opponent was Sanballat, governor of the province of Samaria. Two other formidable opponents included Tobiah, governor of Ammon, and Geshum the Arab, whose kingdom extended from the Sinai to southern Judah and included Edom and the Negev. Nehemiah was therefore surrounded by enemies on all sides. Each of these opponents resisted the reestablishment of Judah as a viable and powerful pro-Persian rival loyal to Artaxerxes.[220]

The conspiracy against Nehemiah involved six strategies. First was mockery, obviously to undermine morale (Nehemiah 4:1–3). Second, his enemies employed gangs of Arabs, Ammonites, and Philistines to terrorize Jerusalem and the surrounding towns in Judah (4:7–12). Nehemiah shrewdly divided his work crews into those who worked and those who provided security.

Third, the opponents attempted to lure Nehemiah from Jerusalem, ostensibly for negotiations, but obviously to murder him. Fourth, his enemies threatened to inform Persia that Nehemiah was guilty of sedition and a threat to Artaxerxes (6:5–9). In effect, Nehemiah dared them to contact Artaxerxes.

Fifth, within Jerusalem were the relatives of Tobiah the Ammonite, who kept the conspirators informed of Nehemiah's activities, sowing distrust within the city. Finally, they hired a "prophet" to lure Nehemiah into the temple out of fear of Sanballat, which Nehemiah rejected as an act of cowardice (6:10–14).[221]

Nonetheless, after fifty-two days, the walls of Jerusalem were completed. Even Nehemiah's enemies recognized God's providential hand in this project (6:16).

As governor of the province of Yehud (Nehemiah 5:14), Nehemiah embarked on reorganizing the province. Yehud was much smaller than the Judah before the exile, only extending from an area north of Hebron to Bethel, and from the Dead Sea in the east to Gezer in the west.

The economic situation was desperate. Due to the political instability fostered by opposition to Persia, food shortage was acute.

This was exacerbated by the exploitation of the poor by the rich Jewish nobility and political officials of the province. No doubt as a result of the turmoil that had accompanied the building of the wall, food prices were exorbitant. Because of the hardships of high-priced food and high Persian taxes, many of the needy borrowed at high interest rates from the wealthy. When they could not meet the payments, their children entered into various forms of indentured servitude to meet the family obligations (Nehemiah 5:1–10). Nehemiah insisted that these usurious practices and indentured servitude end. To set an example, Nehemiah modeled the compassion of a servant leader through his actions as the governor, even refusing remuneration (5:14–19).

Because of Jerusalem's devastation from the Babylon invasion, few Jews were willing to live in the city (Nehemiah 7:1–4). Nehemiah's Jerusalem was only about thirty-seven to thirty-eight acres, smaller than David or Solomon's city. Now that the city was secure, Nehemiah embarked upon building private homes. He ordered that research into genealogical records be used to determine who came from families that had lived in Jerusalem. Once determined, members of these families, chosen by lot, were to repopulate Jerusalem (7:5–73). With Jerusalem again fortified and populated, it attained respectable status as the provincial capital of Yehud. Its importance in subsequent years would only grow.[222]

Finally, Nehemiah fostered the spiritual renewal of the Jewish people in Yehud. In October 445 BC, he called the people together. Ezra read from the Law, while the Levites circulated among the people to ensure that they understood (Nehemiah 8:1–8). For nearly six hours, the people stood and listened—and then began to weep. Sorrow for sin and covenant rebellion against God, led, under the leadership of Ezra and Nehemiah, to the joy of covenant renewal (8:9–12). They celebrated the Feast of Booths together and, after another period of confession and worship, reaffirmed in writing their covenant commitment to Yahweh (9:13–18). The community leaders signed the document (Chapters 9–10). With astonishing worship, loud singing, and offering of sacrifices, Nehemiah dedicated the walls of Jerusalem (12:27–43). Although they were in the land as a vassal of Persia, the Jewish people were now a people of the Book, not only of the temple.

We do not know how long Nehemiah remained the governor of Yehud. Nehemiah's first term as governor lasted twelve years. For reasons that are unclear, he returned to Susa and remained there for about three years (ca. 433–430 BC). During his absence, his old enemy Tobiah the Ammonite moved into the temple precinct under the sponsorship of Tobiah's relative, the priest Eliashib. Nehemiah returned to Jerusalem and forced Tobiah out. Because Tobias was a foreigner, Nehemiah purified his chambers. Nehemiah also reaffirmed acceptable Sabbath practices, a key element of the Mosaic covenant that the people were to follow (Nehemiah 13:15–22). Finally, he condemned the ongoing practice of mixed marriages (this time to Moabites, Ammonites, and Philistines) as a violation of the covenant, which the people had renewed only a few years earlier. That covenant stipulated that they must focus on their distinctiveness as a nation. Because their syncretism had contaminated them as a holy nation and produced the exile, reestablishing their purity as a people was Nehemiah's central concern.

In many ways, Ezra and Nehemiah had saved the Jewish community in Yehud from extinction. In doing so, they also reestablished the Israelites' major characteristic as God's people—covenant purity. "They must heed the covenant stipulations in the Torah given by Moses. The Temple worship must be carried out as the Lord mandates, and Israel must purify itself from uncleanness. Israel has compromised with pagans to prosper financially and to enjoy sexual relations with women from cultures where other gods are worshiped. They must renew their covenant with the Lord, for the Lord, despite all of Israel's sin, has not abandoned Israel."[223]

The Impact of the Exile and the Restoration to the Land

The Jewish people were back in their land, albeit as a vassal of Persia. But the exile had profoundly changed the Jewish people in many ways:

1. Through the work of both the major and minor prophets, the exile forced the Jewish people to reflect on why Yahweh had sent them into exile and to ensure that this would never happen again. Most definitely, the exile cured them of their penchant for idolatry. But would they remain a unique covenant people dedicated to the Lord God?

2. The influence of Babylonian culture on the Jewish culture was profound. Jewish names were now replaced with Babylonian names. Also, Aramaic was the lingua franca of the Babylonian Empire and became the dominant language of the Jewish community during and after the exile.

3. As a formal religion, Judaism was born during that exile. The Law became central to the Jewish community after the exile. Increased study of the Law became a passion. Becoming "people of the Book" changed their focus. The Jewish community thereby reemphasized their commitment to absolute monotheism. This was evident in the singular statements in Isaiah (44:46), Jeremiah (1:16; 2:13; 8:19) and Ezekiel (20:32). Syncretism and idolatry would not be tolerated. Their passion for the Law also enhanced a stricter observance of the Sabbath. Finally, as Ezra and Nehemiah illustrated, contact and assimilation with pagan cultures were not tolerated. The danger of syncretism was too great, for this was one of the reasons for the exile in the first place. How to interact with the pagan cultures all around them would define the Jewish community for the next five hundred years.

4. A theological tension was now evident, especially in the prophets immediately before and after the exile. God's covenant loyalty (His *chesed*) was obvious, for, as promised,

He returned them from Babylonia. Yet the new covenant promised by Jeremiah 31 and Ezekiel 36–37 was not fulfilled. The coming of the righteous "Branch" of Jeremiah 23:5 and 33:15 was not fulfilled. The various Servant Songs of Isaiah (42; 49; 50; 52–53) awaited completion. Isaiah 65 spoke of a new heaven and new earth. The twelve (the minor prophets) were laced with language and prophecies that spoke of an age that did not fit with their vassalage under Persia. The mysterious temple of Ezekiel 40–48 certainly did not fit Zerubbabel's temple. Their prophets spoke of a day of the Lord, a day filled with horrible wrath and judgment, but also a day of astonishing blessing. This day would be connected with God's Spirit (e.g., Joel 2:28–29; Ezekiel 36:27), who was also connected with the new covenant.

The perplexing book of Daniel added to these tensions, for it spoke of human kingdoms but also of God's kingdom and "one like the son of man" who would rule over God's kingdom (7:13). The future for the Jewish community was now focused on a new David, the son of man, the servant of the Lord, who would bring in the triumphant kingdom of God. That One would fulfill the promises God made to Abraham and David completely and perfectly. He would be their messianic King.[224]

The Jewish community had a new hope, a hope centered on a Messiah, God's anointed One, who would bring them salvation and restore Israel to its prominence among the nations. The Davidic ideal now had a future orientation, one filled with immense promise and hope. Their future as God's people depended on Him.

Chapter 9

The Hellenistic Challenge

About four hundred years separated the close of the Old Testament canon with Malachi and the opening of the New Testament canon with Matthew. Although there were no inspired texts written during this period, Judea played an increasingly important role in the geopolitical forces shaping the eastern Mediterranean. It was caught in a confrontation between the emerging power of the West, Greece, and the last major force of the East, Persia.

As Alexander the Great and his successors won that struggle, the clash between the Greek and Hebrew worldviews shaped the Jewish community. They found it more and more difficult to endure as an isolated and pure community. Greek presence in the eastern Mediterranean produced a further fragmentation of Judaism and heightened the expectation—and hope—of a Messiah who would deliver Israel from a new western power, the mighty Roman Empire.

VanGemeren summarizes the change: "Judaism at the end of the Old Testament writings was confined and comfortable, but Judaism some four hundred years later was cosmopolitan and constantly adjusting to change. The Jewish world in the time of Jesus and the apostles was in flux and hence shows little in common with the era of Ezra and Nehemiah."[225]

This chapter is the story of that change.

157

The Late Persian Empire, 400–331 BC

After the death of Artaxerxes in 424 BC, Persia consolidated its control of the Greek city-states on the western coast of Asia Minor (Turkey), largely due to the two Peloponnesian Wars (460–404 BC), which utterly decimated the Greek city-states. But from 404 to 338 BC, Persia began to decline. The western satraps were in rebellion, and Persia's control over Egypt was weakening. The rise of Macedonia (north of Greece) under Philip II would challenge Persian rule everywhere.

During these latter years of Persian rule, several important developments occurred in Judea. The tightness Judaism achieved through the reforms of Ezra and Nehemiah widened the split between the Jews and the Samaritans. The political separation occurred when Nehemiah was made governor of Yehud. There was no hope for Samaria under Sanballat to absorb ancient Judea into its province. Further, the spiritual renewal under Ezra and Nehemiah made the religious division inevitable. The Samaritans could no longer worship in the temple at Jerusalem. Thus the Samaritans built their own temple on Mount Gerizim during the reign of Darius III of Persia (336–330 BC). The Samaritans only accepted the Pentateuch as sacred, and this exacerbated the growing split.[226]

The province of Yehud during this time was somewhat of an autonomous province; there is evidence that it could strike its own coins and levy its own taxes. There are also fragmentary pieces of evidence indicating that the high priest in Jerusalem was becoming a political as well as a religious leader. Further, although Hebrew remained the language of religious and theological discourse, Aramaic, the lingua franca of the western satraps of Persia, was becoming the preferred spoken language of Yehud.[227]

The Hellenistic Period, 331–63 BC

***

Excursus on Daniel

The Old Testament book of Daniel is quite central to understanding the period discussed in this chapter. Daniel was exiled to Babylon during the first wave taken by Nebuchadnezzar in 605 BC. Daniel served in the courts of Babylonia and early Persia. The first eight chapters of Daniel's book, written in Aramaic, outline the contours of Gentile world history, positing four great empires, followed by a final form of the fourth empire, and culminating in the kingdom of God ruled by one "like a son of man" (7:13). Chapters 9 to 12, written in Hebrew, itemize the prophecies that focus on the people of Israel and detail their future from the end of the exile through the culmination of history in God's kingdom.

The vision Daniel received in 11:2–12:13 is astonishing, for it provides a detailed overview of history. For the faithful followers of God, this vision affirmed His sovereignty and providence over history. This is a summary of the historic details prophesied in Daniel's vision:

- 11:2—three more Persian kings (Cambyses, Smerdis, Darius I Hystaspes) would follow Cyrus the Great of Persia, followed by a fourth (Xerxes), who would attack Greece.
- 11:3—Alexander the Great would destroy Persia.
- 11:4—upon his death, his generals would divide his kingdom into four parts.
- 11:5-20—two of the four generals and their descendants, "the kings of the north" and "the kings of the south" (the Ptolemies and the Seleucids), would fight one another for the control of the land.
- 11:21–38—the appalling reign of Antiochus IV Epiphanes, whose brutality and self-elevation produced the Maccabean Revolt.

- 11:39–12:13—Israel's suffering and persecution associated with "the time of the end" under Antichrist would be followed by the triumph of God's kingdom.

The material in Daniel was important information for the Jewish community as they returned from the exile. Even though they could return to their land, they were still a vassal state of Persia—and would remain subjects of Greece, then Rome and all future conquerors through AD 1948, when the modern nation-state of Israel was created. Daniel gives comfort, hope, and an assurance that indeed God will fulfill His covenant promises to Abraham and David.

**

Since Darius I and Xerxes I had invaded Greece in the fifth century BC, hostilities between Persia and Greece were ongoing. With Philip II of Macedon, those tensions took a different turn. Philip trained a formidable army, united the Greek city-states, still reeling from the disruptive Peloponnesian Wars, and launched a sacred war of revenge against Persia.

When Philip was assassinated in 336 BC, his son, Alexander, seized the throne and invaded the East. In 333 BC, Alexander defeated Darius III of Persia at Issus. He then moved along the coast and, according to the ancient Jewish historian Josephus, went up to Jerusalem and offered sacrifices to Yahweh. This story is probably apocryphal, but he did evidence a degree of favoritism toward the Jews. He then conquered Egypt, declared himself pharaoh in 332 BC, and founded the important city of Alexandria on the Nile Delta. In 331 BC, Alexander decisively defeated the armies of Darius III at the battle of Gaugamela, thereby bringing the Persian Empire to an end.

He continued his conquest east, going as far as the Hindu Kush Mountains. When his armies would go no farther, he returned to Babylon, where he died unexpectedly in 323 BC. He was thirty-three. His conquest broke down most of the political and cultural boundaries that had existed for centuries in the eastern Mediterranean world and throughout much of southwest Asia.

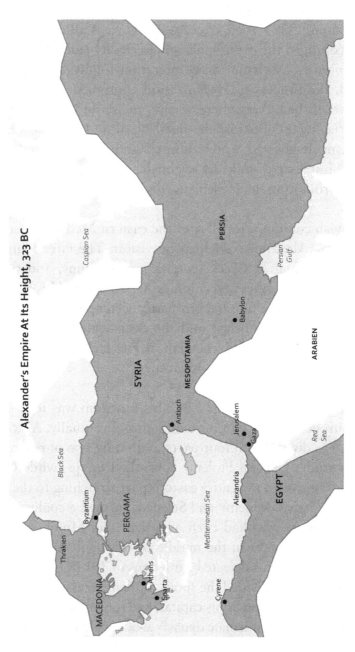

Alexander's vision was to unite the world around Greek culture—
its architecture, language, philosophy, thought, and ethics. Tutored
by the philosopher Aristotle, Alexander believed in the superiority
of the Greek way of life, and that Greek culture (*Hellenism*, from
Hellas, the Greek word for Greece) would be the unifying center
of his empire. He settled veterans of his wars all over his empire
and encouraged the overpopulated Greek city-states to migrate to
these colonies. A virtual mass migration followed. Even though
he died, the process of Hellenization continued. Greek colonies
were established everywhere, each "an island of Hellenism."[228]
lexandria, Egypt, became the intellectual and cultural center of
Hellenism. It boasted a great library, and its intellectual climate
fostered impressive works by scientists, philosophers, and historians, all promoting the Hellenistic worldview.

The Jewish communities all over the eastern Mediterranean were
affected by Alexander's Hellenistic vision. The Greek language,
plus the building of Greek temples, gymnasiums, and theaters,
characterized the cities and colonies Alexander and his successors
founded. Increased trade and prosperity accompanied Hellenism.[229]
Could Jewish monotheism and the deep-seated spiritual forces
reawakened by Ezra and Nehemiah survive Hellenism's onslaught?
Or would Hellenism change Judaism?

When Alexander died in 323 BC, his kingdom was torn by civil
war as his generals fought for dominance. Eventually, Alexander's
empire was divided into four parts, with only two of real concern
for this study: General Ptolemy controlled Egypt, while General
Seleucus controlled the entire eastern part stretching to the Hindu
Kush Mountains. Ptolemy and Seleucus formed a coalition to defeat Antigonus, who had been awarded Asia Minor. Judah and
Samaria were caught in the middle of this civil war. Eventually,
Ptolemy and Seleucus defeated Antigonus in 301 BC, and these two
powerful generals divided the spoils. Ptolemy reasserted control of
Egypt with Alexandria as his capital, and took control of Phoenicia
and Palestine. The Ptolemaic dynasty would rule Judah for the next

one hundred years. Seleucus claimed everything to the east. The Ptolemaic dynasty and the Seleucid dynasty would fight five major wars over the land of Israel.[230]

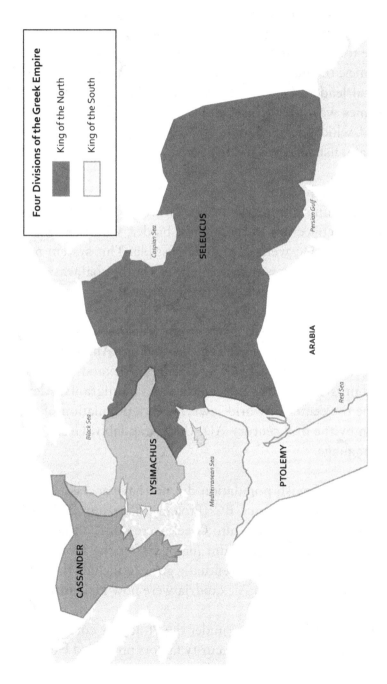

The Ptolemies' Rule Over Israel, 301–200 BC

Under the Ptolemies, the Jews enjoyed a status similar to that under the Persians. But taxes were high, and the high priest in Jerusalem had the responsibility for tax collection and paying the annual tribute to Alexandria. Since Judea was a "temple state" under the Ptolemies, the high priest in Jerusalem was both the spiritual and political leader. This comparative religious autonomy under the Ptolemies was in contrast with a significant degree of economic control, which included trade, finance, and agriculture. Dates, olive oil, grain, fish, cheese, and fruit were regularly exported to Egypt.

The most important dimension of economic control was the Ptolemaic innovation called "tax farming." The Ptolemies franchised tax collection to the highest bidder, who then was free to collect taxes that were as high as possible. This system produced significant oppression and exploitation, for the goal was always "to maximize profit for the court in Alexandria."[231]

The Jewish population in Egypt swelled during this period. Indeed, Ptolemy I, in 312 BC, during the war against Antigonus, resettled a large number of Jews from Jerusalem to Alexandria. Other Jews settled in Alexandria as mercenaries and immigrants. Alexandria became the center of world Jewry, with a population of over one million by the first century AD. Understandably, Greek was their first language.

Because this Jewish population did not have access to Scripture, during the third century BC (Ptolemy II's reign, 285–247 BC), translations of the Torah into Greek were done, and this translation, known as the Septuagint (named after the seventy scholars who did the translation), eventually grew to include the entire Old Testament. The Jews in Alexandria were now Hellenized Jews.

The Hellenization of Judea under the Ptolemies continued. Brisco writes that "economic and security factors promoted Hellenization in many cities, especially along the coasts and in the Transjordan. Ptolemais (Acco), Gadara, Philadelphia (Rabbah), Philoteria (Beth-yerah), and other cities surrounded Jerusalem as something of a Hellenistic border."[232] In addition, when Onias II, the high priest under Ptolemy III, refused to collect the taxes, he was replaced by the Tobiads, a wealthy Jewish family that traced its origin back to Nehemiah's time (2:10; 6:1–19). The Tobiad family became the chief driver of Hellenized Judaism; they sought to minimize Jewish law and maximize the Greek way of life. Jewish leadership was thus inextricably linked to Alexandria. But that was about to change, for the Seleucids would challenge Ptolemaic rule of Judea.

The Seleucid's Rule Over Israel, 200–162 BC

Because of its sheer size, the Seleucid Empire was much more difficult to rule. Its boundaries were not as easily defined as in the Ptolemaic Empire. Further, there were rebellions in the eastern provinces, and by the mid-third century, the Seleucids had lost control of parts of Asia Minor. The Seleucids established Antioch in Syria as their key administrative center in the western part of their empire, and Seleucia on the Tigris River as their key administrative center in the east. As with the Ptolemies, the Seleucids envisioned Hellenization as the unifying force for their vast empire.[233]

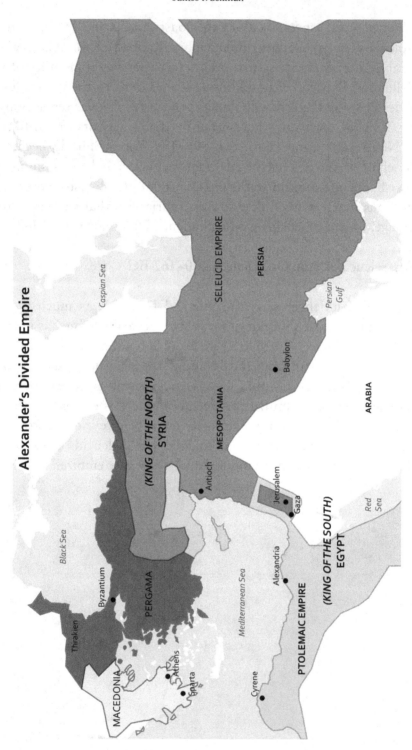

Alexander's Divided Empire

The reign of Antiochus III (223–187 BC) was a watershed for Seleucid rule, for he regained control of much of the previously lost territories from Asia Minor to India. His two wars with the Ptolemies of Egypt (the Fourth, 219–217 BC, and the Fifth, 202–195 BC, Syrian wars) drove the Egyptians out of Asia. Antiochus III thereby gained control of all of Palestine. (See Daniel 11:10–16.)

The Jews welcomed their new rulers and had indeed fought on their side against the Ptolemies. As a result, Antiochus III released all Jewish prisoners and issued a decree permitting the return of Jewish refugees to their homes. He allowed the Jews to affirm the supremacy of their Law in Judea, financially supported Jewish religious leaders with tax revenue, and exempted most religious personnel from Seleucid taxation. He also decreed that temple repairs were to be done at Seleucid expense.[234]

However, Seleucid fortunes were changing. A new power was rising in the west—Rome—and the Parthian menace to the east was also a new rival. The Seleucids lost significant parts of their empire to both powers. For example, in his last years, Antiochus III suffered a humiliating series of defeats at the hands of Rome, which now established itself as the formidable power of Asia Minor. (See Daniel 11:17–19.) Financially weak and threatened on all sides, the Seleucid Empire had begun its decline.

The Seleucid loss of much of Palestine centered on the reign of Antiochus IV (later called Antiochus Epiphanes, "god manifest"; see Daniel 11:21–23). That loss began with rivalry over the high priesthood in Jerusalem. Onias III was the high priest, and in 174 BC Antiochus IV deposed him, replacing him with his brother, Jason (Joshua). The hereditary nature of the priesthood was now over. Future high priests would be appointed by whoever was ruling Judea at that time, the post often going to the one who paid the highest bribe.

The Hellenization of Jerusalem accelerated under Jason. He facilitated the incorporation of Jerusalem as a Greek city (a *polis*) and established a Greek *gymnasium* (an educational institution) in Jerusalem. The Jerusalem gymnasium championed a classical educational curriculum. Because one competed in athletic games naked, and circumcision was embarrassing, circumcision was no longer regularly practiced in Jerusalem. Some men even had surgery to conceal their circumcisions.

As Bright shows, "Since Greek sports were inseparable from the cult of Heracles, or of Hermes, or of the royal house, membership in the gymnasium inevitably involved some degree of recognition of the gods who were its protectors."[235] The decree of Antiochus III granting Jews the right to live according to their Law had been abrogated—and with Jewish help. For that reason, more orthodox Jews and most of the people began to charge the leadership with apostasy. Even the sacrifices were "blemished and unacceptable."[236]

Although Jason's sympathies were clearly Hellenistic, after three years, Antiochus IV appointed Menelaus high priest because he offered a larger bribe. To pay the bribe, he looted the temple. Jerusalem was now a Hellenistic temple state, and the high priest was its chief, albeit corrupt, political figure.[237]

Antiochus IV twice invaded Egypt. In 170 BC, he defeated Ptolemy VI, plundering Egypt as a result. (See Daniel 11:24–27.) After this victory, on his return home in 169 BC, he stopped in Jerusalem and, with the total support of Menelaus, put down an insurrection led by the former high priest Jason, killing 80,000 Jews. He then looted the temple. (See Daniel 11:28.) In 170 BC, Antiochus again invaded Egypt, conquering Memphis and then attacking Alexandria. Rome, allied with the Ptolemies, ordered him to leave Egypt, which he did in humiliation and defeat. (See Daniel 11:29–30.) In early 167 BC, Antiochus directed his rage against Jerusalem.

Because he felt threatened by Rome and because Jerusalem was seething with rebellion, Antiochus began a policy of forced

Hellenization in Jerusalem. To that end, later in 167, he dispatched Apollonius, a commander of his mercenaries, to Jerusalem. Apollonius was ruthless. He tore down some of the walls of the city, savagely butchered many of its citizens, and set up a military fortress in Jerusalem called the Acra.

The temple was no longer the property of the Jewish people; it now belonged to the Seleucids. As Bright argues, Apollonius, working with the apostate Menelaus and his colleagues, removed "all barriers to the thoroughgoing Hellenization of the Jewish religion ... It was apparently the aim of these renegade priests to reorganize Judaism as a Syro-Hellenic cult in which Yahweh would be worshiped in identification with Zeus, and [Jerusalem] a place provided for the royal cult in which the king was Zeus Epiphanes."[238]

Apollonius further banned orthodox Jewish practices: sacrifices, observation of the Sabbath, and traditional feasts. Circumcision was outlawed. Altars to Greek gods were built and sacrifices were offered. On the Temple Mount altar to Yahweh, an idol of Zeus was erected, and pigs were sacrificed on that altar. To show their loyalty, Jews were required to participate in these sacrifices.

In addition, Antiochus IV was to be worshipped as a god— Antiochus Epiphanes, or "god manifest." (See Daniel 11:36–38.) From 167–164 BC, these edicts were enforced by troops from the Acra. Jews who circumcised their children were murdered. Those who observed the Sabbath were slaughtered.

The Maccabean Revolt, 167–142 BC

Most Jews followed a course of passive resistance to Antiochus IV, but not all. The active resistance boiled into the Maccabean Revolt, which began in the tiny village of Modein, northwest of Jerusalem. An elderly man of priestly lineage named Mattathias lived there, along with his sons John, Simon, Judas, Eleazar, and

Jonathan. Because Mattathias was a priest, a Seleucid emissary ordered him to offer sacrifices on a pagan altar as a sign of loyalty to Antiochus. Mattathias refused. When another priest offered the sacrifice, Mattathias killed him and the Seleucid officer.

Mattathias and his sons fled and organized a revolt. (See Daniel 11:33–35.) He and his sons were joined by an anti-Hellenist group called the Hasidim (the pious ones), who were devoutly loyal to the Law. Together they sought to purify the land by focusing on apostate Jews, the destruction of pagan altars, and the requirement that all male Jews be circumcised. When Mattathias died in 166 BC, leadership of this revolt passed to his son Judas, who was called Maccabeus ("the hammer").[239]

Judas led his supporters in a guerilla war against the Seleucids. Attacking the Seleucids in narrow mountain passes all around Jerusalem, Judas won a series of impressive victories. In 167, he defeated the army of Apollonius near Lebonah, north of Jerusalem. In 166 BC, Judas defeated the commander Seron at Beth-horn, a pass northwest of Jerusalem. The next year, he routed a considerable army under the command of Nicanor at Emmaus, west of Jerusalem. Finally, in 164 BC, Judas delivered a crushing defeat to the commander Lysias at Beth-zur, south of Jerusalem.

In December 164 BC, Judas marched into Jerusalem, barricaded the Syrian forces in the Acra, and then entered the temple. Judas and his supporters destroyed the altar to Zeus and built a new altar. The entire temple area was purified, the sacrificial system was restored according to the Law, and a new priesthood was installed. On 25 December 164 BC, the festival of Hanukkah was instituted to commemorate the dedication of the temple and the reinstitution of the sacrificial system.

In 164 BC, Antiochus Epiphanes died and a power struggle for control ensued. To win the support of the Jewish community, in 162 BC, Seleucid general Lysias rescinded all previous edicts against the Jewish religion. The Hasidim, allies of the Maccabees, accepted this gesture and ended their armed struggle.

Demetrius I won the power struggle for control of the Seleucid Empire, executed Lysias, and sought to reassert control over Judea. Judas Maccabeus responded in two ways. First, in 161 BC, he signed a treaty of alliance with Rome, which was aggressively pursuing its desire to influence the eastern Mediterranean. Second, he continued his guerilla warfare tactics. Fighting the growing Seleucid military presence, Judas was killed in 160 BC at Elasa, northwest of Jerusalem.[240]

Jonathan Maccabeus succeeded Judas. Because of the mounting military presence of the Seleucids and because many had given up on the armed struggle, Jonathan withdrew to the Judean desert. The guerilla warfare tactics continued from there, especially against the new Seleucid general Bacchides.

A truce between the two forces was reached, and Jonathan relocated to Michmash in the Judean desert. There Jonathan changed tactics and engaged in diplomacy, taking sides between the contending powers for the Seleucid throne. He reaffirmed the alliance with Rome that Judas had signed. In 152 BC, Jonathan was declared high priest and given control over much of Judea and Samaria. Tragically, in 143 BC, Jonathan was executed by a rival Seleucid general Trypho.

Simon Maccabeus, who succeeded his brother Jonathan, was a watershed figure in Jewish history. In the ongoing struggle for control of the Seleucid Empire, Simon sided with Demetrius II, who won the struggle. Because of his allegiance, Simon was awarded the independence of Judea and Jerusalem. Demetrius exempted Judea from taxation, and the high priesthood, which had been a political appointment, was now under the hereditary custody of the Maccabean family. Simon was declared high priest and ruler of his people (the "ethnarch").

The Maccabean goal of independence had been achieved. Simon was in effect the founder of a new dynasty of rulers, the Hasmonean dynasty. Simon was murdered in a coup attempt led by his son-in-law in 135 BC.[241]

The Hasmonean Dynasty, 142–63 BC

Simon's son John Hyrcanus succeeded him and ruled for thirty years (135–104 BC). As the power of the Seleucids was receding and as the protective alliance with Rome provided cover, John Hyrcanus significantly expanded Hasmonean territory. In 129 BC, he attacked Medeba, east of the Dead Sea, and in 128 BC he subdued Samaria to the north, razing Shechem and the Samaritan temple on Mount Gerizim. He conquered Idumea to the south, forcing everyone there to convert to Judaism and to practice circumcision. Finally, he added southern Galilee up to the Valley of Jezreel to his expanding kingdom.

Although his conquests were notable, John Hyrcanus took on the trappings of a Hellenistic king. He employed mercenaries as a part of his army. He gave his children Greek, not Hebrew names. His increasingly Hellenistic style of rule caused a significant rift with a new religious sect emerging within Judaism, the Pharisees. Another new sect, the Sadducees, who came from the upper class, were some of his strongest supporters.

Aristobulus, eldest son of John Hyrcanus, ruled briefly (104–103 BC) but was the first Hasmonean to use the title "king." He also completed the conquest of Galilee, seizing the entire upper region from an Arab tribe called the Itureans and forcing them to adopt Judaism, including circumcision.

The remaining Hasmonean rulers reflected the rapid decline of the independent Jewish state. Alexander Jannaeus (103–76 BC) extended the new state's holdings to almost the footprint of Solomon's empire. But his personal debauchery earned the antipathy of the

Pharisees, who organized popular support against Alexander. In return, he massacred hundreds of Pharisees, including their wives and children.

Alexander was succeeded by Salome Alexandra, his wife, who ruled from 76 to 67 BC. Most notably, she brought the Pharisees back into favor, who then turned on the Sadducees. She appointed her son, Hyrcanus II, the high priest, but her other son, Aristobulus, was a strong supporter of the Sadducees and rejected his appointment. When Salome died in 67 BC, a virtual civil war developed between her sons.

When it looked as though Hyrcanus was defeated, Antipater II, governor of Idumea (appointed by Alexander Jannaeus), intervened and provided Hyrcanus protection in the Nabatean kingdom at Petra. The Nabatean king, Aretas, promised Hyrcanus support. The Hasmonean dynasty was now hopelessly divided: Hyrcanus II had the support of the Pharisees, Antipater, and Aretas of Nabatea, while Aristobulus II had the support of the Sadducees.

While the Hasmonean dynasty was self-destructing, Rome was on the march. Seeking to establish Rome's presence firmly in the eastern Mediterranean, the great Roman general Pompey had invaded Syria in 64 BC. His legions were just north of the warring Hasmonean kingdom. Both Hyrcanus and Artistobulus appealed to him. Pompey's legions marched from Damascus and conquered Judea, laid siege to Jerusalem for three months, and conquered it. Pompey then entered the Holy of Holies on Temple Mount, desecrating it as far as the Jews were concerned. Pompey established Hyrcanus as high priest, to the delight of the Pharisees and Antipater of Idumea, who shrewdly saw that Rome was the future. (He was the father of Herod the Great). The Hasmonean dynasty had come to an end; Judea was now a subject of Rome.[242]

James P. Eckman

Excursus on 1 and 2 Maccabees

Two important books in the Apocrypha are 1 and 2 Maccabees. Of the two, 1 Maccabees is the most important. It is a reliable history of the period from 175 to 134 BC, covering the reign of Antiochus Epiphanes, the success of the Maccabean revolt, and the rule of John Hyrcanus. Originally written by an anonymous writer in Hebrew, it was translated into Greek. Although it gives important historical details of this period, its clear intent is to elevate the Maccabees as the champions of orthodox Judaism against the paganism of Seleucid Hellenism. Much of what we know of the revolt and early Hasmonean rule comes from this book.

The second book of Maccabees is less reliable. Although it covers some of the same material as 1 Maccabees, there are chronological and factual errors, and it is therefore not as valuable. But there are still valuable historical details about this period that can be gleaned from 2 Maccabees.

**

Developments Within Judaism during the Hellenistic Period

During the period of what is normally called Diaspora Judaism (the Jews of the exile), the synagogue system developed. Its exact origins are obscure. For those Jews who lived a considerable distance from Jerusalem and the temple, the need for some kind of religious center was obvious. Hence, the synagogue emerged as a meeting place, a place for prayer, and a place for instruction in Scripture. It was distinctly separate from the temple, its ritual, and its priesthood. As David O'Brien argues, "the shift from a priestly to a popular religious center was radical. It was a first step toward the democratization of Judaism."[243]

By the time of Jesus, there were literally hundreds of synagogues in Judea and Galilee (e.g., Capernaum, Nazareth), as well as in

Jerusalem and Alexandria in Egypt. Wherever Jews settled, synagogues developed. Those who attended were governed by a council of elders. As the synagogue system matured, there was a structured time for the reading of Scripture, with most males participating in the reading. During the Hellenistic period, the synagogue became a central element of Judaism.

Also during the Hellenistic period, Judaism began to fragment. Sometime before the Hasmonean independent state, the national council, or the Sanhedrin (from the Greek word for "council"), had begun to meet. The Sanhedrin was apparently made up of the key advisers to the high priest when Judea was a temple state under the Ptolemies and then the Seleucids. Two parties of Judaism dominated the Sanhedrin—the Pharisees and the Sadducees.[244] The origins of both are wrapped in a good deal of obscurity.

- **The Pharisees.** They first appear in the work of the early Jewish historian Josephus, who cites them when they lost favor with John Hyrcanus. They broke with Hyrcanus because of his penchant for Hellenistic elegances. There is little doubt that their origin was in some way connected with the Hasidim, who had supported the Maccabees in the early periods of their revolt. The Pharisees were separatists who saw the Law as sacred. Thus, for the Pharisees, the laws of ritualistic purity, tithing, observing the Sabbath, and the feast days of Judaism were equally sacred. Over time, in their study of the Law, they constructed an oral tradition of interpretation and application, that became as sacred as the written Law. This oral tradition became as rigid and unbending as the law of Moses.[245] The Pharisees were extremely popular with the people, who were loyal and devoted to them. As O'Brien comments, "The Pharisees were the party of the synagogue, deriving authority from the interpretation of Scripture and the rigor of their adherence to that interpretation."[246]

Sadducees

Priests

Worked in the Temple

Did not believe in resurrection

Did not believe in angels

Rejected the idea of Oral Law (added scholarly interpretation of the Torah) and insisted on a literal interpretation of the original Law/Torah given at Mt. Sinai.

Main focus of Sadducee life was rituals associated with the Temple

vs.

Pharisees

Teachers of the law

Taught in Synagogues

Believed in resurrection

Believed in angels

Believed Oral Law (added scholarly interpretation of the Torah) was equal to the original written Law/Torah given at Mt. Sinai

Main focus of the Pharisees was teaching the application of priestly laws to non-priests, commoners

- **The Sadducees.** They surface first in their support of the Hasmoneans from John Hyrcanus on. The term "Sadducee" is perhaps connected to the Greek term for "counselor," as they were counselors of the Hasmoneans; or from the Hebrew for "Zadok," the priestly clan; or from the Hebrew word for "righteous." What is certain is that the Sadducees enjoyed significant power during the Hasmonean period, almost always at the expense of the Pharisees. They were the most loyal supporters of the Hasmonean dynasty until Salome Alexandra turned on them. Their support came from the upper-class families and priestly clans of Jerusalem, and they were much more comfortable with Hellenism than the Pharisees. The Sadducees rejected the oral law of the Pharisees, focusing exclusively on the Pentateuch. They rejected the doctrine of the resurrection and were skeptical about the existence of angelic beings. They were the dominant political force in Judea prior to the Roman conquest, and they were intimately linked with the temple. High Priest Caiaphas and his family during the time of Jesus were Sadducees. The Sadducees went out of existence in AD 70 when General Titus destroyed the temple.[247]

- **A Word About the Essenes.** The Essenes are a difficult group to understand. They are mentioned by Philo, the Alexandrian Jewish scholar, by Pliny, the Roman historian, and by Josephus, the Jewish historian. That they existed is certain, but there is immense controversy about them. They deserted Jerusalem, apparently because of the corruption of the city during the Hellenistic period, and, preparing for an apocalyptic end to history, lived separatist lives of personal piety in small communal living arrangements throughout Syria and Palestine. Josephus depicts Essenes living in harsh, simple conditions, in communities that renounced pleasure. The Essenes performed significant purification rites using water. (See also *The Manual of Discipline* found among the Scrolls at Qumran.) In all likelihood, one of their communities was at Qumran on the west side of the Dead Sea. Whether the Essenes were the authors/copiers of the Dead Sea Scrolls is today controversial and less than certain. If the Dead Sea Scrolls are from the Essenes, they have much to tell us about apocalyptic thought in early Judaism. Also, the Dead Sea Scroll copies of Isaiah, Habakkuk, and other Old Testament texts are exceedingly valuable for biblical studies. Among other things, they validate the accuracy of the Old Testament books. The Essenes were apparently destroyed by the Roman legions during the Jewish revolt of AD 67–73.[248]

As the Hellenistic challenge faded and was replaced by a new challenge—the challenge of Rome, we are left with the haunting silence of the Old Testament. Schreiner best summarizes that silence: "The OT clearly leaves us with an unfinished story. The serpent was not yet crushed. The promise that Israel would dwell in the land was contradicted by the exile, and even when Israel repossessed the land, they were either under the thumb of foreign powers or barley hanging on to independence. The promises of the new covenant, the new exodus, the new creation, and the new David obviously were not realized."[249]

But that silence was soon to be broken. The apostle Paul declared that in the "fullness of time," God sent His Son (Galatians 4:4). Hellenistic Greek thought, Rome's imperial conquest, and Jewish messianic expectations were all part of that "fullness." God's redemptive plan was on schedule and His covenant promises were about to be fulfilled—and that fulfillment would be wrapped around the Lord Jesus Christ.

Chapter 10

Rome, Messiah, and the New Order

The Jewish world into which Jesus was born was entirely different from the postexilic world of Ezra and Nehemiah. The exile had cured the Jewish people of idolatry, but Hellenism was a new form of idolatry that was much more seductive and powerful. As the last chapter has shown, many Jews learned that by "acculturation to the Greek way of life and thinking, one could obtain power and wealth."[250]

The Hellenization of the eastern Mediterranean dramatically affected the Jewish community and Judaism in particular. The response to Hellenism produced the fragmentation of Judaism. Consequently, today it is impossible to talk about what the Jewish people believed as a group in the first century AD. A religious order that involved the Pharisees, the Sadducees, and the Essenes was evidence of a religion very much in a state of flux. In addition, after Pompey's success in 63 BC, the Jewish community had a new master: the Roman Empire, an empire of order, structure, and ruthless power. The Jews would not willingly submit to their new master.

The combined message of John the Baptist and Jesus was, "Repent, for the kingdom of heaven is at hand" (Matthew 3:3; 4:17). A new order was dawning, and the anticipation of the Old Testament was resolved in the fulfillment of the New Testament. Thomas Schreiner captures this well:

> The OT closes on a note of anticipation, and the NT opens on a note of fulfillment. The kingdom of God

has come, and this is evident because Jesus is raised from the dead, and "all authority in heaven and earth" is his (Matthew 28:18). The very first verse of Matthew resonates with OT themes and covenants: "The book of the genealogy of Jesus Christ, the son of David, the son of Abraham" (1:1) ... The references to David and Abraham hearken back to OT covenants.[251]

Jesus Christ would fulfill the covenant commitments God had made to Israel and, as the prophets had declared, would usher in the kingdom of God. In that context, the mighty Roman Empire was merely God's instrument to accomplish His purposes. This chapter is the story of how God used Rome for those purposes.

The Rise of Rome

The beginning of Rome is wrapped in myth and legend, especially the stories of Romulus and Remus, which traditionally date Rome's founding in 753 BC. The "city of the seven hills" was ruled by a monarchy, which, legend has it, was begun by Romulus. As Rome developed, the influence of the Etruscans to the north and the Greeks to the east was significant. Rome synthesized these various cultures, ideas, and practices to best suit its needs; this ability to synthesize became a distinctive Roman trait.

According to Roman tradition, 509 BC was the founding date of the Roman Republic. Rome was no longer ruled by a monarch; rather, various representative bodies, which would develop into the Senate and other assemblies, ruled the people of Rome. Tensions between the patricians—the wealthy, landholding families—and the plebeians—the lower classes of Roman society—defined the early republic.

As a result of a deadly invasion in 390 BC by the Gauls from the north, Rome was determined to rule the entire Italian peninsula. Therefore, through a series of wars (334–264 BC), Rome basically won control of most of Italy. In 312 BC, Rome constructed its first road, the Appian Way or *Via Appia*, which connected Rome with its military outposts to the south. This was the beginning of the famous road system that would eventually connect the entire Mediterranean world.

As the Roman Republic consolidated its control of Italy, it faced a significant rival for control of the western Mediterranean—Carthage, which was an old Phoenician colony founded in 814 BC. Between 264 and 146 BC, three major wars (called the Punic Wars) were fought between Rome and Carthage. (The Second Punic War involved the famous Carthaginian general Hannibal, who unsuccessfully invaded Rome from the north.) By the end of the third war in 146 BC, after more than a hundred years, Rome had conquered Carthage's empire and completely destroyed the city, becoming the most powerful state of the Western Mediterranean.

With the end of the four Macedonian wars (214–148 BC)—which were fought concurrently with the Punic Wars—and the defeat of the Seleucid king Antiochus III the Great in the Roman-Syrian War in 190 BC, Rome was now the dominant Mediterranean power. When Pergamum's King Attalus III willed his kingdom to Rome in 133 BC, Rome's colonies extended from Asia Minor in the east to Spain in the west.

Serious social crises at home, piracy threats on the Mediterranean, and instability on the frontier (e.g., the 88 BC revolt of Mithradates in Asia Minor) demonstrated the incompetency of the Senate to rule. The political structures of the republic were failing. Thus three famous generals, Pompey, Julius Caesar, and Crassus, formed the First Triumvirate to bring political and social order to Rome. After Crassus and Pompey were killed, Caesar emerged as the sole ruler, declared by the Senate to be dictator in 44 BC. The Roman Republic had come to an end.

When Caesar was assassinated on the Ides of March in 44 BC, his grandnephew, Octavian, hunted down Caesar's assassins and by 27 BC had emerged victorious in the wars with Antony and Cleopatra. The Senate then gave Octavian the title of Augustus; he was known as "Divine Augustus Caesar, Son of God, and Savior of the world." The Roman Empire had begun, as had the Pax Romana, a two-hundred-year period (27 BC through AD 180) of internal and external peace. During the Pax Romana, Jesus Christ was born, the Christian church was founded, Rome totally destroyed Jerusalem during the Great Jewish Revolt, AD 67–73, and the Jews were dispersed throughout the Mediterranean world.[252]

Pompey, Julius Caesar, and King Herod

By 67 BC, Pompey had cleared the Mediterranean of pirates, and by 65 BC had put down the revolt of Mithradates in Pontus (Asia Minor). Because Syria was basically in a state of anarchy, Pompey moved his troops into the region, conquered Damascus, and annexed Syria in 64 BC. Pompey then intervened in the civil war raging between the Hasmonean rivals, Hyrcanus II and Aristobulus II, siding with Hyrcanus II. Aristobulus's supporters resisted Pompey's troops as they moved into Jerusalem by taking refuge on Temple Mount. From the Pools of Bethesda, Pompey besieged the temple for three months. On the Sabbath, his troops stormed the temple, killing the priests who guarded the Holy of Holies. Surprisingly, Pompey entered the Holy of Holies, inspected this sacred center of Judaism, but did not loot the temple, including the two thousand talents deposited there. Graciously, he permitted the temple to be purified and the offering of sacrifices to resume.[253]

Pompey reinstated Hyrcanus as high priest, but gave him the title of ethnarch, not king. Pompey razed the walls around the temple and the city of Jerusalem. Roman taxation was imposed, and the territory of the Jewish state was reduced to four districts in which Judaism was the dominant religion—Galilee, most of Samaria, Judea, and part of Idumea. Pompey also established the Decapolis, a league of ten Greek cities, nine of which were on the east side of the Jordan River. Pompey's strategy was to reduce the Jewish state's ability to trade and to humble it by reducing its status and territory. It was not annexed, but it was now a vassal of Rome and a buffer to the hazardous Parthians lurking to the east.

Antipater, ruler of Idumea and the real power behind Hyrcanus II, was devastated by Pompey's settlement. He dreamed of ruling an independent kingdom through Hyrcanus as his puppet. But he quickly concluded that there was no future in opposition to Rome.[254]

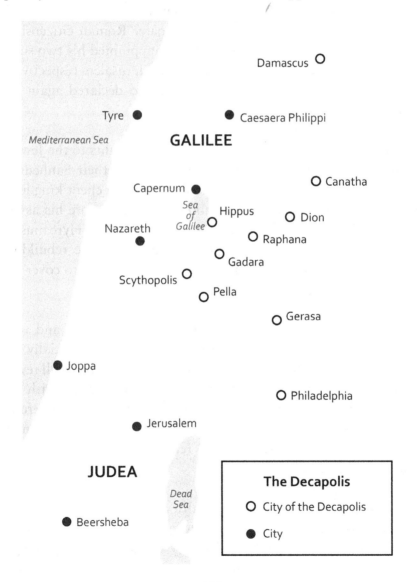

Though Pompey and Julius Caesar had been allies in the First Triumvirate, when Crassus, the third member, was killed in 53 BC, war broke out between the two. Caesar pursued Pompey to Egypt. Pompey was killed by the Egyptians in 48 BC, and Caesar's long affair with Cleopatra began.

Hyrcanus and Antipater realized that their fortunes now rested with Julius Caesar, so they pledged loyalty to him and gave him additional military aid for his campaign in Egypt. As a reward, Caesar traveled to Judea, granted Antipater Roman citizenship, and appointed him procurator. Antipater appointed his two sons, Herod and Phasael, tetrarchs of Galilee and Jerusalem respectively. Hyrcanus was reaffirmed as high priest and declared again the ethnarch of the Jews.

Caesar also granted significant privileges and rights to the Jewish people in terms of their Law and the power of their Sanhedrin. Caesar confirmed that the Jewish territory was a client kingdom, not a Roman province. Finally, about a month before his assassination, Caesar received a special delegation from Hyrcanus in Rome and, with senatorial approval, authorized the rebuilding of the walls of Jerusalem and a reduction in taxation to cover the expenses of doing so.[255]

Herod's rule as the tetrarch of Galilee was successful and won him friendship with Rome, but the Jewish leaders, especially the Sadducees, stood opposed. Herod ruthlessly crushed a small revolt in Galilee led by one Hezekiah, further alienating the Jewish nationalists. Instability increased, as did court intrigue, after Herod's father, Antipater, was assassinated in 43 BC. Mark Antony, now ruling in this part of the empire, reaffirmed the tetrarchies of Phasael and Herod.

By 40 BC, the old Hasmonean rivalries were again stirring. The son of Aristobulus II, Antigonus, negotiated an agreement with the Parthians to the east, by which they would install him as high priest and ruler of the Jews. The subsequent Parthian invasion resulted in Phasael's suicide and Herod's flight to the fortress at Masada, where he left his family. Herod's only hope was direct intervention from Rome, so he made his way to Rome.

Both Mark Antony and Octavian supported Herod as he appeared before the Roman Senate in 40 BC. At the urging of Anthony, a pivotal decision was made: Herod would be named "King of the Jews." Political power in the Jewish territory would now be separated from spiritual leadership. Herod was thereby assured political superiority over the high priest. In addition, the Senate awarded him control over Judea, Galilee, Samaria, and all of Idumea.

Herod returned to the eastern Mediterranean with the unbridled support of Rome. It took him three years to subdue his enemies. While Rome neutralized the Parthian threat, Herod's army of Idumeans and mercenaries defeated forces loyal to Antigonus. Jerusalem fell to Herod in 37 BC, and at Herod's insistence, Antigonus and many of his Sadducee supporters were executed. The Hasmonean dynasty had come to an end. Herod was now the undisputed king of the Jews, ruling, as a client of Rome, over a territory that included Judea, Samaria, Idumea, Galilee, and Perea.[256]

Because Herod was an Idumean and not a Jew, few in his new kingdom were supportive. He needed to consolidate his rule. The Hasmonean factions certainly did not support him, so the possibility of revolt was real. Hence, as support for Herod, Rome left a legion in Jerusalem. For obvious political reasons and to ingratiate himself with the Jews, the shrewd Herod, before he conquered Jerusalem in 38 BC, had married Mariamne, a Hasmonean and the niece of Antigonus. Mariamne's mother-in-law, Alexandra, did not support the marriage and sought to elevate her own sons instead. So Alexandra turned to Cleopatra for help.

Cleopatra's ambition was to reconstitute the Ptolemaic Empire, so she pursued the support of Antony, her lover. Antony remained loyal to Herod, but did give Cleopatra Jericho, the Decapolis, and, most importantly, the port city of Joppa, thereby denying Herod access to the Mediterranean. Because he feared Cleopatra, Herod could not decisively challenge her growing intrusions into his kingdom. However, Antony and Cleopatra were defeated by Octavian at the Battle of Actium in 31 BC. With their subsequent suicides, Herod's position changed. (Eventually, Herod had Mariamne, Alexandra, and virtually all of their family murdered).

Herod was uncertain about his new master, Caesar Augustus. Summoned to Rhodes, Herod presented his case that he was a loyal subject of Rome. Octavian accepted this pledge of loyalty and not only reaffirmed that Herod was king of the Jews, but also restored all the lands taken by Cleopatra. Between 23 and 20 BC, Augustus also added to Herod's kingdom Trachonitis, Batanea, Auranitias, Gaulanitis, Panias, and Ulathan, with the result that Herod ruled virtually everything from the southern Dead Sea to the borders of Syria. Herod's kingdom was thus an invaluable buffer state for Rome against the Parthian threat to the east.[257]

Herod the Great, King of the Jews, 37–4 BC

Herod had the confidence of Rome during his entire reign. Everything about his kingdom both served his own personal aggrandizement and evidenced his loyalty to Rome. The most significant index was his building program. Even today, the mark of Herod is everywhere in modern Israel.

1. **Caesarea Maritima.** Herod took an old Phoenician town (the Greeks called it Strato's Tower) and, using quarried stone and hydraulic cement, built a magnificent port facility that linked his kingdom to the entire Roman world. It was his "window to the world."[258] Built between 22 and 9 BC,

Caesarea was a deep-water port facility capable of accommodating the largest Roman cargo vessels. Caesarea was a typical Greco-Roman city with a hippodrome, a theater, and an aqueduct that provided fresh water.

2. The fortresses at **Herodium and Masada,** along with several others, were built to provide security and safety for Herod in times of political unrest. The Herodium was a mountain fortress eight miles southeast of Jerusalem. Herod's engineers took off the top of the mountain and built a cylindrical cone of four towers. Herod's remains were recently discovered in the Lower Herodium. At Masada, Herod renovated existing Hasmonean structures and added two palaces, one on the northern side and one on the southern side. It was on Masada where the Zealots made their last defensive stand against Rome in AD 73.

3. **The Temple in Jerusalem.** Although Herod transformed Jerusalem with a new palace on the western side, a new theater, and a hippodrome, and with additional aqueducts for fresh water, it was the temple that was his lasting achievement. It was begun in 19 BC and was not completely finished until AD 64. Herod pulled down the existing second temple built by Zerubbabel. Herod's engineers then dug down to bedrock. He expanded the esplanade of Temple Mount, filling in the space with a substructure supported by pillars and vaulted arches. The result was a massive platform, enlarged to the north, south, and west. Lebanese cedar provided the lumber, and massive ashlar stones from the quarries around Jerusalem were used to build the vast retaining walls that supported the platform. (The Wailing Wall on the western side of Temple Mount today is one of those retaining walls). Herod's Antonia Fortress, with its four distinctive towers, dominated the northwestern corner of Temple Mount. Montefiore describes the finished product: "Dazzling and awe-inspiring, Herod's Temple was 'covered all over with plates of gold and at the first rising

of the sun reflected back a fiery splendor' so bright that visitors had to look away. Arriving in Jerusalem from the Mount of Olives, it reared up 'like a mountain covered with snow.'"[259] The entire space Herod enclosed amounted to forty acres. This was the temple where Jesus worshipped and prayed, and which He prophesied would be destroyed (Luke 21:5–6).[260]

The last decade of Herod's life was marked by quarrels and intrigue among his family members and within his kingdom. He severely punished over six thousand Pharisees who refused to swear an oath of allegiance to him and Augustus. He executed two popular rabbis and their students when they protested his placement of a golden eagle over the temple doorway. Because of his growing insecurity and evident paranoia, in 7 BC, Herod executed his two sons with Mariamne, Alexander and Aristobulus. Only five days before his own death, he executed his son with Doris, Antipater. Of course, at the birth of Jesus, his execution of Jewish boys two years and younger in Bethlehem evidenced his growing paranoia.

During the last two or three years of his life, Herod was suffering from an acute illness that caused mental instability and several physical pain. (Stomach or colon cancer has been suggested, as has arteriosclerosis). Herod died in his palace in Jericho in March or April 4 BC, after countless vain attempts to alleviate his pain. He was buried at the Herodium.[261]

Herod's last will and testament was presented to Caesar Augustus. It stipulated that Archelaus was to be king over the entire kingdom, with Antipas and Philip serving as subordinate tetrarchs. After a somewhat lengthy and detailed challenge to the will by Antipas, Caesar Augustus accepted the terms of Herod's will, with important modifications: Herod Archelaus was declared ethnarch (not king) of Judea, Samaria, and Idumea; Philip was declared tetrarch of north and east of the Sea of Galilee; and Herod Antipas was declared tetrarch of Galilee and Perea. Each was to rule his assigned territory independent of the others.²⁶²

The news of Herod's death and the elevation of Archelaus precipitated a significant revolt in much of Judea. Herod's palace at Jericho was destroyed, and many of Herod's troops defected to the rebels. But under the ruthless leadership of the Syrian legate, Varus, the revolt and all of its components were crushed, with two thousand rebels crucified as punishment. Varus left a legion in Jerusalem to support Archelaus.²⁶³

Herod's Successors, 4 BC–41 AD

Archelaus, 4 BC–AD 6. Of Herod's three sons, arguably Archelaus had the most difficult charge. Despite all of Herod the Great's accomplishments and the prosperity and employment opportunities his building program generated, he remained deeply unpopular. The distrust and hatred of the Jews toward Herod the Great was transferred to Archelaus. Because Archelaus sponsored no significant building programs other than rebuilding Jericho, and because there was a concomitant drop in tax revenue, discontent with his rule grew. Further alienation from the Jews resulted from his incestuous marriage to Glaphyra, widow of his half brother. Because she had had children with her dead husband, Jewish law forbade such a marriage.

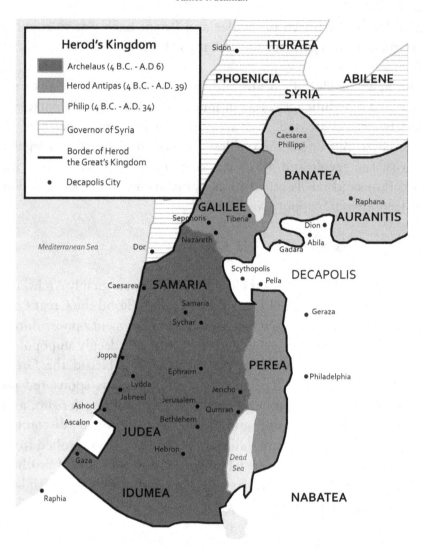

Archelaus was also known for his brutality and tyranny. A n
example of his ruthless reputation comes from Matthew 2:22.
When Joseph heard that Archelaus had been made the ruler over
Judea, where Bethlehem was located, Joseph took Mary and the
child Jesus to Nazareth in Galilee, where Herod Antipas ruled.

Because of this brutality and his general incompetence, in AD 6,
a joint complaint from Jews and Samaritans was sent to Caesar

Augustus, who summoned Archelaus to Rome. Augustus launched an investigation into his rule. At a formal hearing in Rome, Augustus deposed Archelaus and sent him into exile at Vienne in Gaul, where, within ten years, he died. Augustus then declared Archelaus's territory (Judea, Samaria, and Idumea) to be a Roman imperial province, renaming it simply Judea, to be governed from Caesarea by a Roman prefect (later procurator).[264]

Between AD 6 and 41, during what is called the First Procuratorship, there were seven procurators of Judea, the most famous of whom was Pontius Pilate, who ruled from AD 26–36. Caesar Claudius ended the procuratorship when he appointed Herod Agrippa I king, thereby ending direct Roman rule.

Philip, 4 BC–AD 34. Philip's kingdom, north and east of the Sea of Galilee, was mainly non-Jewish in its population. Hence, he did not face the contentious religious issues that undermined Archelaus's rule. All indications are that he was a skillful ruler. He expanded his capital Panias and renamed it Caesarea Philippi. He also enlarged and fortified the village of Bethsaida on the northern end of the Sea of Galilee, renaming it Julias after Augustus's daughter. The apostles Peter and Andrew came from Bethsaida, and Jesus frequently journeyed into Philip's kingdom. Philip ruled his kingdom until he died in AD 34.

Herod Antipas, 4 BC–39 AD. Antipas, who became Herod Antipas after Archelaus was deposed, ruled over Galilee and Perea, territory on the east side of the Jordan River. Antipas rebuilt Sepphoris, north of Nazareth, into a beautiful Roman-style city. It was his capital until AD 18. He built his new capital city on the west side of the Sea of Galilee and named it Tiberius, after the Roman emperor. Since he ruled Galilee, Herod Antipas, whom Jesus once called "that fox" (Luke 13:32), was the focal point for several key events in the Gospels. He had married the daughter of the Nabatean king Aretas IV, but divorced her to marry Herodias, the wife of his half brother Herod Philip. (King Aretas would wage a successful war against Antipas in AD 36 to avenge his daughter's humiliation). John the Baptist publicly denounced this marriage as unlawful. Fearing insurrection because of John's popularity, Antipas arrested him and, about one year later, at the demand of Herodias and her daughter, executed John (Mark 6:14–28). When Pilate was attempting to avoid condemning Jesus, he sent Him to Herod Antipas because Antipas ruled Galilee, where Jesus' principal ministry was located. Antipas sent Him back to Pilate (Luke 23:6–16).

Antipas played a strategic role as a mediator between Rome and the Parthians to the east. For example, an important treaty resulted from his role in AD 36 between Rome and the Parthians. But when Caesar Tiberius died in AD 37, Antipas lost favor with Rome. His nephew Agrippa won the favor of Caesar Caligula (Gaius), who deposed Antipas in AD 39, banishing him to Gaul, where he died.[265]

The Life and Ministry of Jesus the Messiah, 4 BC–AD 33

This chapter provides the historical backdrop for the incarnation of Jesus. As Rome's iron-fisted rule dominated all that was occurring in the eastern Mediterranean, "in the fullness of time" God sent His Son, the Messiah of Israel, to Bethlehem, a tiny village in Judea (Galatians 4:4). A new order was dawning that would center on God fulfilling His promises to Israel and offering redemption to the world. Schreiner summarizes the magnificence of this new order:

> [The Gospels] proclaim that the king has come, that Jesus of Nazareth is the Son of Man, the Son of God, the Messiah, the final prophet, the true Israel, and the Lord of all. Jesus fulfills the promise made to David that his dynasty would never end, that a king would always sit on the Davidic throne. By virtue of his resurrection and exaltation he is now seated at God's right hand and reigns from heaven ... The age

to come has invaded history, for Jesus is risen from the dead ... The presence of the kingdom manifested itself in Jesus' healings, exorcisms, and nature miracles. These miracles anticipate the new creation that is coming, the day when all that is wrong with the world will be made right.[266]

In the early second century AD, Jesus was briefly mentioned by the Roman historians Suetonius, Tacitus, and Pliny. Titus Flavius Josephus, an important Jewish historian of the first century, also referred to Jesus in his *Antiquities of the Jews*, written in the late first century.[267] But it is the four Gospels of the New Testament that provide the details of Jesus' public ministry and His death, burial, and resurrection. None of the Gospels are exhaustive, chronologically tight biographies. Instead, they present firsthand testimonies about Jesus Christ, His words, and His works, all designed to prove that He is the Messiah of Israel, God's Son, and the Lord of the universe. Luke even makes it clear that his gospel was carefully researched (Luke 1:3–4). All four Gospels are inspired and infallible, and are therefore historically reliable accounts of Jesus Christ.

Jesus was born in Bethlehem in the winter of 5/4 BC. Mary, his mother, and Joseph, his earthly father, traveled from Nazareth, their home, to Bethlehem, to register for a tax census mandated by the Syrian governor Quirinius. Such a census was common in the Roman Empire, for it provided the necessary data for levying taxes in the provinces.[268]

Until Jesus' public ministry began, we know very little about His life. The few things we do know are summarized below:

- Mary, Joseph, and the baby Jesus fled Herod's butchery of male children in Bethlehem by traveling to Egypt (Matthew 2:13–15) and remaining there until Herod died. The assumption is that the gifts of the magi financed this trip and stay in Egypt (Matthew 2).

- To avoid the ruthless rule of Archelaus, the holy family did not return to Bethlehem, but went back to Nazareth in Galilee, where Jesus apparently spent the first thirty years of His life (Matthew 2:19–23).
- According to Luke 2:41–51, Jesus traveled to Jerusalem with His family to celebrate the festivals of Israel, which would have included offering the necessary sacrifices.
- Since Herod Antipas rebuilt Sepphoris, north of Nazareth, it is possible that Joseph and Jesus might have been employed as carpenters in that project.[269]
- John the Baptist, who proclaimed a baptism of repentance in the Judean wilderness, was the forerunner of Jesus. He also declared the necessity of repentance because the kingdom of heaven was at hand (Matthew 3:2). John baptized Jesus (Matthew 3:13–17), which was followed by His temptation by Satan in the Judean wilderness (Matthew 4:1–11; Luke 4:1–13).

During Jesus' earthly life, a major change occurred in the Roman Empire: Caesar Augustus died in AD 14 and was succeeded by his stepson, Tiberius, who reigned for twenty-three years. He was the Caesar during the entire public ministry of Jesus and was the one responsible for appointing Pontius Pilate the prefect (procurator) over the Roman province of Judea. When Jesus established Capernaum, on the north side of the Sea of Galilee, as His base of operations, He was in the territory governed by the tetrarch Herod Antipas. Except for His few recorded trips into the territory of Philip (e.g., Caesarea Philippi in Matthew 16), the Decapolis, and Jerusalem, most of Jesus' public ministry was in the triangle of towns around the sea of Galilee—Capernaum, Chorazin, and Bethsaida. (See Matthew 11.)

Because Judea was a Roman province, several important events in Jesus' life were affected by Roman policies. Judea was typical in that Rome allowed the normal administrative affairs and practices to be handled by local authorities. That meant Jewish law was the norm in Judea and that the Sanhedrin had authority in all administrative and judicial matters relating to Jewish affairs.

The power of capital punishment was restricted, for the Roman prefect had the singular authority over life and earth. But apparently in capital issues relating to Jewish law, the Sanhedrin had limited power to issue execution orders (e.g., the case of the woman caught in adultery in John 8 and the case of Stephen in Acts 7). The Roman prefect (e.g., Pontius Pilate) had to ratify the order and could overturn it.

In addition, people in Judea paid the land tax (*tributum soli*), the personal head tax (*tributum capitis*), and various customs duties and taxes. The tax census that caused Joseph and Mary to travel to Bethlehem was the *tributum capitis*. Perhaps because it symbolized living under Roman occupation, no issue was more resented by the Jews than Roman taxation.[270]

***

Excursus on Pontius Pilate and the Zealots

The rule of Pontius Pilate as procurator of Judea, AD 26–36, is important for understanding the trial of Jesus and also for understanding the deteriorating relations between the Jews and Rome. Little is known of Pilate before Caesar Tiberius named him prefect. As procurator, Pilate had full authority in Judea and was in charge of the army of occupation stationed in Caesarea, which included a small garrison stationed at the Antonia Fortress on the northwest corner of Temple Mount. Pilate did a number of things during his rule that antagonized the Jews:

1. Previous prefects made certain that the Jerusalem garrison at the Antonia Fortress never carried the medallion busts of Caesar on their standards. For Jews, these were symbols of the imperial cult and virtual objects of worship. Pilate had

his garrison use the medallion busts and, to coincide with the Day of Atonement and the Feast of Tabernacles, entered Jerusalem with that garrison. Significant demonstrations ensued, which ultimately resulted in Pilate withdrawing the garrison to Caesarea.

2. To improve the water supply to Jerusalem, Pilate built an additional aqueduct, but used money from the temple treasury to fund it. Huge demonstrations followed this outrage, with Pilate dispatching his troops to crush the demonstrators. Many were killed. Perhaps Luke's reference to Pilate's killing of Galilean pilgrims occurred at this time. (See Luke 13:1.) If not, then the killing of the pilgrims is further evidence of Pilate's anti-Jewish policies.

3. Pilate executed a number of Samaritans near Mount Gerizim. The Samaritans had gathered there expecting a miraculous apparition of their redeemer as Moses, who would lead them to a new home, accompanied by their sacred vessels from their tabernacle. The Samaritans had been quite loyal to Rome, but under Pilate, they joined with the Jews in protesting his rule. They turned to the Roman Syrian governor, Vitellius, who forced Pilate's hand. Caesar Tiberius ordered Pilate to appear in Rome to answer the charges of the Samaritans.[271]

4. Pilate was a close friend of Sejanus, an intimate confidant of Caesar Tiberius. All evidence indicates that Sejanus was a virulent anti-Semite and might have strongly influenced Pilate's policies. When Sejanus was executed by Tiberius for plotting a coup, this perhaps marked the decline of Pilate's favor with Tiberius.

All of these activities provide a framework for the obvious tension between Pilate and the Jewish leadership at the time of Jesus. This framework might also give fuller meaning to the accusation that Pilate was "no friend of Caesar" (John 19:12). Shortly after Tiberius died, Pilate was deposed as prefect in AD 36 by Caesar Gaius (Caligula).[272]

The radical movement called the Zealots was founded by Judas the Galilean, who led a revolt against Rome in AD 6. Judas and his supporters opposed payment of tribute to Rome on the grounds that, because Caesar was a pagan emperor, this was treason against God. Apparently the name "Zealot" was chosen because they followed the example of the Maccabean Mattathias and his sons, who manifested uncompromising zeal for God against Antiochus IV. The revolt of Judas in AD 6 was crushed, but the Zealot spirit lived on and played a major role in the Jewish revolt of AD 66–73, culminating in the Zealot holdout at Masada. One of Jesus' disciples was Simon the Zealot.[273]

***

Jesus' public ministry began in the summer or autumn of AD 29 and ended at Passover in AD 33. Because John's gospel organizes Jesus' ministry around Passover celebrations, this provides a helpful framework for dating Jesus' ministry.

- Ministry before the First Passover: Jesus' baptism and temptation began His public ministry in AD 29. Other events of this year include the call of His first disciples, the Cana wedding feast, the journey to Capernaum, and the journey to Jerusalem to attend the first Passover (7 April AD 30) of His ministry.
- Ministry from Passover of AD 30 to Passover of AD 31: His ministry during this period was largely in Jerusalem and Judea. When John the Baptist was arrested and imprisoned, Jesus moved toward Galilee, passing through Samaria (John 3 and 4).
- Ministry from Passover of AD 31 to Passover of AD 32: As Jesus retuned to Galilee, He preached the Sermon on the Mount. Jesus returned to Jerusalem for the Feast of Tabernacles in October AD 31. John the Baptist was executed, causing Jesus to withdraw. The feeding of the 5,000 preceded His return to Jerusalem for Passover in April AD 32.

- Ministry from Passover of AD 32 to Passover of AD 33: The gospel accounts give most focus to this year. Among some of the highlights are His ministry in Tyre and the Decapolis, Peter's confession at Caesarea Philippi, and the Mount of Transfiguration. The Gospels record several visits to Jerusalem during this period, including one for the Feast of Tabernacles and another for the Feast of Dedication in December (Hanukkah), and then a separate ministry in the Perea and Samaria regions. He went again to Jerusalem, and at Bethany raised Lazarus from the dead. After returning once again to Galilee for additional ministry, He made His final journey to Jerusalem for the Passover, which led to His arrest, His trials, and His execution.[274]

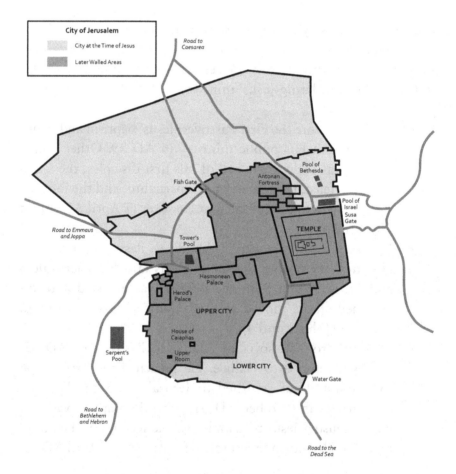

The arrest, trials, and execution of Jesus occurred in early April AD 33. During the first Sunday of Passion Week was His triumphal entry into Jerusalem, during which He presented Himself to Israel as their Paschal Lamb. Dating precisely all that occurred during Passion Week is quite difficult, but it included the following: the (second) cleansing of the temple; debates and discussions with the Pharisees; The Olivet Discourse (Matthew 24–25), in which Jesus taught about the end times; the meeting with His disciples in the upper room, teaching them significant truths about His return to the Father and the coming of the Spirit (John 14-16); His arrest in Gethsemane, precipitated by Judas's betrayal; and His six trials.

Trials of Jesus

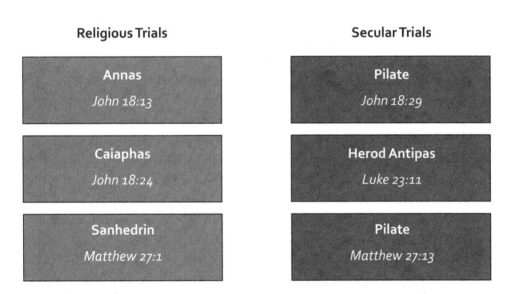

Religious Trials	Secular Trials
Annas *John 18:13*	**Pilate** *John 18:29*
Caiaphas *John 18:24*	**Herod Antipas** *Luke 23:11*
Sanhedrin *Matthew 27:1*	**Pilate** *Matthew 27:13*

On Friday, 3 April AD 33, about nine o'clock in the morning, Jesus Christ was crucified. He died at about 3 p.m., at the very time Israel was celebrating the slaughter of the Passover Lamb. Three days later, on 5 April AD 33, Jesus was resurrected from the dead.[275]

The New Testament declares forcefully that Jesus' death was a substitutionary death as prophesied in the Suffering Servant passage of

Isaiah 53:13–53:12. God the Father poured out His wrath on His Son as an act of His magnificent grace. Redemption was thereby secured and justification (the declaration of God's righteousness) was now available by faith and faith alone. Although Rome carried out the execution, it was merely the instrument God used to accomplish His stunning act of salvation. Jesus' subsequent resurrection validated that the payment had been made and salvation procured. Death no longer had authority, and its power had been broken.

In Galatians 3:7–9, the apostle Paul argued that when God said to Abraham, "In you all the nations will be blessed" (Genesis 12:3), He was speaking of the blessing of salvation, now available to every human being through faith in Jesus Christ. For that reason, Jesus Christ understandably bifurcates human history, connecting the covenant promises of the Old with the fulfillment in the New. Things would never be the same.

It is John's gospel that most connects Jesus' death, burial, resurrection, and ascension with the new order. Not only was Jesus the fulfillment of the Davidic covenant and the Abrahamic covenant, He was also the agent for the inauguration of the new covenant. In the Upper Room Discourse of Jesus (John 14–16), He declared that His ascension was absolutely essential, for then the Holy Spirit would come. God's law would be on the hearts of His people, and the Spirit would indwell, teach, guide, and fill those who followed Christ.

The language of this discourse resonates with the language of Jeremiah 31:31–37 and Ezekiel 36:22–32. The coming of the Spirit of Truth was nothing less than the dawning of a new order. There would be a new dynamic to prayer, spiritual sustenance, and intimacy with God, such that His people would now call Him "Abba." Spiritual enablement and nourishment would flow as between a vine and its branches. From the Spirit as Helper and Counselor would come a new power, a new energy, and a new obedience, all motivated by deep-seated love for God. A new order had indeed begun.

Chapter 11

The Jews Revolt Against Rome: AD 66-73 and 132-135

C hristianity was born out of Judaism. Jesus and Paul were both Jews, as were virtually all the early church leaders. Spreading first from Jerusalem and then throughout Judea and Samaria, the church exploded across the Mediterranean world. (See Acts 1:8.) It changed the Roman Empire.

Rome at first tolerated Christianity as a separate sect of Judaism (e.g., Acts 18:12–15), but as the church grew, by the AD 60s Rome regarded Christianity as a separate religion. In some areas, it persecuted the church as ruthlessly as it persecuted the Jews. As Rome increased its persecution, the church spread even more rapidly.

Jewish resistance to Roman authoritarianism produced the First Jewish Revolt (AD 63–73) and, a generation later, the Bar Kochba Revolt (AD 132–5). The First Jewish Revolt ended with the complete destruction of Jerusalem. The Bar Kochba Revolt ended with Jews totally banished from Jerusalem and much of Judea.

With the temple destroyed, much of the priesthood dispersed, and Diaspora Judaism now the norm, Judaism evolved into what is often called Rabbinic Judaism. As the church grew and Rabbinic Judaism took hold, Christianity and Judaism separated decisively and completely.

The Growth of Christianity

Unlike any previous period, under the Roman Empire, the Mediterranean world was united. The imperial legions of Rome maintained this unity by a forced peace—the famous *Pax Romana* (30 BC–AD 180). As the army defended the empire from its enemies, as well as robbers and pirates, trade flourished on both land and sea. Prosperity and wealth followed. Rome brought stability and order to its cities, with free food and public games at taxpayers' expense. Further, the Roman roads provided an infrastructure that knit the empire together. As a result, the legions could be anywhere in the empire within a few weeks, and communication between Caesar and the provinces occurred with a speed unheard of in previous empires. In God's providence, the early church utilized this communication and travel network to spread the gospel.

As the imperial legions moved with ease through Caesar's domain, they carried out his orders with efficiency and discipline. But the gospel also penetrated the army. For example, Paul spoke of believers in the Praetorian Guard, an elite force closest to the emperor (Philippians 1:13). Also, Christianity first came to Britain through Roman soldiers. So significant was the impact of Christianity on the legions that they were often referred to as the "mouthpiece of the gospel."[276]

As previous chapters have shown, the Roman world was also a Greek world. Rome conquered the Greeks militarily, but the Greeks conquered the Romans intellectually and culturally. The common language of the day in the first century was *koine* Greek, the language of Alexander's vision of Hellenization. *Koine* was also the language of the New Testament. In addition, Greek philosophy heavily influenced the way the Roman world thought. Greek philosophers wanted to know truth and the place of human beings in the universe. Despite the variations among Greek philosophers, most of them shared the belief that there was a realm beyond the physical world, the domain of the transcendent.

Christianity took advantage of this hunger for truth and for transcendent reality: witness the apostle Paul's argument with the philosophers in Acts 17, his presentation of Jesus in Colossians 1, and John's philosophical arguments in his gospel and first epistle. The Greco-Roman world was intellectually "set up" for the gospel.

The Roman world also pulsated with religious exhilaration and anticipation. Josephus, the first-century Jewish historian, spoke of Eastern cults, false messiahs, and religious fervor that permeated the empire. Many in Israel envisioned the Messiah coming at any moment. The Zealots plotted a revolution against Rome. The Essenes longed for a prophet of light who would overcome the darkness of evil. The Pharisees yearned for a nationalist leader who would restore the Law and free Israel from Rome's oppression. Further, because of the Diaspora, the synagogue system signified a Jewish presence in most major cities. Each time the apostle Paul entered a city, he first preached the gospel in the synagogues, then to the Gentiles.[277]

Pentecost (fifty days after the crucifixion and ten days after the ascension of Christ) marked the birth of the church. Peter emerged as the spokesperson for the early church. At Pentecost, he preached the Spirit-inspired sermon that produced three thousand converts. He cut through the fog of exclusive Judaism by declaring of Jesus that there is salvation in no one else (Acts 4:12). He performed miracles, defied the Sanhedrin, disciplined Ananias and Sapphira, and established deacons as helpers so the apostles could study and preach. Despite his slip at Antioch when he withdrew from fellowship with Gentile converts (Galatians 2:14), he championed the gospel's penetration into the Gentile world. As the decisive speaker at the Jerusalem Council (AD 49) in Acts 15, he brilliantly defended Gentile church membership.

As one of the pillars of the Jerusalem church (Galatians 2:9), John, brother of James and the son of Zebedee, was Peter's coworker. John's most significant contribution to the church was his writing.

His gospel is unique. Only 8 percent of it is related to the synoptic gospels of Matthew, Mark, and Luke; the remaining 92 percent is original with John. Most exceptional is his instruction regarding the deity of Christ—He is the eternal Logos (1:1–18) and the great "I am" (8:58). John likewise gave emphasis to the Spirit, especially in the Upper Room Discourse of Jesus (14–16). Finally, the book of Revelation, written on the island of Patmos where the Roman emperor Domitian had exiled him, constitutes the framework for understanding events surrounding the second coming of Jesus Christ. Emperor Nerva apparently released John from exile sometime between AD 96 and 98.

The other decisive leader of the apostolic church was Paul, in whose life three great ancient traditions intersected. Religiously, he was a Jew; culturally, he was a Greek; and politically, he was a Roman. He was born in Tarsus, a major university town and the principal city of the Roman province of Cilicia. Paul was trained in Pharisaism at the rabbinic school in Jerusalem headed by Gamaliel (Acts 22:3; Philippians 3:5). His familiarity with Greek authors (Acts 17:28; 1 Corinthians 15:33; Titus 1:12) and his use of Greek argumentation (Romans 2:1–3:20; Colossians 1:15–20) evidenced his Greco-Roman training.

Approximately thirteen years separated Paul's conversion on the Damascus road (AD 35) and his first missionary journey (AD 48). Paul claimed to be *the* missionary to the Gentiles. The missionary journeys documented by Luke in Acts bear this out. Through his three missionary journeys, Paul took the gospel throughout the Mediterranean world, probably even going to Spain after his release from prison in Rome. He was arrested again at the heights of Nero's persecution and executed by decapitation, most likely in AD 68.[278]

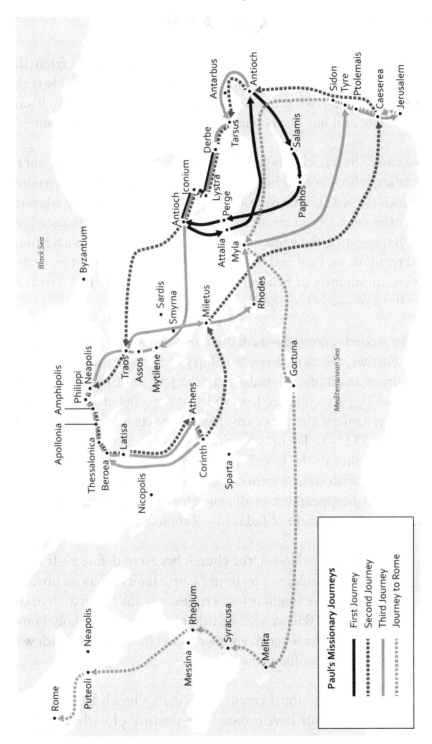

Paul's Missionary Journeys

First Journey
Second Journey
Third Journey
Journey to Rome

The Separation of Christianity and Judaism

The fundamental difference separating the Christian from the Jew remains the messiahship of Jesus. Christians believe He is the Messiah; most Jews do not. Today, this gap is seemingly insurmountable and has been compounded by the realities of history.

The early church, clearly Jewish, was successful in reaching out to Gentiles, which in turn led to the landmark ruling of the Jerusalem Council (Acts 15). That decision in AD 49 released Gentile converts from the necessity of circumcision and adherence to Mosaic law. By championing the cause of Gentile freedom from Jewish rituals and regulations, Paul and other apostolic leaders in effect produced a new community of believers. Could Jew and Gentile Christians live harmoniously together?

As the second century dawned, this harmony became more problematic. Further, the move from worship on the Sabbath to the Lord's Day drove an additional wedge between Jew and Christian. Finally, the growing persecution of Jews widened the split between Christian and Jew. During the two early Jewish revolts against Rome (AD 66–73 and 132–5), Jewish Christians refused to fight, compromising their allegiance to the Jewish community and their identity within the early Jewish state. Further, the destruction of Jerusalem in AD 70 and the disappearance of all major Jewish sects but the Pharisees forced a reformulation of Judaism—Rabbinic Judaism.

As the separation widened, the church began to define itself using non-Jewish terminology. The term "Christianity" was an obvious example, for it gave singular focus to Jesus as the "Christ" (Greek) or the "Messiah" (Hebrew). The title of Christianity's holy book, the Bible, was a Greek term, another signal that this new faith was stepping away from Judaism.

In addition, by the third century, the early church had taken on an increasingly anti-Jewish tone. The posture of early Christian writings was decidedly against the synagogue system. Whereas one Gentile nation after another responded positively to the Christian message, Jews continued to cling stubbornly to their ancestral faith. The later leaders of the church taught that the unfaithfulness of the Jewish people resulted in a collective guilt that made them subject to the permanent curse of God. As the church grew, there was growing contempt for Jews and Judaism.

By the fourth century, when Emperor Constantine made Christianity a legitimate religion of the empire, Jews experienced a further wave of discrimination and persecution. They lost many of their legal rights. In 339 it was made a criminal offense to convert to Judaism. The break was complete and final.[279]

The First Jewish Revolt, AD 66–73

After the new Caesar, Gaius (Caligula), deposed Pilate in AD 36, the relationship between the Jews and Rome continued to deteriorate. During the winter of AD 39–40, a group of Greeks in the Jewish town of Jamnia, along the coast, erected an altar to the imperial cult. Because it was contrary to Jewish law, the Jews demolished it.

Meanwhile, Caesar Caligula, now convinced he was indeed a god, ordered that Temple Mount should have a "shrine of the imperial cult, with a colossal statue of himself in the guise of Jupiter in the Holy of Holies."[280] He also ordered the Syrian legate, Petronius, to use between two and four legions to enforce his order.

Massive Jewish demonstrations met Petronius as he entered Palestine. The Jewish leaders told him of an imminent revolt if he proceeded, and, as a part of the revolt, that the Jews would destroy all the crops and fruit trees of the land. Petronius sought several ways to delay following the emperor's orders.

Agrippa I was in Rome and, when he heard of Caligula's schemes, wrote a well-reasoned and articulate letter to the emperor. Agrippa begged Caligula to follow the precedent of previous Caesars, who always respected the sanctity of the temple. Caligula followed Agrippa's counsel and ordered Petronius to cease all efforts regarding the statue. Rumors persisted that Caligula was still going to erect the statue, but he was assassinated by the Praetorian Guard on 24 January AD 41, ending the prospect of a Jewish revolt at that time.[281]

Herod Agrippa I, King of the Jews, AD 37–44. The debacle over Caligula's statue brought Herod Agrippa I to the forefront. (The book of Acts refers to him as merely "Herod.") Agrippa was born in 10 BC, the son of Aristobulus and thus the grandson of Herod the Great. Agrippa spent much of his early life in Rome and befriended the prominent leaders of Roman society, including Caesar Tiberius and two future emperors, Gaius and Claudius. When Gaius (Caligula) became the Caesar in AD 37, he gave Agrippa the tetrarchy of Philip, who had died in AD 34. In AD 39, when Herod Antipas was deposed, Agrippa inherited his tetrarchy as well. Finally, also in AD 41, the new Caesar, Claudius, added Judea, Samaria, and Idumea to Agrippa's holdings. Herod Agrippa I ruled over a kingdom roughly comparable to that of his grandfather. Rome gave him the title of king. For now, its direct rule over Judea had come to an end.

Because Agrippa had intervened with Caligula over his plans for the statue on Temple Mount, Agrippa initially enjoyed good relations with the Jews. Because of his grandmother Mariamne, the Jewish leaders saw him as a Hasmonean and as a buffer against further intrusions from Rome. Claudius gave him the right to appoint the high priest, and he appointed three new high priests in as many years. His actions indicated a desire to control that important office. He also sought to defend Jewish rights in other parts of the eastern Mediterranean. He defended religious liberty issues for the Jews in Alexandria, and for those in the Greco-Syrian city of Dora.

But as Smallwood demonstrates, Agrippa's attitude toward Judaism and the Jews was only a façade: "With his Roman upbringing he was as much a pagan at heart as the rest of his family." He wished to be regarded "as a normal Hellenistic king receiving divine honors."[282] He struck coins for his realm that had his own head on one side and on the other depicted his son on horseback. Even in the heavily Jewish parts of his kingdom, he struck coins showing the head of a city goddess and a pagan temple.

Apparently to placate the Jews, Agrippa also dealt with the early church in a hostile manner. He executed James, the son of Zebedee (Acts 12:2) and had Peter imprisoned in Jerusalem (Acts 12:3–19). The book of Acts details Agrippa's gruesome death (12:20–23). In AD 44, he was presiding in Caesarea over an imperial festival, adorned like a Greek god in a robe of silver and gold. The crowds in the large theater there hailed him as a god. God struck him, and in five days he was dead.

Herod Agrippa II, AD 44–66. The young Agrippa was sixteen when his father died, so Emperor Claudius deemed him too young to succeed his father. Therefore, Claudius reconstituted the Roman province of Judea to be administered, as before, by a procurator based in Caesarea. This new province was much larger, for it included not only Judea, Samaria, and Idumea, but also Galilee and Perea. The most famous of these procurators from the New Testament perspective were Antonius Felix, AD 52–60, and Porcius Festus, AD 60–2. In Acts 24–25, the apostle Paul appeared before both in Caesarea.

Eventually, what the second Agrippa did rule was largely Gentile territory. In AD 50, Claudius gave the young Agrippa Chalcis, in the very northern region, and in AD 53 added the territory of Philip's old tetrarchy, also to the north. In AD 56, his friend, the Caesar Nero, added the area north and west of the Sea of Galilee to his kingdom. In fact, Agrippa renamed Caesarea Philippi Neronias, and promoted his friendship with Nero by issuing coins with Nero's portrait on one side and "Philo-Caesar" (friend of Caesar) on the back.

Between AD 48 and 66, Agrippa had the authority to appoint the high priest and manage the temple.[283] Hence, for the next twenty-five years, the temple and Jerusalem were administered by both Agrippa and the Roman procurators—a confused and messy relationship. When the apostle Paul, who had been arrested in Jerusalem, was taken to Caesarea, he appeared before Agrippa II and his incestuous lover Berenice. Paul proclaimed the gospel to them, pleading with them to become Christians (Acts 26). Agrippa was almost persuaded (26:28).

The Origins of the First Revolt. Once Rome reconstituted direct rule over the enlarged province of Judea, trouble began. Jewish nationalists began to plot widespread attacks. Between AD 44 and 66, the seven procurators were largely tax collectors and administrators, which led to oppression, corruption, and mismanagement. The procurators had no military power; that came from the legions stationed in Syria under the Roman legate's authority. A whole series of incidents during this period heightened the tensions between the Jews and Rome, and led to the outbreak of the First Jewish Revolt in AD 66:

1. In AD 44, a pseudo-messiah by the name of Theudas gathered a following in the Jordan valley, promising to part the river as Moses had parted the Red Sea. The procurator, Cuspius Fadus, feared an anti-Roman demonstration and ordered a massacre. The cavalry unit beheaded Theudas and killed dozens of his followers. Such state terror antagonized the Jews and heighted their bitterness toward Rome.
2. The procuratorship of Ventidius Cumanus (AD 48–52) marked a turning point. During Passover, when the Roman garrison at the Antonia Fortress patrolled the streets and was positioned on the rooftops, a Roman soldier exposed himself, which caused a major Jewish riot and stone throwing. The Roman soldiers panicked, and hundreds of Jews were killed by the soldiers during the subsequent stampede. Shortly thereafter, a Roman soldier, part of a cohort dealing

with a robbery, took a copy of Scripture, tore it, and burned it in front of a group of Jews. Jewish leaders demanded that Cumanus discipline him, which Cumanus did, having him beheaded. Temporary calm was restored. Finally, a bitter dispute between a group of Jewish Galilean pilgrims and Samaritans, which resulted in the Jews being killed, deteriorated into a brutal confrontation. Cumanus refused to discipline the Samaritans, and a group of Jewish rebels burned several Samaritan villages, killing dozens. Cumanus then took five of his military units and attacked and killed most of the Jewish rebels. Those who were not killed went into hiding. Influential Jews, with the help of Agrippa, appealed to Caesar Claudius, who deposed Cumanus and appointed Antonius Felix as the new procurator.[284]

3. Antonius Felix, procurator from AD 52–60, in an act offensive to Jewish law, took Agrippa II's sixteen-year-old sister, Drusilla, away from her husband, Azizus I of Emesa. After AD 52, the growth in the number of Jewish rebels in the Judean province accelerated. As Felix suppressed them, the rebels developed a new method of terror. They dressed as pilgrims, with daggers hidden in their clothing. As they mingled in the crowds, they killed prominent Jewish officials who collaborated with Rome. One of the early assassinations of these *sicarii* ("dagger men") was the ex-high priest Jonathan, who had befriended Felix and was his personal counsel. The *sicarii* spread from Jerusalem to other prominent districts of Judea. Smallwood summarizes the breadth of their impact: "The religious and political fanatics joined hands to terrorize the country, not only plundering the estates of the wealthy who were likely to be 'collaborators' for economic reasons and inciting people to revolt, but firing and pillaging villages which refused to support their anti-Roman campaign."[285] Jewish rebellion spread throughout the province, and the last procurator, Gessius Florus, because of his inept, corrupt, and oppressive administration, could not restore order.

4. The outbreak of the revolt began in the summer of AD 66 in Caesarea, between Jews and Greeks, over a long-simmering dispute about the meaning of citizenship in this largely Greek city. Caesar Nero rejected all Jewish appeals. Tensions between Jews and Greeks in Caesarea mounted. When a group of Jews went to the synagogue on the Sabbath in Caesarea, they found a Greek mocking Jewish law with an improvised altar at the synagogue's entrance—an upside-down chamber pot containing sacrificed birds. A bloody riot ensued. The incompetent Florus rejected appeals by the Jews concerning this incident and demanded seventeen talents from the temple treasury as a much-needed "tax." The Jews of Jerusalem refused, and Florus sent a cohort of troops to Jerusalem. Dreadful violence resulted with many Jews beaten, killed, or crucified. To no avail, even Queen Berenice directly appealed to Florus to end the violence.

5. Two events that summer sent a message of open Jewish rebellion against Rome's authority. A group of Zealots (the *sicarii)* seized Masada and murdered the Roman garrison there. Hearing of events In Jerusalem, these Zealots also seized weapons from the arsenal at Masada. Led by Menahem, they marched on Jerusalem and occupied the western part of the city. Second, the captain of the temple, Eleazar, son of the ex-high priest Ananias, ended all daily sacrifices for the Caesar's well-being—an unacceptable affront to Rome. Eleazar and Menahem were now rival leaders of the growing insurrection, and fighting between them resulted. Menahem was captured and executed by Eleazar's forces, and the remaining Zealots fled back to Masada, where they would stay until AD 73.[286]

The Jewish War of AD 66–70. The early months of AD 66 were marked by bitter and bloody conflicts between the various Jewish factions. Even though most Pharisees and Sadducees did not support the revolt and often joined the high priests in a "peace party," some Jewish leaders advocated "no master but God" and called for the reestablishment of the theocracy. Some even argued that the revolt would be the harbinger for the Messiah coming.[287]

Jewish insurgents that summer did capture key facilities in and around the temple. In early September, a Roman garrison holding Herod's citadel agreed to surrender if promised safe passage out of the city. They surrendered, but were slaughtered by the rebels. When the Roman legate in Syria, Cestius Gallus, marched the Twelfth Legion into Judea, he effectively captured key towns but could not take Jerusalem. As Gallus and his legion retreated, over five thousand of his troops were killed at the Pass of Beth-horon. A tipping point had been reached; Rome would now respond with vengeance.

Why did the Jewish insurgents believe they could succeed against the mighty power of Rome? After these initial successes, the "peace party" faction had few supporters. Most insurgents believed that God was on their side, that He would fight for them as He had for the Maccabees in their initial victories against Antiochus Epiphanes. As God had brought down the powerful forces of Antiochus, so He would bring down the forces of seemingly invincible Rome. As F.F. Bruce demonstrates, the initial success against the forces of Gallus at Beth-horon "discredited the moderates and leaders of the peace-party in the public eye, and encouraged the insurgents to organize the whole Jewish population of Palestine for a war of liberation."[288]

Several key developments followed the victory at Beth-horon. First, the high priests and other spiritual leaders, who had been forces of moderation, now joined the revolutionary cause. The Sanhedrin, in effect, became the executive leadership of the quasi-republic, with a re-formed popular assembly as the legislative branch with final governmental authority. It met in the temple court. Second, the revolutionary leadership divided the country into seven districts, each led by a military governor. The governor of Galilee was Joseph ben Mattathias, better known as Josephus. Third, the new nation began to mint its own coins. The leaders minted various denominations, many made of bronze, but some of silver, which was significant because Rome did not permit its provinces to issue silver coins. During the war, many of these silver coins bore the following inscriptions: "Jerusalem is holy," "Jerusalem the holy," "The freedom of Zion," and "For the redemption of Zion."[289]

***

Excursus on Josephus

Joseph ben Matathias, also known as Titus Flavius Josephus (AD 37–ca. 100), was a Jewish scholar and historian, born in Jerusalem to a father of priestly descent and a mother who claimed royal ancestry. During the First Jewish Revolt, he was the military governor of Galilee and initially fought against the Romans, surrendering in AD 67 to Rome after the six-week siege of Jotapata. The Romans destroyed the city, killing thousands. The survivors committed suicide. According to Josephus, he was trapped in a cave with forty of his companions. The Romans (commanded by Flavius Vespasian and his son Titus, both future Roman emperors) asked the group to surrender, but they refused. Josephus suggested a method of collective suicide: they drew lots and killed each other. The sole survivor of this process was Josephus, who surrendered to the Roman forces and became a prisoner.

Josephus claimed that the Jewish messianic prophecies made reference to Vespasian, and later, in a speech, he predicted Vespasian would become emperor. After the prediction came true, Vespasian released Josephus from prison, but kept him as a hostage and interpreter. When Vespasian became emperor in AD 69, he granted Josephus his freedom, at which time Josephus assumed the emperor's family name of Flavius. He referred to himself as "Josephus."

He became an advisor and friend of Vespasian's son Titus, serving as his translator when Titus laid siege to Jerusalem. After Rome destroyed the Jewish state, Josephus went to Rome. While in Rome, and under Flavian patronage, Josephus wrote both of his known works: *The Jewish War* (ca. 75) and *Antiquities of the Jews* (ca. 94). *The Jewish*

War is an indispensable account of the First Jewish Revolt; *Antiquities of the Jews* recounts the history of the world from a Jewish perspective. Much of what we know about the First Jewish Revolt and key elements of the intertestamental period come from Josephus's books.

Of Josephus, Smallwood writes:

> [Josephus] was conceited, not only about his own learning but also about the opinions held of him as commander both by the Galileans and by the Romans; he was guilty of shocking duplicity at Jotapata, saving himself by sacrifice of his companions; he was too naive to see how he stood condemned out of his own mouth for his conduct, and yet no words were too harsh when he was blackening his opponents; and after landing, however involuntarily, in the Roman camp, he turned his captivity to his own advantage, and benefited for the rest of his days from his change of side.[290]

***

Caesar Nero responded to the insurrection by dispatching Vespasian, an experienced military officer, who was accompanied by his son Titus, another experienced officer. At Ptolemais (Acco), they assembled an army of three legions, plus several auxiliaries, for a total of 60,000 soldiers. As the campaign developed, three additional legions were added. A massive concentration of Rome's military might—nearly one-fourth of its twenty-six legions—was needed to crush the Jewish revolt.

Vespasian then invaded Galilee with the main invasion force. Josephus was the commander of the Jewish forces in Galilee and was (apparently) the sole survivor of Vespasian's siege of Jotapata. (See the above excursus.) In October, east of the Sea of Galilee in the Golan region, heroic fighting occurred during the long siege at the fortress of Gamala, where thousands of Jews were killed or committed suicide. By late AD 67, Vespasian had crushed the revolt in Galilee. Vespasian then had his troops secure key coastal cities—Joppa and Azotus (Ashdod)—and, in AD 68, he began the campaign to isolate Jerusalem. His troops conquered Perea, Idumea, and western Judea. Vespasian ordered the Tenth Legion to secure its base at Jericho and the Fifth Legion to do so at Emmaus, west of Jerusalem. With all but eastern Judea in Roman hands, Zealots fled to three fortresses—Herodium, Machaerus, and Masada.

General Vespasian convened a war council in Caesarea to finalize plans for the assault on Jerusalem. It was there that he received news that Caesar Nero had committed suicide on 9 June AD 68. An intense and brutal power struggle ensued throughout the empire. Because Nero had appointed him, Vespasian had to suspend his plans to capture Jerusalem while he waited for confirmation from the new Caesar. During the famous "year of the four emperors," Galba, then Otho, and then Vitellius claimed the throne of Rome. But, when the legions of the eastern empire gave their support to General Vespasian in December AD 69, he assumed the role of emperor. He then named his son Titus the commander of the legions in the east, with the goal of finally ending the Jewish revolt.

During the year's respite from fighting, the Jewish leadership in Jerusalem fragmented. Fighting between the Jewish forces resulted in three separate leaders claiming three separate areas in Jerusalem. A group of 2,400 Zealots led by Eleazar, son of Simon, controlled the inner courts of the temple. John of Gishala's forces of 6,000 controlled the outer court and part of the lower city; and Simon bar Giora's forces of 15,000 controlled the upper city and most of the lower. One of the most serious effects of this infighting was the destruction of grain. Thus, when the siege began, starvation resulted.

With a combined army that probably totaled over 80,000, Titus began his siege of Jerusalem in AD 70. As with virtually all invaders of Jerusalem, Titus came from the north. By late May, the first and second walls to the north had been breached. By mid-June the

Antonia Fortress at the northwest corner of Temple Mount fell to Titus. Titus then ordered a siege wall built around the entire city. In late August, the Roman troops burned the walls surrounding the inner court, and on 28 August the entire temple was burned. Titus and his army carried back to Rome the golden furniture, the trumpets, the table of shewbread and the seven-branched menorah. (In Rome, the Arch of Titus, built to commemorate Jerusalem's destruction, bears evidence of these objects.) By 30 August, after horrific street fighting, the upper and lower cities were secured. Finally, by the end of September, all of Jerusalem was under Roman control.[291]

Due to famine and Roman slaughter, Josephus estimated that 1.1 million Jews were killed during the siege. This is probably an inflated figure; a more realistic number is 600,000. Despite such slaughter, thousands of Jews survived. Titus chose seven hundred of the tallest and most handsome for his victorious processional. The remainder were divided into several categories for speedy removal from Jerusalem. Surviving rebels were immediately executed; healthy men over the age of seventeen were sent to work in the Egyptian mines or kept for use in the wild animal shows or gladiatorial contests; children under seventeen were sold as slaves; and the old and sickly were also instantly executed. To finalize the humiliation, Titus ordered that the remaining temple enclosure wall and the entire circuit of Jerusalem's city walls be razed. He only left Herod's three towers. The destruction of the walls was so complete that Jerusalem was completely unrecognizable.[292]

Jesus predicted this thoroughgoing devastation of Jerusalem in Luke 21:20–24 and Matthew 24:2. He declared that Gentile domination of the city would last until the "times of the Gentiles are fulfilled." Only with the victory in the 1967 war did Israel regain control of Temple Mount.

General Titus delegated to other Roman officers the task of subduing the three remaining Zealot fortresses. The fortresses at

Herodium and Machaerus fell quickly to the Roman legate Lucillus Bastus. The fortress at Masada was another story; the Zealots there held out for three years. The Roman general, Lucius Flavius Silva, leading the Tenth Legion, organized the siege of Masada on the west side of the Dead Sea.

Eleazar the Galilean led the *sicarii* and Zealots within Masada. The Roman legion surrounded Masada and built a wall and then a siege ramp against the western face of the plateau. This formidable siege ramp was completed in the spring of AD 73, with the Romans breaching the wall of the fortress on 16 April.

As the Romans completed the siege ramp, Eleazar addressed his men and their families:

> Where is this city [Jerusalem] that was believed to have God himself inhabiting therein? We long ago my generous friends resolved never to be servants to the Romans nor to any other than God Himself. We were the first that revolted against them; we are the last that fight against them and I cannot but esteem it as a favor that God has granted us that it is still in our power to die bravely and in a state of freedom, in a glorious manner, together with our dearest friends. Let our wives die before they are abused and our children before they have tasted slavery.[293]

According to Josephus, when Roman troops entered the fortress, they discovered that its 960 inhabitants had set fire to all the buildings but the food storerooms, and had committed mass suicide rather than surrender. With Masada's fall, the First Jewish Revolt had come to an end.

Caesar Vespasian was determined not to repeat the past errors of Rome that had helped produce the revolt in the first place—inept procurators and an inadequate military. To that end, Vespasian appointed competent governors and reorganized the entire military structure of the eastern Mediterranean provinces. Instead of four legions in Syria, there were now three, plus one in Judea. Caesarea remained the capital of the imperial province, but the Tenth Legion garrisoned in Jerusalem, not Caesarea. As a further humiliation for the Jews, the legionary emblem of the Tenth Legion was a boar—to the Jews, an unclean animal.

To facilitate communication and easy troop movements, an extensive network of roads was built throughout the province.[294] When Agrippa died in AD 92, Rome annexed his largely Gentile holdings in the north and made them part of the imperial province of Judea. Evidence of Rome's tyrannical rule was now everywhere in the eastern Mediterranean.

Jewish Life After AD 70

The temple-state, which had characterized Judea since the return from the exile, was gone. The spiritual and political center of Jewish life, the temple and the entire sacrificial system, was totally destroyed.

The Sanhedrin, comprised of the chief priests, elders, Pharisees, and Sadducees, with the reigning high priest as president, was no more. With no functioning priesthood, the Sadducees went out of existence. Unlike the previous rule under the procurators, internal Jewish affairs were now under the purview of the governor in Caesarea, not the Sanhedrin.

Rome did not prohibit Jews from resettling in Jerusalem, but after AD 70, the half-shekel tax paid annually by Jews to support the Jerusalem temple, went to the temple treasury of Jupiter Capitolinus in Rome. Unlike the temple tax, this tax (now called a *didrachmon*) was levied on women and children three years and older, and the upper age limit of fifty was abolished. Understandably, this tax was a heavy burden for large families, causing some to even pay it installments. But to Jews of all economic levels, "it [was] a psychological burden, marking them out as members of a defeated race punished for their nationality."[295] While this tax was a special insult to the Jews, over the years, it became a source of considerable income for the Caesars.

Yet all was not lost. Yohann ben Zakkai of the Hillel rabbinic school pledged loyalty to Vespasian and received special permission to establish a rabbinic school at Jamnia in western Judea, which became in effect a functioning Sanhedrin. With little administrative authority politically, this new Sanhedrin organized Jewish law and its accumulated tradition of oral interpretation. Bruce summarizes the important role this school played over the next hundred years: "The work of codification was prosecuted by successive leaders of the school—notably Rabbi Aqiba and Rabbi Me'ir—until, towards the end of the second century, under Rabbi ben Judah the Prince, the completed work was reduced to writing in the corpus of religious jurisprudence which is called the Mishnah."[296] With the temple and all it represented gone, the new Sanhedrin articulated a practical truth for Judaism after AD 70: "New occasions teach new duties."[297]

The new Sanhedrin, largely made up of Pharisee rabbis, exercised its religious authority over Jewish life through the synagogue system. To establish a degree of uniformity in Judaism, the Sanhedrin revised the Jewish prayer book for use in the synagogues. Among other things, this revision sought to expose "heretics" (i.e., Jewish Christians) who could no longer publicly recite the Jewish prayers.

In addition, the Jamnia council affirmed the canonical status of the thirty-nine books of the Old Testament, rejecting all other Hebrew and Aramaic texts. Further, because so many copies of the Old Testament had been destroyed during the revolt, the Jamnia rabbis began work on the meticulous copying of the Hebrew text, with an accuracy that ensured near perfection of the copies. Finally, the rabbis standardized the reading of the Old Testament texts in the synagogue liturgy. For example, in some liturgies the select sacrificial passages from Leviticus and the fourth Servant Song from Isaiah 52–53 were omitted because Christianity claimed these as prophecies pointing to Jesus' sacrifice on the cross. Rabbinic lines of interpretation also excluded all messianic exegesis favored by the Christian church. There was to be no connection whatsoever between Judaism and the Christian church.[298]

Rome evidenced a near obsession with any future threats to its iron rule of the enlarged province of Judea. Between AD 70 and 117, there were three specific attempts by Rome to extinguish the royal line of David. The first occurred after Jerusalem's destruction when Vespasian ordered a search for living members of David's royal line. Since messianic hopes contributed to the Jewish revolt, Rome needed to ensure that there would be no further messianically fueled resistance.

The second occurrence was under Domitian's rule, which also apparently involved some persecution of Christians as well as Jews. His cruel oppression of Jews and Christians partially stemmed from the growing emperor cult and their unwillingness to worship Domitian. The apostle John was one of his victims, exiled to the island of Patmos.

The final episode occurred in Caesar Trajan's reign, when Simeon, bishop of Jerusalem, was described as a cousin of Jesus. He was crucified.

We lack significant details on the nature of each of these attempts, but they indicate that Rome was "on the alert to guard against incipient messianic movements and to pounce on anyone who looked like a potential trouble-maker."[299]

The Jewish Revolt of AD 115–7

Another Jewish uprising took place in AD 115–7, but this time primarily among the Diaspora Jews of the Roman Empire. In

115, the Roman emperor Trajan attacked Armenia and the kingdom of the Parthians. His military operations were a magnificent success. However, after he had created the new Roman provinces of Armenia, Mesopotamia, and Assyria, several messianic revolts broke out simultaneously. Jews of the Diaspora in Egypt, Cyrenaica, and Cyprus were among the rebels, but Jews of the newly conquered region of Mesopotamia were involved too.

As Trajan's army advanced victoriously through Mesopotamia, Jewish rebels began attacking the small garrisons left behind. A revolt in far-off Cyrenaica soon spread to Egypt and then Cyprus, inciting a smaller revolt in Judea. A widespread uprising centered at Lydda threatened grain supplies from Egypt.

Trajan ordered the commander of his Mauritanian auxiliaries, Lusius Quietus, to crush the Jews in these various provinces. Quietus slaughtered many Cypriote, Mesopotamian, and Syrian Jews, in effect wiping them out; as a reward, he was appointed governor of Judea.[300]

In a much broader sense now, Jews were viewed as hostile to the entire Roman Empire. The Roman historian Tacitus wrote of the Jews, "They regard as profane everything we hold sacred, while they permit all we abhor."[301]

Trajan had attained his military goals in the East. On his return home, he fell ill and died on 8 August 117. His successor Hadrian gave up the newly conquered provinces and dismissed Lusius Quietus, who was killed in the summer of 118.

The Bar Kokhba Revolt AD 132–5

The final revolt of the Jews against the oppression of Rome occurred under the leadership of Simon bar Kosebah, whom Rabbi Akiba declared to be the Messiah. Hence, his followers named him Simon Bar Kokhba ("son of a star"), viewing Simon as the fulfillment of the messianic passage in Numbers 24:17.

During the reign of Emperor Hadrian (AD 117–38), two decisions by Rome precipitated the revolt. First, Caesar Hadrian issued an empire-wide ban of the barbarous practice of castration. The application of this edict apparently included circumcision— the most sacred of Jewish practices, for it was the sign of the Abrahamic covenant. Such an application ran counter to the long-established Roman practice of protecting Jewish religious liberty.

Second, Caesar Hadrian sought to make Jerusalem a Greco-Roman city, which went with his larger policy of the Hellenization of the imperial Judean province, as seen previously in Sepphoris and Tiberias. It also involved a name change from Jerusalem to Aelia Capitolina. In effect, Hadrian sought a deliberate secularization of the sacred capital. Both of these proposals were an affront to everything the Jews regarded as sacred. It is difficult to imagine anything more offensive.

But why did the Jews rise in revolt under Simon? Why did they believe they would be successful this time? Smallwood argues, "Conceivably Hadrian's abandonment of most of Trajan's eastern conquests immediately after his accession was taken by the Jews of Palestine as a sign of a decline in Roman power which they could turn to their advantage."[302] Thus the Jews began to seize towns around Jerusalem and fortify them with walls and subterranean passages. Under Simon Bar Kokhba, the Jews captured approximately fifty strongholds in Judea and 985 undefended towns and villages, including Jerusalem, which they held for two years. As a symbol that Simon had established an independent Jewish state, the Jews minted coins with slogans such as "the freedom of Israel" and "the Redemption of Israel" written in Hebrew. Simon attempted to extend his rule into Galilee, but he found little support there.

The turning point of the war came when Hadrian dispatched one of his best generals from Britain, Julius Severus. Hadrian took up residence in Palestine as well. Under Julius Severus, there were twelve Roman legions in Judea. Slowly, the Roman forces under Severus destroyed all fifty Jewish fortresses and 985 villages.

By the third year of the revolt, Simon had to abandon Jerusalem, and he and his forces fled to Bether, seven miles southwest of Jerusalem. In 135, Hadrian's army besieged Bether, and by the end of summer, the city fell. Every Jew in Bether was killed, including Simon Bar Kokhba.

Following the fall of Bether, surviving rebels fled to Judean desert caves, which Severus methodically surrounded. All survivors were eventually executed.

The consequences of the Bar Kokhba Revolt were utterly devastating for the Jews. Hadrian executed Rabbi Akiba, who had declared Bar Kokhba the Messiah, and many other prominent Jewish leaders. The ancient historian Dio estimated that the death toll of Jews killed during the revolt totaled 580,000, with the majority of the remaining Jewish population of Judea either killed, exiled, or sold into slavery. Judean settlements were not rebuilt. Jerusalem was turned into a pagan city called Aelia Capitolina, and the Jews were forbidden to live there. The sacred scroll was ceremonially burned on the Temple Mount, and Hadrian built a pagan temple to Jupiter and another to himself as Olympius on Temple Mount.

Brisco summarizes other changes to Jerusalem: "Hadrian added a monumental triple gateway to the northern defenses of the city ... A large open piazza behind the [Damascus] gate continued in a single large column capped with a statue of the emperor. A main north-south street (the Cardo) extended southward to the camp of the Tenth Roman Legion located in the area of the Upper City.

North of the Temple Mount, Hadrian's architects built a forum entered by means of the triple gate."[303]

Hadrian also changed the name of the province from Judea to Syria Palestina, a humiliating change, for the Jews' homeland was now named after their ancient enemy, the Philistines.

In the years following the revolt, Hadrian issued a series of decrees forbidding the study of the Torah, Sabbath observance, circumcision, Jewish courts, meetings in synagogues, and other ritual practices.[304] Judea would not be a center of Jewish religious, cultural, or political life again until the twentieth century.

Chapter 12

Constantine, the Byzantine Empire, and the Diaspora, AD 300-636

Due to the near-genocidal polices of Hadrian, the dispersion of the Jews entered its final phase. Much of Judea was depopulated, and Jews were basically banned from Jerusalem. Significant Jewish presences in Alexandria, Rome, Mesopotamia, and other parts of the Mediterranean world meant that there was no longer a geographical center of Judaism.

Before the Bar Kohkba Revolt, the Sanhedrin met in Jamnia. After that revolt, eventually Tiberias on the western coast of the Sea of Galilee replaced Jamnia as the seat of Sanhedrin, before the Sanhedrin completely disappeared. Throughout the empire, persecution of Jews often accompanied that of Christians (e.g., in AD 49, Caesar Claudius decreed that all Jews leave Rome; see Acts 18:2).

With the emergence of Constantine in the early 300s, the role of Christianity in the empire changed. It was no longer persecuted; it was embraced. Christians came into the Roman government, and the government's geographical center switched from Rome to Constantinople. As the Western Roman Empire collapsed, the church, now called the Roman Catholic Church, replaced the empire in the West as the defining institution of what became medieval civilization.

For this book, most importantly, the theology of the institutionalized church witnessed a significant change. The separation of

Christianity and Judaism was now complete, and a growing hostility of the church toward the Jews was finalized. This hostility helped to legitimize pogroms and the genocidal persecution of Jews throughout the Mediterranean world and into what became Christian Europe.

Judaism Before Constantine

After Hadrian, Aelia Capitolina (Jerusalem) became a backwater town of less than ten thousand people, two-fifths its former size. Montefiore describes the pagan city of Aelia: "[Aelia] had two forums, the Temple of Jupiter on the site of Golgotha, two thermal baths, a theater, a nymphaeum (statues of nymphs around the pool) and an amphitheater, all decorated with colonnades, tetrapylons and statues, including a large one of the Tenth Legion's very unkosher boar."[305]

With the reign of Roman Emperor Antonius Pius (138–61), there was a partial reversal of some of Hadrian's most atrocious policies. Although Jews were still banned from Aelia and were now a significant minority in Judea, the circumcision ban for Jews was relaxed. The largest concentration of Jews in the expanded Roman province was now in Galilee. The rabbinic school switched from Jamnia in Judea to Sepphoris and then Tiberias in Galilee, which became the permanent center of rabbinic scholarship and teaching. Further, in the later part of the second century, the Sanhedrin also moved to Tiberias. Thus, to a degree, these changes produced the reestablishment of a central authority for Judaism, something quite critical for Diaspora Jews because, without the temple, there was no authority to prescribe uniform worship and a common calendar. In Tiberias there was now an official, recognized head to prescribe these things. A semblance of uniformity for Judaism was achieved.[306]

The reconstitution of the Sanhedrin also meant the reconstitution of the *Nasi* or patriarch of Judaism, recognized as such by emperors

Septimus Severus (193–211) and his son Caracalla (211–7). The patriarch maintained a degree of control over Diaspora Judaism by sending his personal emissaries to oversee the local Jewish communities and to collect the annual tax, which supported the patriarch and which replaced the temple tax. Smallwood describes how important this position of patriarch had become: "As the head of a worldwide religious community, holding an official position recognized by Jew and Roman alike and in the course of time acquiring the title of *vir illustris* as a dignitary in the Roman system,"[307] the patriarch of Judaism was as powerful as a political ruler. This position within Judaism survived until the first quarter of the fifth century.

Nonetheless, the Hellenization of the expanded Roman province of Judea continued. Aelia remained a thoroughly pagan city, while other cities in the region were transformed. For example, since AD 72, the ancient city of Shechem had become Neapolis; in 130 Hadrian renamed Sepphoris Diocaesarea; Lyyda became Diospolis; and Emmaus became Antoninopolis. This process of urbanization meant that more and more land was brought under Gentile control—a key facet of the Hellenization of Palestine.[308]

The third century witnessed the beginning of the decline of the Western Roman Empire. Rome could no longer defend its borders, inflation was becoming a problem, and, to support growing military defense needs, taxation increased.

The eastern Mediterranean was not exempt from these challenges. Roman legions were constantly traversing Palestine, defending the eastern border against a vigorous new Persian Empire, which had replaced the Parthians. Urban life was decaying, and the Hellenization of the East ended.

Under Emperor Diocletian (284–305), the empire was reorganized. Among other things, it was divided into two parts, East and West, with one ruler in Rome and the other in Byzantium. In addition,

Diocletian unleashed one of the most ruthless persecutions of Christianity in Rome's history. But the Christian church did not go out of existence; instead, it thrived. Diocletian's successor, Constantine, would effect a veritable religious revolution in the Roman Empire.

Constantine

For the first three centuries of the early church, many Christians and Jews living in the Roman Empire faced martyrdom and persecution. Refusing to bow to the emperor as god, early Christians proclaimed "Jesus [not Caesar] is Lord." During the reign of Diocletian (284–305), Christians were martyred by the thousands, Bibles were burned, and churches were destroyed. But Constantine's triumph as emperor in 312 was in many ways a triumph for the church, thereby altering the relationship of Christianity to the empire.

Constantine (ca. 283–337) was born into a military family. Raised in military camps and devoid of formal education, he nevertheless evidenced a quick mind, boundless energy, and unswerving ambition. He spent twelve years in the court of Diocletian in Byzantium, where he witnessed imperial power and relentless attacks on Christianity. But when Diocletian abdicated the throne in 305, the complex politics of the empire broke down and civil war ensued. When Constantine's father, Constantius, died, the troops proclaimed Constantine the new Augustus. By 312 he was at war with Maxentius, his main rival for control of the empire.

As the armies of Maxentius and Constantine amassed near Milvian Bridge over the Tiber River in Italy in October 312, Constantine's life was about to change. His opponent relied on magic and the old gods for his power, but this did not satisfy Constantine. According to Constantine's contemporary biographers, Eusebius and Lactantius, God revealed Himself to Constantine in a vision. Specifically, He gave him the instruction, "In this you shall conquer," referring to a new standard (the labarum) his soldiers were to place on their shields. (The labarum is the superimposition of two Greek letters, *chi* and *rho*—the first two letters of Christ's name in Greek). Because Constantine obeyed the vision and won the battle, his standard and the battle of Milvian Bridge became powerful symbols of the political and military triumph of Christianity. After defeating Maxentius, Constantine went on to unite the entire empire under his rule.

Shortly after his victory, Constantine issued the important Edict of Milan (AD 313), which established Christianity as a legal and officially recognized religion of the empire. Persecution of Christians ended, church property (including cemeteries) was returned, and— for the first time in history—Christianity enjoyed the blessing of the Roman Empire. Gradually, Constantine sought out Christians as advisers, granted exemption from military and civic obligations to the clergy, financed the building of new churches, commanded legal observance of Sunday, and even saw that his children received a Christian education. For him, Christianity was the unifying thread of his empire.

The nature of Constantine's faith, however, is quite problematic and a bundle of contradictions. After Milvian Bridge, he apparently continued to offer sacrifices to pagan gods; in fact, it was only on his deathbed that he was baptized. Was he therefore an opportunist, merely using Christianity to bring unity and power to his empire?

The best explanation seems to be that Constantine slowly grew in his understanding of the Christian faith. Several pieces of evidence lend credence to this. First, following the New Testament teaching, he decreed that worship of the "Supreme God" was to be on Sunday. Second, he called the pivotal church council at Nicea in 325 to deal with the heretical teachings of Arius, who taught that Jesus was created and therefore not eternal. The product of the council, the Nicene Creed, declared forthrightly the deity of Jesus Christ.

Third, Constantine moved the capital of the empire to Byzantium (Istanbul today) and renamed it Constantinople. By doing so he thwarted the growing power of the pagan-worshipping politicians of Rome. He ordered the looting of the old temples and the building of great churches in the empire, especially the majestic basilica he founded in the new capital. The city of Rome was inevitably diminished, the Praetorian Guard abolished, and administrative offices moved to the east. In addition, he and his mother, Helena, herself a devout Christian, committed themselves to finding and restoring many of the historic sites in Palestine associated with Jesus.

The larger question of Constantine's effect on the church is much easier to deal with. The consequences were immense. First, the end of persecution allowed the church a degree of freedom and security it had never enjoyed. But this was a mixed blessing. Gradually, the church became institutionalized, impersonal, and formal. With the removal of the thumb of persecution, the church accommodated itself more and more to its culture rather than separating from its evils.

Second, before Constantine, churches were simple and very functional by necessity. But with the influence of Constantine and his mother, the churches of the empire became large edifices, called basilicas. They reflected the imperial desire for grandeur and beauty. For centuries, churches were modeled after the great basilicas of Constantine, and the formal liturgies that became a part of these great churches forever changed the nature of Christian worship. With the institutionalization of the church came the development of a clerical aristocracy that eventually replaced the old imperial aristocracy.

A final effect centers on Eusebius, "the Father of Church History." Eusebius of Caesarea published his *Church History* in 325 to show that Christianity was the culmination of history, and that the conversion and subsequent actions of Constantine were critical to this goal. God had decreed that His church and Christ would triumph in human history; Eusebius believed that had been accomplished in the person of Constantine. As a result, the doctrine of the imminent return of Jesus for His church was gradually set aside. To Eusebius, His triumph had already come through Constantine.[309]

The role of Constantine's mother, Helena, is important for our study. Constantine commissioned his mother to travel to Palestine to discover the holy places associated with Christ. He bankrolled her efforts from the imperial treasury. Hadrian had erected a temple over the site where Jesus was crucified and buried. So Helena investigated the entire area and interviewed countless people who had knowledge of the oral tradition associated with Jesus. She was purported to have found the cross of Jesus, the nails, and a plaque that read "Jesus of Nazareth, King of the Jews."[310] (This cross was the origin of the relic tradition that pervaded medieval Catholicism).

With her son's support, she ordered the demolition of Hadrian's temple and erected the Church of the Holy Sepulchre, which took ten years to build. It enclosed Golgotha. Above the site of the resurrection was a dome, which had an oculus open to heaven. As Peter Leithart argues,

> Set in Jerusalem ... the church was more than the center of the city. It was conceived as the new temple, the *umbilicus mundi* ... Jerusalem was, in imagination if not in administration, the hub of Constantine's Eastern empire, so much so that he celebrated his *tricennalia* in Jerusalem rather than in Constantinople. Medieval maps that show Jerusalem as the center of the world perpetuated the Constantine vision. With the Christianization of the architecture of Jerusalem, the baptism of public space was complete. At the space where ancient sacrifices had been offered, in a building that rivaled the splendor of Solomon, Christians now gathered to offer their bloodless sacrifice of praise.[311]

Christian pilgrims from all over the world now flocked to Jerusalem to visit the sites associated with Jesus. Jerusalem was no longer a Hellenized pagan city nor a Jewish city; it was the spiritual capital of Christendom.

Constantine intensified the growing shift in how Christians viewed the Jews. When the cross of Jesus was supposedly discovered by Helena, the symbolic center of Christianity shifted from the resurrection to the cross, and perceptions of the Jews subsequently altered. Jews were "Christ-killers," an ugly phrase that symbolized the growing contempt Christian leaders had for Jews.

Evidence abounds that Constantine personally had contempt for Jews. The language of his decrees was "violently prejudicial."[312] He prohibited Jews from attacking converts to Christianity and threatened to burn them if they did. Jews could not own Christian slaves, and he strengthened the laws prohibiting circumcision. Because Passover was a Jewish holiday, he did not want to celebrate Easter on Passover, a practice widely observed in the early church. He therefore decreed that Easter would be celebrated on the first full moon Sunday after vernal equinox. In 331, he decreed that Jews who served in the government were required to fulfill their duties even if those duties conflicted with Jewish religious traditions and customs. His immediate successors in 339 banned intermarriage with Jews, which they called a "savage, abominable disgrace."[313]

Constantine's contempt for the Jews and Judaism reflected what was happening throughout Mediterranean Christianity. Although the great theologian Augustine (354–430) cautioned against persecution of the Jews ("Do not slay them"),[314] within early Christianity a disdain for Jews and Judaism was deepening, and it was rooted in Christianity's developing theology. The Jews no longer had a place in redemptive history. Indeed, theologian Alister E. McGrath argues that a "wide consensus" prevailed in the early church that "the church is a spiritual society which replaces Israel as the people of God in the world."[315]

Within the developing church, from the middle of the second century, this theological view was prevalent. For example, the great Origen (ca. 185–254) declared that "we say with confidence that they [the Jews] will never be restored to their former condition. For they committed a crime of the most unhallowed kind." Lactantius (ca. 304–13) asserted that the Jews were abandoned by God because of their disobedience: "For unless they [the Jews] did this [repent], and laying aside their vanities, return to their God, it would come to pass that He would change His covenant, that is, bestow the inheritance of eternal life upon foreign nations, and collect to Himself a more faithful people of those who were aliens by birth ... On account of these impieties of theirs He cast them off forever."[316]

Theologically, this meant that the church was the "new Israel." The covenant promises God made to Abraham and his descendants were superseded by the church. A corollary was that because the Jewish people rejected Jesus as their Messiah, God was finished with them. His covenant promises to Abraham and David were to be fulfilled in the church. National, ethnic Israel would never be restored to the land, and the new covenant of Jeremiah 31 would no longer apply to the Jews. Today, this view is normally referred to as *supersessionism* or replacement theology, and is the official position of the Roman Catholic Church.

The ugly label "Christ-killers" began to work itself into the language of the church. (Its popular application would justify innumerable persecutions of Jews). For example, Augustine developed the idea that the Jews were the "witness people." By this he meant that, just as Cain slew Abel and was forced to wander the earth as a testimony of his evil, so God marked the Jews when they murdered their brother, Jesus. The dispersion of the Jews and the misery they suffered were a testimony of their evil and a perpetual witness of God's judgment.

A contemporary of Augustine, John Chrysostom (347–407), the preacher with "golden tongue," wrote a series of "Homilies Against the Jews." In one of these homilies, he wrote, "The Jews are the most worthless of all men. They are lecherous, greedy, rapacious. They are perfidious murders of Christ. They worship the devil, their religion is a sickness. The Jews are the odious assassins of Christ, and for killing God there is no indulgence or pardon. Christians may never cease vengeance, and the Jew must live in servitude forever. God always hated the Jews. It is incumbent upon all Christians to hate the Jews."[317]

What was the effect of this kind of teaching? Such teaching dramatically affected medieval Christianity (AD 600–1500). For example, for Jewish people during this time, Holy Week was often horrific. As the church remembered Jesus' passion, fallacious charges were leveled against Jews. Two were particularly heinous.

The "blood libel" charge was one of ritualistic murder. Jews were charged with kidnapping Christian children, especially on Good Friday. In a reenactment of Jesus' murder, the Jews were alleged to kill the children. The blood was used to make Passover matzoh (unleavened bread).

The "host desecration" was the other. Jews were charged with stealing the host, a wafer of unleavened bread used in the Mass. The doctrine of transubstantiation stated that the host, upon consecration, became the body of Christ, and the charge was that Jews would stab the stolen wafer countless times until it "bled." (Pope Innocent III officially accepted this charge at the Fourth Lateran Council in 1215.)

The result of these two charges throughout Christian Europe was that Jews, fearing for their lives, would go into hiding during Passion Week.[318]

Alongside the escalating Jewish persecution within Christendom, the Jews in Babylonia (then under Persian rule) were thriving, enjoying a reasonable amount of autonomy and prosperity. Many

Jews in Palestine fled to the relative security and protection of
Persia. In a sense, the Rabbinic Judaism of Babylonia became
Diaspora Judaism.

There, the Babylonian Talmud was compiled and became one of
the most influential collections of Jewish writings. (The Talmud has
two components: the Mishnah, the written compilation of Jewish
oral law, and the Gemara, a collection of rabbinic interpretations
of the Mishnah.) Among the Babylonian rabbis, the ceremonial
laws dealing with agriculture, purity, and the sacrifices were set
aside and were replaced with the theological and legal teachings
of the rabbis. The family, the synagogue, and the rabbi were now
the centers of Diaspora Judaism.

The End of the Western Roman Empire

As the above material on Constantine has shown, after 330, the
Roman Empire changed its character. Not only was the old aristocracy replaced by a new one—the church—but the entire focus
shifted to the East. With Constantinople as the new capital and the
division of the empire into East and West complete, the concern of
the emperor was no longer Gaul, Spain, or Africa, but Egypt and
Syria. The Rhine River was not as important as the lower Danube.
Increasingly, the Western provinces were abandoned as impossible
to rule. Although the Eastern Empire endured for another thousand
years, the collapse of the Western provinces of the empire (i.e. the
Western Roman Empire) is traditionally dated at 476.

This collapse of the Western provinces was the result of a long
decay. The normal factors usually cited for this decay include
the decadence of Roman society, monetary and price inflation,
overtaxation, an incompetent and inefficient bureaucracy, and
agricultural decline. No doubt all played a role in the collapse.
But perhaps the most decisive was imperial "overstretch," especially as its relates to the Germanic migrations.[319] Norman Davis
summarizes:

The Germanic peoples were on the move throughout the imperial period. The Gothic federation left its resting-place on the lower Vistula in the second-century AD, drifting slowly south-eastwards against the main migratory current. Two hundred years later, the Visigoths were established on the Black Sea coast north of the Danube delta. The Ostrogoths lay further east, in the Crimea and on the Dnieper steppes, precariously close to the advancing Huns. In that fourth century, some of the Frankish tribes were invited into the Empire as imperial *foederati*, and charged with the defense of the Rhine.[320]

What was the empire's response to this massive migration? The empire's strategy was to absorb the barbarian challenge rather than decisively deal with it. The emperors exacted tribute, settled them in the lands they demanded, and employed them as part of the army charged with defending the borders.

The Western provinces gradually were overrun by the various Germanic tribes. From the 370s into the late 400s, they dismembered the Western Roman Empire, and the entire area was abandoned by the eastern Roman legions. These barbarian tribes included the Ostrogoths and Lombards (Italy); the Vandals (northern Africa); the Visigoths (Spain); the Franks (Gaul); and the Burgundians, Bavarians, Alemans, and Bulgars (Rhine, Rhone, and Danube regions). The Roman imperial government in the West had lost so much land and taxes that it was bankrupt by the time it was extinguished in 476.

The Christian church replaced the imperial institutions of the West. Christianity was decidedly egalitarian; Galatians 3:28 was manifestly true. For example, in third-century Rome, the church included "a powerful freedman chamberlain of the emperor; its bishop was the former slave of that freedman; it was protected by the emperor's mistress, and patronized by noble ladies."[321]

Peter Brown summarizes the remarkable appeal of the church and its gospel in the West: "The Christian community suddenly came to appeal to men who felt deserted. At a time of inflation, the Christians invested large sums of liquid capital in people; at a time of increased brutality, the courage of Christian martyrs was impressive; during public emergencies, such as plague or rioting, the Christian clergy were shown to be the only united group in the town, able to look after the burial the dead. In Rome, the Church was supporting fifteen hundred poor and widows by 250."[322]

Further, the appeal of Christianity was the sense of community it provided, for it absorbed people from all walks of life, regardless of socioeconomic status. As Brown concludes, "Christianity had become a church prepared to absorb a whole society."[323]

Finally, with bishops such as Ambrose and Augustine, the monastery became central to the church. The monks took vows, had a distinctive dress, and were educated in Scripture, not in classical education. They were the new professional elite—and their bishops the new "senate" of Rome. The church had become the "new Rome."[324]

The Byzantine Empire and the Jews

The Byzantine civilization that emerged in the East was far different than the civilization of the West. Davies nicely summarizes the difference: "[A]s established by the ninth century, [it] possessed several inimitable features which set it apart both from contemporary states in the West and from the earlier Roman Empire. The state and the church fused into one indivisible whole. The Emperor, the *autokrator*, and the Petrarch were seen as the secular and the ecclesiastical pillars of divine authority. The Empire defended the Orthodox Church, and the Church praised the Empire. This 'Caesaropapism' had no equal in the West, where secular rule and papal authority had never been joined."[325]

Although Emperor Julian (called the Apostate) ruled from 360 to 363 and offered to rebuild the temple in Jerusalem for the Jews, his short rule was followed by further Jewish persecution by the Byzantine Empire. Two other Byzantine emperors shaped the Eastern Empire and its religious polices, especially those associated with the Jews—Theodosius I (379–95) and Justinian (518–27):

Theodosius I. Two significant developments occurred during the reign of Theodosius (379–95)—the treaty of coexistence with the Visigoths and establishing Christianity as the religion of the empire.

1. Between 379 and 380, Theodosius sought first to rebuild the army, and then to consolidate Rome's position on the Balkan Peninsula. Recognizing that the barbarians, who had invaded the provinces as early as 375, could no longer be expelled by force, he concluded a treaty of alliance with the Visigoths in the fall of 382. The Goths, who pledged loyalty to the empire, were given territory between the lower Danube and the Balkan mountains. As a result, the eastern provinces of the empire saw little threat from the Germanic migrations that eventually destroyed the West.

2. In 391, Emperor Theodosius made Christianity the empire's official state religion. The strong linkage between state and church had begun. This momentous decision was preceded by a theological controversy of some importance in the East over the Nicene Creed, which had declared that Jesus was of the same essence as God the Father ("begotten not created"). On February 28, 380, Theodosius decreed that only those who believed that God the Father, Son, and Holy Spirit were of the same essence could be considered Christians. Trinitarian Christianity had won the support of the emperor. This principle had a direct impact on the Jews in the East especially, for they were not Trinitarians. Furthermore, it established clearly the emperor's authority in matters of faith.[326]

Justinian (518–27). As a Christian, Justinian's ambition was to restore the Roman Empire to its former glory. Justinian maintained his eastern provinces virtually intact in spite of the vigorous offensives of Persia. Seeking to rule over the barbarian kingdoms of the West, he reconquered Italy, North Africa, and Spain. The Frankish kings of Gaul even recognized his authority. Justinian was the embodiment of absolute power. The glory of Rome was restored, and the Mediterranean was once again a Roman lake—but it was only a superficial glory. Once Justinian died, it fell apart, exposing Italy to Lombard conquest.[327] Further, the empire was exhausted, in dire financial shape, and losing territory to the Persians, even briefly losing control of Jerusalem to the Persian ruler Khusrau II.[328]

As the supreme legislator, Justinian codified Roman law and established the strong tradition of jurisprudence and rule of law. Because of the church-state linkage, Justinian promoted good government in the church and upheld orthodox teaching. Like Theodosius, he enforced Trinitarian Christianity. Many of his codified laws dealt with religious problems. For example, pagans, heretics, and Samaritans were not tolerated. He demoted Judaism from a permitted religion of the empire, banned Passover if it fell before Easter, transformed synagogues into churches, and baptized Jews against their will. In 537, when he dedicated the great Hagia Sophia in Constantinople, he declared, "Solomon, I have surpassed you."[329]

Under Justinian, Jerusalem became a city dominated by Orthodox Christianity. In 543, Justinian and his queen, Theodora, built the enormous basilica, the Nea Church of St. Mary Mother of God, facing away from Temple Mount, "designed to overpower Solomon's site."[330] Orthodox pilgrims flooded into Jerusalem. Montefiore summarizes the Jerusalem of this period: "The city was set up to host thousands of pilgrims: the grandees stayed with the patriarch; poor pilgrims in the dormitories of Justinian's hospices which had beds for 3,000; and ascetics, in caves, often old Jewish tombs, in the surrounding hills."[331]

After the division of the Roman Empire into east and west, finalized in 395, the Byzantines redrew the borders of the land of Palestine. The various Roman provinces (Syria Palestine, Samaria, Galilee, and Perea) were reorganized into the three dioceses of Palaestina. The use of Hebrew as the spoken language gradually declined after the Bar Kokhba Revolt, but did survive as a literary language. During the Byzantine period, the Jewish population in northern Israel remained large for several centuries, particularly in Eastern Galilee. Western Galilee began to take on a more Christian character. The coastal plain, central Judea, and southern Samaria had already become largely pagan. Southern Judea remained mostly Jewish for several centuries, and northern Samaria remained Samaritan until after the Muslim conquest.

The ambitious policies of Emperor Justinian were costly for the Eastern Empire. From a financial and military vantage point, the empire was drained. Despite the temporary successes of Emperor Heraclius (610–41), the empire began to break up. The Arabs conquered Syria, Egypt, North Africa, and Armenia. Italy fell to the Lombards, and the empire was reduced to Asia Minor and the Balkan Peninsula. The eastern Mediterranean was about to face one of its greatest challenges—the rise of Islam. Muhammad changed the face of almost everything associated with the world of Christianity and Judaism; today we are still reeling from Islam's impact.

Chapter 13

Islam and the Crusades 570-1291

I slam changed everything. Between 632 and 732, all the major centers of historical Christianity were lost to this new, militantly aggressive monotheism. While in 732 Christian Europe stopped Islam's western advance, the Eastern Empire centered in Constantinople was the barrier securing Eastern Europe from Islam's onslaught.

By the eleventh century, Catholic Europe was determined to liberate the Holy Land from "the infidel." Once again, Jerusalem was on the center stage of world history. These waves of Crusades ended the West's isolation and laid the groundwork for the modern era.

While these momentous changes swept across Eurasia, Diaspora Judaism was growing. Although eight hundred years separate the twenty-first century from the end of the Crusades, Islam and the legacy of the Crusades still dramatically impact our lives today.

The Rise of Islam

The founding and early history of Islam revolves around the prophet Muhammad (AD 570–632). Muhammad was born about 570. Because he lost his father near the time of his birth and because his mother died when he was six, Muhammad was cared for briefly by his grandfather and later by his uncle, Abu Talib. Abu Talib was a merchant, so Muhammad traveled extensively with him in the thriving caravan network that traversed Arabia and Syria and into

India and northern Africa. No doubt these journeys first exposed Muhammad to Christianity and Judaism.

At the age of twenty-five, Muhammad led a trading expedition to Syria for a wealthy widow named Khadijah. So impressed was she with Muhammad that she sought his hand in marriage. Though she was fifteen years his senior, he accepted, and they began a life of devotion to one another. The marriage produced six children. Although he married several women after she died, he maintained a monogamous relationship with her throughout their life together.

According to Muslim tradition, the year 610 changed Muhammad and thereby the world. On the seventeenth night of the month of Ramadan, Muhammad was in solitary meditation in a cave at the foot of Mount Hire, near the city of Mecca, when he suddenly saw a vision. The angel Gabriel commanded him to "recite." Not understanding what he was to recite, Muhammad heard Gabriel exclaim that he was the prophet of God (Allah).

Muhammad's newfound monotheism was controversial among the polytheistic tribes of Mecca. Resistance from Mecca intensified, and his life was in danger.

According to Muslim tradition, Allah confirmed Muhammad's prophethood in 620, miraculously bringing him at night to the "Furthest Sanctuary." Although it is not mentioned in the Qur'an, later generations of Muslims would teach that this was Jerusalem. There he conversed with Jesus, Moses, and Abraham. Then he and Gabriel were taken by a ladder to the seventh heaven. Muslims believe that the Dome of the Rock is built on the site of this ascension.

But this confirmation did not facilitate acceptance of his monotheistic message. Muhammad continued to condemn the paganism of the polytheistic Arabian tribes. In Mecca there was a massive stone shrine called the Kaaba, which attracted pilgrims from all over Arabia. Fifty feet high and nearly forty feet square, it housed one idol for each day of the year. Some said it had been built by Adam and Eve after their expulsion from the garden. Others claimed that Abraham and Ishmael had built it. Arabian pilgrims came to kiss or touch the smooth black stone that glistened in the southeastern corner.

So severe was Muhammad's persecution that he took his wife and small group of followers and fled to Medina, about 250 miles north of Mecca. For Muslims, this momentous event, called the Hegira, is year 1 in the calendar.

While in Medina, Muhammad found acceptance and began to build his army of Islam. He had become a military leader. Eight years after the Hegira, Muhammad and his army of 10,000 reentered Mecca in triumph. Thronged by his followers, the sixty-two-year-old Muhammad led a glorious pilgrimage to the Kaaba, now the focal point of Islamic worship. There, in 632, he announced the perfection of a new monotheistic faith—the worship of Allah. Before he died, Muhammad established complete dominion over the Arabian Peninsula.

What was Muhammad's relationship with the early Christians and the Jews? Muhammad was not really familiar with Christianity or the Bible. The Qur'an, the 114 chapters of Archangel Gabriel's revelations to Muhammad, refutes Christian claims that Jesus died on the cross, that He was God's Son, and that God is Trinity. Likewise, the Qur'an alludes to other beliefs that are of course demonstrably false—that Mary was a sister of Aaron and Moses and that Mary was part of the Trinity. Therefore, Muhammad denied Jesus' deity, His atoning death on the cross, and the Trinitarian nature of God.

Despite such egregious error and misunderstanding about the truth of Christianity, Muhammad vigorously taught that he and his teachings were heirs to both Judaism and Christianity, which he called "peoples of the book." For that reason, he decreed that

Christians and Jews were to receive protection under Muslim rule. He extended personal hospitality to Christians, less to Jews.

In fact, as Pat Cate argues, when one evaluates the chapters of the Qur'an chronologically, a clear progression exists confirming a growing hostility toward Jews and Christians. During his early years in Mecca, Muhammad confirmed his basic allegiance to Jews and Christians. However, after the flight to Medina, his attitude toward Jews and Christians changed. He turned radically against them, and his teachings about jihad developed (see below).[332]

After Muhammad's death, Islam spread quickly. In only one hundred years (632–732), it swept across the rest of Arabia, Palestine, all of northern Africa, and into Spain, only to be stopped in France in 732.

Why did it spread so quickly? The military vacuum left by the collapse of western Rome and the jihad, or holy war, proclaimed by the Qur'an help to explain the swift conquest by Islam. There was a passion, a dynamic energy that produced the conviction that, as conquerors, they were spreading the final message of Allah. They were building his kingdom. Huge territories, once dominated by Christianity, were lost, many of which have never been recovered.

When Muhammad died suddenly, he had no designated successor. His followers had to decide the succession issue: Was it to be based on heredity or on loyalty to Muhammad? The successors of Muhammad fell into bitter disagreement, causing a fatal division in Islam that has never healed.

According to the Sunni sect (the traditionalists), Medinans elected an aging member from Muhammad's tribe, Abu Bakr, Muhammad's father-in-law. But, according to the Shia sect (partisans of Ali), the Prophet's cousin and son-in-law was the designated successor—Ali ibn Abi Talib. For the sake of unity, Ali ultimately deferred to Abu Bakr, but the split has never healed; Islam today remains divided between the Sunnis and the Shiites.

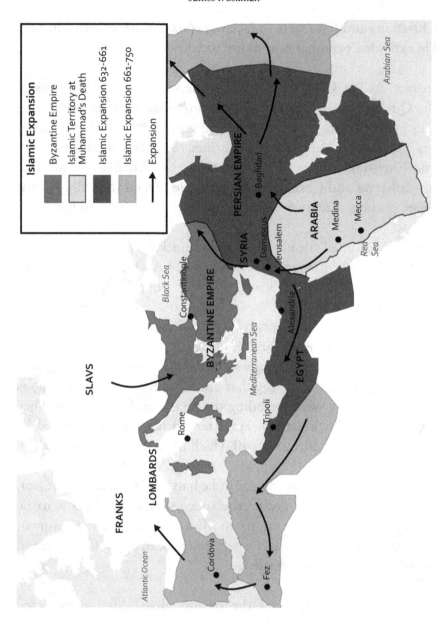

The history of Islam is complex and often difficult to summarize easily. For this study, it can be summarized in the following manner:

- After the first four caliphates (rulers/followers of Muhammad), the Umayyad tribe gained political control of Islam and formed a dynasty, centered in Damascus, that lasted from 661–750. The Umayyads spread Islam across northern Africa and into Spain. Islam remained militant and militaristic during this period.

- The next dynasty, the Abbasids, followed after a successful revolt against the Umayyads. This dynasty effectively lasted from 750 to 1055 and was characterized by peace, not war. (Between the 1050s and 1517, the Abbasids dynasty, though technically still functioning, was ineffectual and weak.) Its political center was Baghdad. The Abbasid courts were filled with luxury and wealth that resulted from prolific trade policies. The Abbasids were the high-water mark of Islamic culture.

- In the 1050s, the Seljuk Turks gained control of much of Islam. Coming from Central Asia, the Turks were brutal and aggressive and destroyed the peaceful court of the Abbasids. They denied Christians access to the Holy Land, which sparked the Crusades, an attempt by Christian Europe to drive the Muslims from the Holy Land.

- The Ottoman Turks succeeded their cousins, the Seljuk Turks, in 1517, conquered the Eastern Empire centered in Constantinople (Istanbul) in 1453, and invaded Europe. Much of Central and Southern Europe fell under Muslim control as a result.

- The modern period of Islamic history (much of the twentieth century) was characterized by a nationalism mixed with Islam that produced the modern Islamic nation-states (e.g., Egypt, Iran, Turkey, Saudi Arabia, Kuwait, Iraq, etc.). Although Islam continues to expand as a faith, it is wrapped up in the larger geopolitical issues of global trade in oil, terrorism, political alliances, and the Israeli-Palestinian conflict. As a faith, Islam is the fastest-growing world religion; as a political/economic force in an age of terrorism, it is at the center of today's world.

Islam as a Worldview: Its Theology and Its Ethics

"Islam" means submission (to Allah) and "Muslim" means one who submits (to Allah). Islam is a remarkable religion of discipline and rigor. Its theology is complex but is central to understanding both its history and its worldview.

God. The Muslim concept of God is summed up in the name "Allah." A critical point for Islamic doctrine is the stress on Allah's unity of being. This dominates the Muslim's thinking about God, and is expressed in the phrase, "There is no God but Allah." He is absolutely unique and inconceivable. An Islamic proverb says, "Whatever your mind may think of, God is not that!" A constant phrase repeated in Muslim prayers is *Allah akbar* ("God is great"); he is far greater than any thought humans can have of him. Allah is so great that he can do what he likes, even break his own laws.

In Islam, Allah has decreed all that will occur. He is the creator of all that is in heaven and on earth. His knowledge is perfect, his will is beyond challenge, and his power is irresistible. All these attributes—omniscience, sovereignty, and omnipotence—are evident in his creation.

Many pious Muslims carry a rosary that has ninety-nine beads, each representing one of Allah's names. The one hundredth name is unknown to humans—known, legend has it, only to the camel.

Allah's might and majesty are tempered with justice. He rewards and punishes, yet he is merciful, a guardian of his servants, defender of the orphan, guide of the wrongdoer, liberator from pain, friend of the poor, and a ready-to-forgive-master (Qur'an, 11:52).

Allah resides in the seventh heaven, far removed from his creation. He is unknowable, but he has chosen to make himself known through the holy books and through his prophets. These books include the Old and New Testaments, and among Allah's many prophets is Jesus.

The Holy Books. Muslims maintain that Allah handed down 104 books, and of these only four are most important. They believe that the Law was given to Moses, the Psalms were given to David, the Gospels were given to Jesus, and the Qur'an was given to Muhammad.

Muhammad made no claim that his teaching invalidated the Jewish and Christian scriptures; rather, he instructed Christians and Jews to follow their respective teachings (5:72,73), and commanded Muslims to believe in and obey the Law and the Psalms (3:78). He taught that the Gospels were sent to confirm and safeguard the Law, which served as guidance and light to those who fear Allah (5:48). The Qur'an safeguards both the Law and the Gospels (5:52).

The Prophets. Muslims believe that Allah sent 124,000 prophets and apostles, but that the three greatest prophets were Moses, Jesus, and Muhammad. Muhammad, the Qur'an teaches, is the last and the greatest prophet, for he proclaimed Allah's final revelation. The heart of his message was one of morality, a call to righteousness. For Muhammad, that meant abandoning the polytheism and paganism of his day and submitting totally to the will of Allah. His message, however, also involved community. Islam would create a new fellowship based on loyalty to Allah and to one another. The old loyalties to clan, tribe, nation, and state were replaced with loyalty to Allah. For that reason, even today, Muslims of all clans, tribes, and nations gather in Mecca for the hajj.

The Day of Judgment. The inevitability of divine judgment permeates the Qur'an . In Sura 2 it is described as the Day of Gathering, when there will be a group in paradise and one in the fire. It teaches that Allah will take a scale and weigh the good and evil deeds of each person. If the good outweighs the bad, the believer will be sent to paradise; otherwise, to hell. But to Muslims Allah is great and merciful, and Muhammad intercedes for them. The result is that Allah's judgment is more related to his will than to his justice. The Qur'an offers little assurance on this matter of eternity.

The Pillars of Islamic Practice. Submission and obedience constitute the vital center of Islam. By good deeds, the Muslim expresses his commitment to Allah. The moral and ritual obligations of Muslims are summed up in the five pillars of Islam:

Pillar 1: The Witness. To make the profession, "There is no God but Allah, and Muhammad is his prophet," is to become a Muslim. By uttering the first part, one becomes a submitter to Allah; by uttering the second, one becomes an adherent of Islam. It cannot be taken lightly. It begins with an affirmation of Allah and his oneness. It continues with the means by which Allah reveals himself to humanity—Muhammad.

Pillar 2: The Ritual Prayers. Every devout Muslim performs the ritual prayers at least five times a day. Ritual prayers are mainly praises to Allah, and are always recited in Arabic. In most Muslim countries, a spiritual leader, called a muezzin, mounts the balcony of the minarets that dot Muslim city skylines and calls Muslims to prayer. The prayer is recited wherever one finds oneself, although urban Muslims usually gather in the mosques of the city. All face the direction of Mecca when they pray, for this reminds them of the birthplace of their faith.

Pillar 3: The Paying of Alms. Paying alms is giving back to Allah a portion of his bounty to avoid suffering in the next life and as a purification of what one retains materially. Alms are not voluntary, but are an obligation to gain favor with Allah.

Pillar 4: The Fast of Ramadan. The fast of Ramadan is an obligatory duty for all Muslims except the sick, pregnant women, travelers under certain conditions, and soldiers in combat. Because Muslims follow the lunar calendar, Ramadan is thirty days long and occurs each year about nine days earlier than the previous year. Each day of the fast begins from the moment one awakes and lasts until sunset. The night is spent eating and drinking. During the day, the Qur'an prohibits eating, drinking, smoking, swallowing saliva, and sex. The fast is a debt owed to Allah. It atones for sin, helps control passions, and merits Allah's favor.

Pillar 5: The Pilgrimage to Mecca. This obligation to Allah is to be performed at least once during a Muslim's life. The pilgrimage is filled with ritualistic observances like stopping at the well where Gabriel heard Hannah's plea for water, stoning Satan, and kissing the sacred black stone of the Kaaba.

A Word about Jihad. The term *jihad* literally means "struggle" or "exertion." In a religious context, it always involves a struggle against evil. That struggle can be one of the heart, in which the Muslim fights the evil of his nature, but it can also be a "jihad of the mouth," in which the Muslim struggles against those who oppose Islam.

The most controversial form of jihad is the "jihad of the sword." Throughout the Qur'an there are calls to physical combat on behalf of Islam. In fact, this doctrine developed over time in Muhammad's teaching. In the Qur'an chapters that focus on his time in Mecca and even early Medina, the militancy of jihad is absent. However, as the opposition to Islam mounted, so did Muhammad's teaching that jihad is military force in the name of Allah. As the doctrine developed, Muhammad taught that those who sacrificed their lives in battle for Allah were guaranteed admission to the highest level of heaven. Jihad had become a violent, military means of spreading the faith, and Allah was thereby glorified. Historically, jihad became the heart of Islam's expansion. Today, Islamic terrorists are trying to resurrect this militant, aggressive form of jihad.[333]

Islam's Effect on Christianity and Judaism

The rise of Islam and its impact on Christian Europe were profound. Norman Davies summarizes this sweeping effect:

> Islam's conquests turned Europe into Christianity's
> main base. At the same time the great swathe of

Muslim territory cut the Christians off from virtually all direct contact with other religions and civilizations. The barrier of militant Islam turned the Peninsula in on itself, severing or transforming many of the earlier lines of commercial, intellectual and political intercourse. In the field of religious conflict, it left Christendom with two tasks—to fight Islam and to convert remaining pagans. It forced the Byzantine Empire to give lasting priority to the defense of its Eastern borders, and hence to neglect its imperial mission in the West. It created the conditions where the other, more distant Christian states had to fend for themselves, and increasingly to adopt measures for local autonomy and economic self-sufficiency. In other words, it gave a major stimulus to feudalism. Above all, by commandeering the Mediterranean Sea, it destroyed the supremacy which the Mediterranean lands had hitherto exercised over the rest of the Peninsula. Before Islam, the post-classical world of Greece and Rome, as transmuted by Christianity, had remained essentially intact. After Islam, it was gone forever.[334]

In addition, language and perceptions changed. Medieval Europeans commonly referred to Muslims as "Saracens," a label derived from the Arabic word *sharakyoun* or "easterner." A strong dichotomy thus developed between the Christian West and the Islamic East—Latin vs. Arabic, canon law vs. Sunnite law, images vs. arabesques. Further, an ethnocentric feeling of superiority in the Christian West led to viewing the Muslim East with utter disdain. They were infidels, destroyers of all that was sacred and holy.[335]

The Muslim conquest of Jerusalem was an epic event for both Christianity and Judaism. After Emperor Hadrian's genocidal policies drove Jews from Judea, Christians since Emperor Constantine had guarded and secured the holy places of Jerusalem. But,

On a February day in the year AD 638, the Caliph
Omar entered Jerusalem riding on a white camel.
He was dressed in worn, filthy robes, and the army
that followed him was rough and unkempt; but its
discipline was perfect. At his side rode the Patriarch
[of Jerusalem] Sophronius as chief magistrate of the
surrendered city. Omar rode straight to the site of the
Temple of Solomon, whence his friend Mahomet had
ascended into Heaven. Watching him stand there, the
Patriarch remembered the words of Christ and mur-
mured through his tears: "Behold the abomination of
desolation, spoken of by Daniel the prophet."[336]

Soon after Jerusalem was occupied by the Muslims, building activity transformed it from a predominantly Christian city into
a triumphant Muslim holy city. By the late seventh century, the
importance of Jerusalem to Islam was well established—the third
most important city in Islam after Mecca and Medina.

Caliph Omar, the conqueror of Jerusalem, was the most venerated
figure in Islam next to Muhammad. Moshe Sharon, professor of
Islamic history at Hebrew University, writes that "Islamic tradition
therefore describes Omar's (the Savior's) entrance into Jerusalem as
a messianic event. Like Jesus, he reaches the city from the Mount
of Olives and Gethsemane, enters through the eastern gate, then
proceeds to the Temple Mount, discovers the place of Solomon's
Temple and restores worship at the ancient place by building a
mosque."[337] This is especially striking because Jerusalem is associated with the second coming of Jesus in Christianity and with
the Messiah's appearance in Judaism. Islam was now claiming
supremacy over both.

Two Christian buildings in Jerusalem represented the centrality of
Christian convictions about Jesus and of His promise to return.
The Church of the Holy Sepulchre was the site established by
Constantine where the death, burial, and resurrection of Jesus

occurred; on the Mount of Olives was the Church of the Ascension, where Jesus ascended into heaven and where He promised to return. Between these two important edifices lay Temple Mount, the site where Abraham offered Isaac on Mount Moriah and the site of Solomon's temple.

Thus, when the Umayyad Caliph, Abd al-Malik (685–705), built the Dome of the Rock, it was the center of the plan to reshape Jerusalem as a Muslim holy city. (Temple Mount is called the Haram al-Sharif, or "Noble Sanctuary," by Muslims). That the Dome of the Rock is higher in elevation than the Church of the Holy Sepulchre challenged the Christian dominance of Jerusalem. Additional evidence points to the intentionality of al-Malik to build a structure indicating Islam's triumph over Christianity and Judaism:

1. Over the eastern and southern gates of the Dome are two inscriptions: "The Unity of God and the Prophecy of Muhammad are true" and "The Sonship of Jesus and the trinity are false." Inside the Dome are inscriptions declaring, "The Messiah Jesus, son of Mary, is indeed a messenger of God"; "So believe in God and all the messengers, and stop talking about a Trinity, Cease in your own best interests!"; and "It is not fitting that God should beget or father a child."[338]
2. Al-Malik's choice of a dome on top of a circular structure surrounded by a double octagonal ambulatory was quite significant. It was common in many of the great churches of Christianity (e.g., the Church of the Holy Sepulchre and the Hagia Sophia in Constantinople) and was commemorative in nature. The Dome of the Rock is sixty-five feet in diameter (the same as the Church of the Holy Sepulchre) but is not a mosque; it is a shrine to the place where Muhammad was taken into heaven for his "night vision." The Dome was thus much greater than and far superior to any church in Christendom. In addition, the Dome of the Rock was

viewed in Islamic tradition as the new Solomonic temple. According to Muslim tradition, Solomon built his temple directly over the rock, and this was the rock from which the prophet Muhammad ascended to heaven. Sharon writes that "Muslims believed the Dome of the Rock symbolized the renewal of Solomon's Temple, and thus served to refute the belief of Christians ... that the site would remain desolate until the Second Coming."[339]

3. Montefiore describes the awe-inspiring beauty of the Dome of the Rock:

> The building has no central axis but is encircled thrice—first by the outside walls, next by the octagonal arcade and then right under the dome, bathed in sunlight, the arcade around the rock itself: this declared that this place was the center of the world. The dome itself was heaven, the link to God in human architecture. The golden dome and the lush decorations and gleaming white marble declared this was the new Eden, and the place for the Last Judgment when Abd al-Malik and his Umayyad dynasty would surrender their kingdom to God at the Hour of the Last Days. Its wealth of images—jewels, trees, fruit, flowers and crowns—make it a joyful building even for non-Muslims—its imagery combined the sensuality of Eden with majesty of David and Solomon.[340]

Before Islam, the Church of the Holy Sepulchre was the most imposing structure in Jerusalem; now it was the Dome of the Rock. Jerusalem was now a Muslim city.

Caliph Abd al-Malik not only built the Dome of the Rock, he centralized and unified Islam. He formulated the double *shahada*, the central belief statement of Islam: "There is no God but God and Muhammad is his prophet." The Prophet's sayings—the hadith— were collected, and Abd al-Malik's edition of the Qur'an become the only legitimate one in Islam. Arabic was now the official language of Islam. Coins of the realm no longer bore human images of any type; they were exclusively decorated with Arabic writing. Abd al-Malik and his son Walid also built the al-Aqsa Mosque on the southern part of Temple Mount, which became the imperial mosque of Islam.[341]

During the early decades of Islam, Jewish life generally improved. Muslims often granted Jews some semblance of protection and freedom to practice their faith. Jews settled back into Jerusalem, living south of Temple Mount and even praying on the Mount. But in 720, the new Caliph Omar II banned Jewish worship on Temple Mount, a stipulation that remained during the entire Islamic rule of Jerusalem. Heavy taxes, abridgment of rights, a change in legal status, and further limitations on religious observances followed. Yet rabbinic scholars and scribes known as the Masoretes still worked in Tiberias in Galilee. One estimate posits 300,000 Jews living in Palestine by the tenth century.[342]

In 750, the Umayyad dynasty was overthrown by the Abbasids, who ruled Islam effectively until the 1050s. Between the 1050s and 1517, they competed with the Fatimids, the Mamluks, and the Mongols for supremacy. The Abbasids shifted the center of Islam from Damascus to Baghdad, and Islam settled down, entering its golden age. Interest in Mecca replaced the importance of Jerusalem during this period. In fact, the Abbasid ruler, Caliph Haroun al-Rashid, exchanged envoys with Charlemagne, the new Holy Roman Emperor, and the Christians in Jerusalem enjoyed a significant amount of protection. Indeed, Haroun permitted Charlemagne to create a Christian quarter around the Church of the Holy Sepulchre, with a convent, library, and pilgrims' hostel, which included 150 monks and 17 nuns.[343]

Christian pilgrims began flooding into Jerusalem during the Abbasid period. When the split in Christendom occurred in 1054, dividing it into Roman Catholicism in the West and Eastern

Orthodoxy in the East, there was new competition between the pilgrims from the West and the East. Hostels and monasteries throughout Jerusalem and other parts of the Holy Land were built to house all the pilgrims. Pilgrimages to the Holy Land became a major means of doing penance during this period, fostering the increasing presence of Christianity in the land.

The Crusades, 1095–1291

While the leadership of early Islam was exclusively Arab, the rise of the Seljuk Turks in the eleventh century is central to understanding the Crusades. They were nomadic tribesman from central Asia who embraced and energized Sunni Islam in the late tenth century. They defeated the Byzantine army in 1071 at the battle of Manzikert and invaded Asia Minor, depriving Byzantium of more than half its realm. They were near the gates of Constantinople, threatening the entire Byzantine Empire.

In addition, the Turks seized control of Jerusalem in 1093. The Church of the Holy Sepulchre was thus vulnerable. There was little the Byzantine Church could do to protect this sacred site. In fact, there was little the church could do without the consent and cooperation of the Muslim authorities. The event that actually triggered the First Crusade was an appeal to Pope Urban II for Western mercenaries (knights) from Byzantine emperor Alexius Comnenus (1081–1118) to halt the advancing Turks. Comnenus had no intention of liberating Jerusalem; his interest was in preserving Byzantium.

Urban's initial response was favorable. He would recruit Christians to aid Byzantium, but he likewise dreamed of reuniting Eastern and Western Christianity and of gaining control of Jerusalem.[344] On 27 November 1095, at the Council of Clermont, Urban gave an impassioned sermon to a large audience of French nobles and clergy, calling for an organized campaign in the East. He explained the great suffering and abuse wrought by the Turks on Eastern

Christendom, but his primary appeal was for the liberation of Jerusalem and the Church of the Holy Sepulchre: "Jerusalem is the navel of the world. Enter the road to the Holy Sepulchere; wrest the land from the wicked race, and subject it to yourself."[345] Urban promised "absolution" from all sins for those who went. But he also added, "The possessions of the enemy, too, will be yours, since you will make spoil of their treasures and return victorious to your own."[346] The enthusiastic crowd responded with cries of *Deus le volt!* ("God wills it!").

Such a massive undertaking as the First Crusade can only be explained by two characteristics of Western Christendom at that time. First was the militarization of medieval society. In the competition between kings and the more regional warlords, the one element that was central was the dominance of the mounted-knight elite. By the time of the First Crusade, they dominated the social and economic life of medieval Europe. Marcus Bull writes that medieval European society's "military organization ... was intricately bound up with wider economic and administrative structures; it was impossible to extract a sizable cavalry force from its cultural and social milieu ... Armies needed support services from grooms, servants, smiths, armorers, and cooks, all of whom could turn to fighting if needed ... And clerics would also be involved to minister to the army and pray for success. This is significant for an understanding of the broad response to the First Crusade appeal."[347]

The second characteristic was the devotional pilgrimage. Because of the theology of Roman Catholicism, Christians believed that doing acts of penance would shorten the time their souls spent in purgatory, eliminate the temporal debt owed to God for sin, and merit God's favor. Pilgrimages were viewed as acts of penance and thus encouraged by the church. This was one of the reasons Pope Urban II's call for a crusade against Islam met with such potent appeal. Urban declared that going on the Crusade was a "satisfactory" penance capable of undoing the debt for confessed sins. As Bull argues, "Here at last was a spiritually effective activity designed specifically for lay people, in particular warrior elites whose sins were considered among the most numerous and notorious."[348]

Enthusiasm for the Crusade was most intense in France, Italy, and western Germany, such that between the spring and autumn of 1096, tens of thousands of Europeans, as a pilgrimage journey for the remission of all sin, took to the road to regain Christ's land for Christianity. There was no more noble cause.[349]

An unintended consequence of the First Crusade was a war on the Jews. It is doubtful Pope Urban had any idea of the extraordinary zeal his words unleashed across Europe. As the news surged across the continent, it created a religious tidal wave that engulfed all "the alien peoples" (Urban's words), including the Jews. Jonathan Phillips quotes contemporary Christians stirred with Crusader fury: "Behold we travel to a distant land to do battle with the kings of that land. We take our souls in our hands in order to kill and to subjugate all those kingdoms which do not believe in the crucified. How much more so should we kill and subjugate the Jews who killed and crucified Him." Or another: "Let us take vengeance first upon them. Let us wipe them out as a nation; Israel's' name will be mentioned no more. Or else let them be like us and acknowledge the child born of menstruation."[350] This was not a European-wide phenomenon, nor was it systematic persecution; but it created havoc and concern, such that church and civil authorities tried to calm down the furor. But it was a sign of what the Crusader knights would do to Jews in the Holy Land. They would show little mercy.

The anti-Jewish impulse unleashed by the Crusades lasted well into the next century. Indeed, the thirteenth century was probably the most violently anti-Semitic of the medieval period. Dan Jones shows that across Europe, kings enacted oppressive measures against the Jews of their respective kingdoms: "Pogroms, massacres, ghettoization, discriminatory laws, persecution, and abuse were on the rise against Jewish people whenever they lived."[351] In England, Henry III taxed Jews for his crusading fund. He outlawed most forms of usury, restricted Jews to living in certain cities, ordered Jews to wear a yellow badge of shame, and levied an annual tax on all Jews over twelve. His son, Edward I, issued the Edict of Expulsion in 1290, which ordered that all Jews leave England on pain of death. The small minority of two thousand Jews left England. Their confiscated land and wealth enriched Edward's treasury.[352]

The Crusaders arrived in Constantinople during the winter of 1096–97. Since Alexius was seeking their help as mercenaries for his fight with the Seljuk Turks, he was aghast when over 50,000 spiritually energized knights showed up in his city. Relations between Alexius and the Crusaders quickly deteriorated, especially when he sought negotiations with the Turks, not war.

The Crusaders moved south into the Levant, progressing into Syria, then Palestine, and eventually, in June 1099, laying siege to Jerusalem, now controlled by the Fatimids of Egypt. After a five-week siege, they entered the city, purging the city of unbelievers through a massacre of Muslim and Jewish men, women, and children. Thousands were slaughtered.

Although many Crusaders returned to Europe, those who remained established the Crusader principality of Antioch, the County of Edessa, the County of Tripoli, and the Latin Kingdom of Jerusalem. Godfrey of Bouillon was named ruler of the Latin Kingdom and "The Protector of the Holy Sepulchre." As a result, relations between the Byzantines and the Crusaders worsened. The Crusaders had replaced an Orthodox bishop in Antioch with a Roman Catholic one, doing something similar in Jerusalem. So bad did this become that the Eastern Orthodox Patriarch Michel II declared, "Let the Muslim be my master in outward things rather than the Latin dominate me in matters of the spirit."[353]

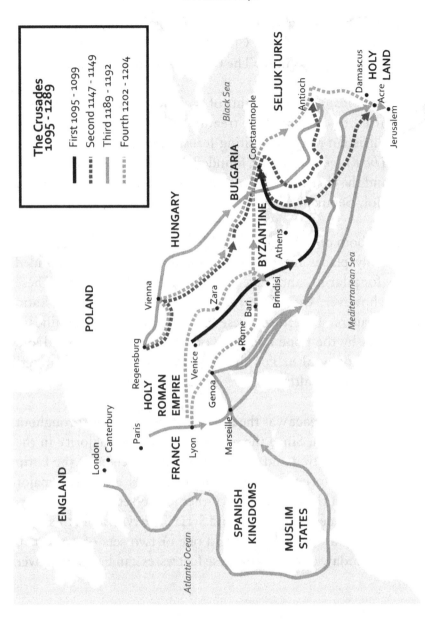

The presence of Western Christians in the Holy Land had a dramatic impact in several ways. First, to defend and protect the sacred places, the religious military orders of Western Christendom emerged. These were unique to Latin Christendom, for members were a combination of monk and knight. These new military orders provided the support structure for the Latin Kingdom and served the Roman Catholic Church, which found its power and authority thereby enhanced. The two most important orders were:

- *The Hospitalers* (Knights of St. John) were originally organized to offer medical treatment and accommodations to Christian pilgrims visiting Jerusalem.
- *The Knights Templar*, founded in 1118, guarded the temple and the churches of Jerusalem, especially the Church of the Holy Sepulchre.

Knights of both orders were totally dedicated to serving the church and its holy places in the Latin Kingdom. They also provided security for pilgrims and travelers throughout the kingdom. These knights, however, were fiercely loyal to the pope, not the Latin Kingdom rulers. Therefore, these orders were granted significant concessions by the pope and were often rewarded with land and other forms of wealth. For that reason, many of these knights because notably wealthy.

A second major impact was the need to build fortresses throughout the Latin Kingdom. Since there was no Christian majority in the Holy Land, protecting and defending the major cities of the Latin Kingdom was a priority. They built fortresses along the major highways and in the major cities. Other fortresses dotted the borders with their enemies—Egypt and Syria. The typical fortress was surrounded by a dry moat and had one or two sets of protective walls. Even today, remnants of these fortresses can be seen all over Israel.

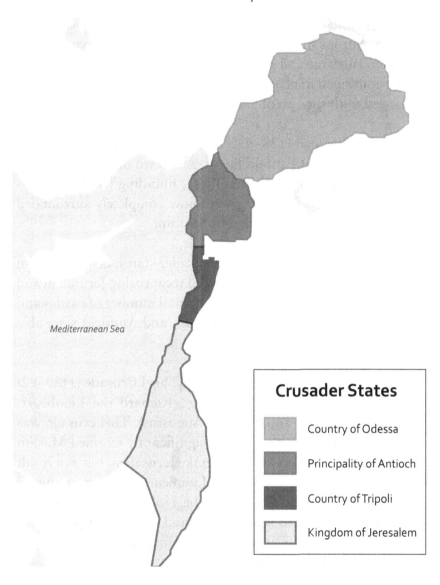

Mediterranean Sea

Crusader States

Country of Odessa

Principality of Antioch

Country of Tripoli

Kingdom of Jeresalem

Because Islam was so fragmented, no Muslim leader organized significant resistance to the Crusaders. For over a century, two rival Islamic empires challenged one another for domination—the Shiite Fatimids centered in Egypt and the Sunni Abassids in Baghdad. (The Seljuk sultan of Baghdad ostensibly served the Abbasid caliph at this time.) As Karsh argues, "They feared and loathed each other as much as they feared and loathed the Christian powers, and this precluded any conceivable collaboration between them against the European invaders."[354] Since the Crusaders were largely confined to Palestine and parts of Syria, Muslim fragmentation and disunity continued unabated during the early Crusader years. This all changed with the rise of Saladin.

In 1169, Saladin (ca. 1138–93), a Kurdish general in the Seljuk army, took control of Fatimid Egypt. A shrewd military tactician, he was able to defeat the Seljuk Turks, founding the Ayyubi dynasty. The Crusader kingdoms were now completely surrounded by a single Muslim empire ruled by Saladin.

In 1187, Saladin made war on the Crusader states, defeating them at the Battle of Hattin (4 July 1187) and recapturing Jerusalem and most of the Crusader territory. Only a small number of castles and well-fortified coastal cities (Tyre, Tripoli, and Antioch) were able to hold out against Saladin.

His conquest of Jerusalem provoked the Third Crusade (1189–92) called the Crusade of the Kings (e.g., Richard the Lionheart, Frederick Barbarossa, and Philip II Augustus). This crusade was effectively a war of attrition, which significantly strained Muslim resources. The Crusaders failed to retake Jerusalem, but as a result of an agreement with Richard the Lionheart, Saladin permitted Christian access to the Church of the Holy Sepulchre. Saladin also encouraged Jews to settle in the land of Israel, especially in the coastal cities. The Crusaders maintained a firm hold on the coastline, especially Acre and Tyre.

The Fourth Crusade of 1204 was a watershed. In 1198 Innocent III (1198–1216) was elected pope and brought new energy to the crusading idea. He believed and preached that crusades should be directed toward enemies from within the church and those outside, principally Islam. He forcefully declared that the Christian church must overcome the loss of Jerusalem and the failure of the Third Crusade. He directed the fury of the mounted knights against heretics in southern France (the Albigensians), against his political opponents, and toward the goal of eliminating "from the Holy Land the filth of the pagans."[355] Hence, the 1204 Crusade was launched. Such Crusader furor also produced the legendary Children's Crusade of 1212, in which thousands of children were either killed or sold into slavery.

The key to the Fourth Crusade was Venice. The Crusaders contracted with the Venetians, who had somewhat monopolized eastern Mediterranean trade, to transport them, for an exorbitant price, to the Holy Land. The Crusaders agreed to enable the Venetians to gain more territory for their trading empire and to place Alexius Angelus on the throne in Constantinople. When the people of that city rejected Alexius, the Crusaders sacked the city. They looted the Hagia Sophia, the spiritual center of Byzantium, of its wealth, including countless relics, which made their way back to Western European churches. The Crusaders slaughtered Eastern Christians and Jews, raped nuns, and defamed the holy places of Eastern Orthodoxy. For a brief time Eastern and Western Christianity were united, but at a terrible price. Orthodox Christianity has never forgiven Western Christianity for the horror of 1204.[356]

There were four more major Crusades, but none of them achieved significant success. The Crusaders were completely driven from the Middle East by the Mamluks, slave-soldiers of the Ayyubi dynasty in Egypt, who overthrew their masters in 1250. In a series of brilliant campaigns, the Mamluks destroyed the crusading infrastructure in Galilee and the coastal plain, finally capturing Acre in 1291, thereby ending all Crusader presence in the region.

But the impact of the Crusades was monumental. The Crusades saw the rise of powerful monarchs ruling nation-states (e.g., France, England, Spain) at the expense of the Roman Catholic Church, which ultimately was weakened by the Crusades. The Crusader spirit eventually produced the expulsion of the Spanish Muslims (the Moors) from Spain by 1492, and helped provide the energy for Columbus and the voyages of discovery. Christianity and Islam shared a holy war ideology and, at various times, used it quite successfully (e.g., Pope Urban in 1096, Innocent III in 1204, Saladin in 1197). The 1204 Crusade widened the gap between Eastern Orthodoxy and Western Catholicism—a gap that remains seemingly unbridgeable even today. Finally, crusading imagery and metaphor survive today and energize al-Qaeda and many parts of radical Islam. Osama bin Laden's fiery rhetoric was laced with the language of "Crusaders from the West," meaning the United States and Europe.

With the Mamluk conquest in 1291, the land of Israel became a desolate place. Most of the cities were deserted, and Jerusalem lay in ruins. Few Jews inhabited the area, and those who did lived in extreme poverty. Between 1291 and 1517, the Holy Land was largely forsaken and neglected.

But all that was about the change. In 1517 a new Islamic power, the Ottoman Turks, seized control of Islam. They would rule this part of the world until the end of World War I. During the Ottoman Empire, the West, especially the United States and Great Britain, began discussions about a homeland for the Jewish people. When the Ottoman Empire collapsed after World War I, forces were already in motion that ultimately led to the creation of the nation-state of Israel in 1947.

Chapter 14

The Ottoman Empire (1517-1919) and the Idea of a Jewish Homeland

The Ottoman Empire was the last great Islamic empire. Its defeat in World War I produced the modern nation-states of the Middle East and the further fragmentation of Islam.

At first, the Ottomans adopted a rather tolerant attitude toward the Jews, and Jews began to return to the land. The Protestant Reformation, the Scientific Revolution, the Industrial Revolution and the subsequent growth of worldwide trade altered Western perceptions about the Middle East and its importance. In addition, virulent anti-Semitism in Europe, pogroms in Russia, and the birth of Zionism in the nineteenth century all contributed to the growing need for a homeland for the Jewish people. The biblical promises that God would regather His people to their land took on a fresh urgency.

After the Ottoman Empire collapsed, a new competition between Arab and Jew for the Holy Land ensued. The West took notice.

The Ottoman Empire: Birth And Expansion, 1517–1815

In the thirteenth century, the imperialistic ambitions of the Mamluks met the growing threat of the Mongol hordes under Genghis Khan ("Universal Ruler"). The Mongols swept across the Asian steppes, conquering northern China and Central Asia, and moved into Southwest Asia, conquering Iraq. By the time Genghis

Khan died in 1227, his empire stretched from the Pacific to the Black Sea. His successors swept into Russia, Ukraine, Poland, Bulgaria, and Hungary. By the 1260s, the Mongols were in northern Syria. But at the 1260 Battle of Ain Jalut, south of the Sea of Galilee, the Mamluks stopped the western advance of the Mongols.[357]

One of the results of the Mongol invasion of Southwest Asia was the complete subjugation of the Seljuk Turks and the emergence of small Turkish principalities in Anatolia (modern-day Turkey). One of these was located in northwestern Anatolia, named after its founder Osman Bey (1291–1326), also known as Ottoman. This frontier position meant that the Ottomans were constantly fighting the Byzantines, and "as they saw it, the constant expansion of Muslim power was a predestined development in which they were chosen to act as Allah's Sword 'blazing forth the way of Islam from the East to the West.' This privileged role made it imperative for them to unify the House of Islam under their command and turned their fight against the Muslim rivals into a quintessential act of jihad."[358]

Osman's son, Orhan (1326–60), carried his father's vision forward and initiated a series of conquests that brought the Ottomans into Eastern Europe and led to the ultimate destruction of the Byzantine Empire. Over the next two hundred years, the Ottomans transformed Southwest Asia and southern Europe.

- In 1354, Orhan occupied the Gallipoli Peninsula, the largest eruption of Islam into Europe since the invasion of Spain in the eighth century.
- Murad I (1360–89) encircled Constantinople by taking Adrianople and the Bulgarian and Serbian territory in 1385 and 1389 respectively.
- On 29 May 1453, the Ottomans conquered the city of Constantinople, ending the Eastern Roman Empire of Byzantium, which had survived the Western Empire by nearly a thousand years: "Constantinople had been the foremost barrier—both physically and ideologically—to

Islam's sustained drive for world conquest and the object of desire for numerous Muslim rulers."[359] The conqueror, Mehmed II, rode into Constantinople on a white horse, making it his new imperial capital. Slaughter and rape throughout the city ensued. Symbolic of the triumph of Islam over Orthodox Christendom, the great Hagia Sophia was turned into a Muslim mosque.

- By the time of his death in 1481, Mehmed II had conquered Greece, Serbia, and all Balkan territories south of the Danube and added the Crimean Peninsula to his holdings. The Black Sea was now "an Ottoman lake."
- Selim I (1512–20) added to the Ottoman advance by taking Syria, Palestine, Egypt, and Arabia.
- Suleiman the Magnificent (1520–66) completed the empire by taking Iraq, North Africa, and Hungary, and gaining a foothold in southern Italy. The Ottomans were at the gates of Vienna.

The Ottoman Empire was now the "single imperial authority of Islam combining the supreme religious and temporal power."[360] The boundary between Islam and Christendom had been re-made. Russia, and more specifically Moscow, gradually replaced Constantinople as the center of Orthodoxy. Russia represented the new force of Eastern Christendom, and its interest in the Holy Land would be energized over the next hundred years.

The Ottoman conquest of Jerusalem effected profound change in this most holy of cities. On 20 March 1517, the Ottoman sultan, Selim the Grim, took possession of Jerusalem and received the keys to al-Aqsa and the Dome of the Rock. His son, Suleiman, transformed the city. In fact, much of the Old City of Jerusalem today is his work. The walls and gates of Jerusalem are his. The walls were built between 1535 and 1538. The total length of the walls is about two and a half miles; their average height is forty feet and average thickness is eight feet. The walls contain thirty-four watchtowers and eight gates.

Suleiman added a mosque, an entrance, and a tower at the citadel near the Jaffa gate. He also built an aqueduct to bring water into the city to fill the nine fountains he built, including the three on Temple Mount. He replaced the "worn mosaics on the Dome of the Rock with glazed tiles [a total of 450,000] decorated with lilies and lotus in turquoise, cobalt, white and yellow as they are today."[361] Jerusalem's population tripled to almost 16,000, with 2,000 of them being Jews.

Two other developments occurred in Jerusalem as a result of Suleiman's reign:

- Islam was clearly the superior and conquering faith in Jerusalem, but he did make provision for Jews to pray. Muslims had a monopoly on Temple Mount, but he assigned a nine-foot street along the retaining wall of Herod's temple for Jewish prayers. Montefiore describes the process as it unfolded: "This made some sense, because it was adjacent to their old Cave synagogue and next to the Jewish Quarter where the Jews had started to settle in the 14th century ... Jewish worship there was carefully regulated; and Jews were later required to have a permit to pray there at all. The Jews soon called this place ha-Kotel, the Wall, outsiders called it the Western or Wailing Wall, and henceforth its golden, ashlar stones because the symbol of Jerusalem and the focus of holiness."[362]
- In 1535, because Suleiman needed French support against the Hapsburgs in Europe, he granted to the Franciscans custody of the Christian shrines in the Holy Land. This included the Church of the Holy Sepulchre. But they needed to share church space with all the other sects of Christendom, a reality that continues today. A degree of religious freedom for Christians characterized this period.

By 1853, Czar Nicholas I declared, "We have on our hands a sick man—a very sick man. It will be ... a great misfortune if, one of these days, he should slip away from us, especially before all necessary arrangements are made."[363] Why did Nicholas characterize the Ottoman Empire as the "sick man?" By the nineteenth century, the question was no longer whether the Ottoman Empire could reform itself and survive, but when would it expire. Its imperial status, its ability to hold its vast empire together and its very survival were all in jeopardy. How did this happen? By the nineteenth century, why was the Ottoman Empire on the verge of collapse?

Ephraim Karsh argues, "No sooner had the Ottoman Empire reached its apogee than it went into a prolonged and steady decline. Centrifugal pressures, degeneration, and bureaucratic and administrative mismanagement, all perennial problems that had plagued past Muslim empires, came to afflict the newest member of the imperial club."[364] The "steady decline" centered on five major developments:

1. As the rise and success of the Ottomans owed much to superb and highly capable sultans such as Suleiman, so its decline is explained by high levels of incompetence. The military is a significant case in point. Whereas the army was the key to early Ottoman success, by the seventeenth century it had deteriorated into a "self-indulgent hereditary caste that would go to almost any length to protect their privileged status, including the overthrow and murder of the sultan. All attempts at reform and modernization were summarily nipped in the bud."[365]

2. The Ottoman economy needed to generate significant wealth and therefore taxes to support the state bureaucracy and the sizable military machine. An agricultural economy with peasants as the mainstay could not, over time, provide resources sufficient enough to sustain the empire.

3. The European economy and the Ottoman economy were inextricably linked, but over time that linkage turned from an advantage to the Ottomans to a disaster. As the developing European economy turned into a net exporter

of commodities, the Ottoman Empire began experiencing significant trade deficits that drained it of its gold, silver, and raw materials.[366]

4. Increasingly the empire found it impossible to control its provinces. Karsh writes, "Ottoman officials were both corrupt and hated. Anarchy and the reign of local chiefs and notables who disregarded the government's orders created widespread confusion, insecurity, and misery. Some of these declared their subservience to the sultan; others refused to recognize any Ottoman authority and openly defied the central government."[367]

5. Because of the internal rot of the Ottomans, external pressures threatened the security of the empire. The Balkans were insecure because the Hapsburgs were inching ever closer to liberating this region from Islam. Russia was an even more serious threat. Under Peter the Great (1672–1725) and Catherine the Great (1729–96), Russia gained control of the Black Sea, giving it access to the Mediterranean Sea.

During the nearly four hundred years of the Ottoman Empire, the Jewish people initially found the Ottomans to be tolerant rulers. They began to return to the land, settling in Jerusalem, Hebron, Tiberias, and Safad (the center of Jewish mysticism). The Ottomans attached the land to the province of Damascus and viewed Israel as a source of revenue for their empire.

But as Ottoman taxation became oppressive, many Jewish families fled the land once again. By 1800, the population of Palestine was about 300,000 (5,000 were Jewish), and much of the land was owned by absentee landlords from Egypt and Lebanon. Because the Ottomans levied a higher tax on land with trees, most of the trees of Palestine were cut down, leaving the land barren and wasted. In addition, the rich agricultural land of northern Galilee became a swamp, and the south saw the desert expand.[368]

But major changes were about to occur which would reverse the deplorable conditions of Palestine and re-energize interest in Israel as a homeland for the Jewish people. It all began with Spain.

The *Reconquista* of Spain and the Division of Diaspora Judaism

After Muhammad's death in 632, the expansion of Islam extended across northern Africa and into Europe. By the eighth century, the Umayyad dynasty of Islam had conquered Spain, but was defeated in 732 at the Battle of Tours in France. They retreated back into Spain, where they remained until the fifteenth century.

By the eleventh century, the power of the Umayyad caliphs had begun to wane, disintegrating into a series of separate Islamic kingdoms. Meanwhile, by the late 1080s, Spanish Christians had recaptured much of central Castile (Toledo, Madrid, and Guadalajara). However, the Christian reconquest, or *Reconquista*, did not gather momentum until the thirteenth century, when the Christian kingdoms united to drive the Muslims out of Spain.

The turning point in the *Reconquista* was the 1212 battle of Las Navas de Tolosa, when the combined armies of Castile, Aragon, and Navarre, along with volunteers from Leon and France, defeated the Muslims. Shortly thereafter Valencia, Cordoba, Seville, and the Balearic Islands all fell to the Christians. Only the tiny Islamic kingdom of Granada survived as Muslim.

With these victories, the separate Christian kingdoms began to merge. Castile and Leon united in 1230, and the marriage of Ferdinand II of Aragon and Isabella I of Castile in 1474 produced the nation of Spain. Ferdinand and Isabella conquered the last Islamic kingdom of Granada in 1492, thereby ending seven hundred years of Islamic rule in Spain.

Later that same year, Ferdinand and Isabella commissioned Christopher Columbus's voyage west, which had the goal of not only finding passage to India, but also the liberation of Jerusalem from the East. Indeed, one of Ferdinand's self-declared titles was King of Jerusalem. Further, Columbus, in his *Book of Prophecies*, dreamed that the Spanish Empire would rebuild Jerusalem and Mount Zion.[369]

Shortly after commissioning Columbus, Ferdinand and Isabella turned on the Jews in Spain. The Spanish government was already coercing Jews to convert to Catholicism, but now, with the advice of the chief Inquisitor, Torquemada, the Spanish king and queen declared that the Jews must convert or be expelled. Some did convert, but between 75,000 and 150,000 were expelled. The monarchy even banished them from settling in Naples.

Over the next fifty years, much of Western Europe followed Spain in banishing the Jews. Out of a narrow and short-sighted conviction that had its origin in bigoted Catholicism, Spain ended the great cultural and intellectual center of Diaspora Judaism. This horrific act is the origin of the Sephardic Jews (*Sepharad* is Hebrew for Spain). As Montefiore so poignantly observes, "In the most searing Jewish trauma between the fall of the Temple and the Final Solution, these Sephardic Jews ... fled eastwards to the more tolerant Holland, Poland-Lithuania and the Ottoman Empire, where they were welcomed."[370]

The Ashkenazi Jews of France, Germany, and Eastern Europe were the other main division of Diaspora Judaism that emerged. The term Ashkenazi is derived from the Hebrew word "Ashkenaz" (see Genesis 10:3), generally referring to the people of the north, often specifically from Germany. Today, most American Jews are descended from Ashkenazi Jews.

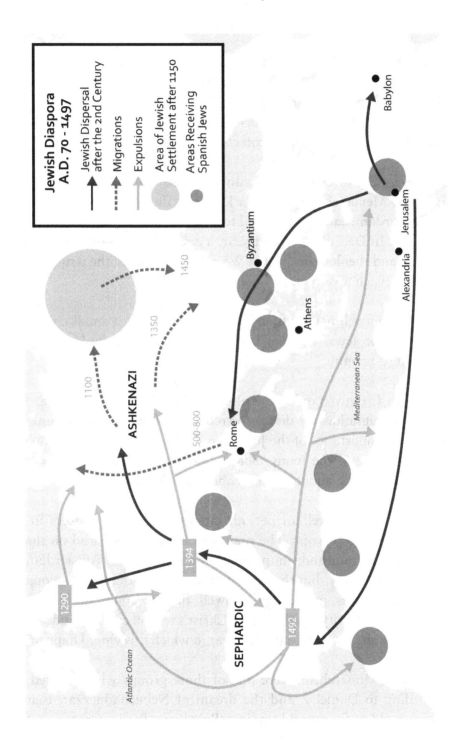

Jewish Diaspora
A.D. 70 - 1497

Jewish Dispersal
after the 2nd Century

Migrations

Expulsions

Area of Jewish
Settlement after 1150

Areas Receiving
Spanish Jews

Babylon

Byzantium

Jerusalem

Athens

Alexandria

Mediterranean Sea

Rome

ASHKENAZI

SEPHARDIC

Atlantic Ocean

1450

1350

1100

500-800

1290

1394

1492

Oliver Cromwell and the Fifth Monarchy Men

In 2006, England observed the 350th anniversary of the readmission of the Jews into England under the Cromwellian Protectorate. (Edward I had expelled the Jews in 1290.) Oliver Cromwell (1599–1658) was the key Puritan leader during the English Civil War and the short-lived, republican Protectorate (1649–60).

However, Cromwell did not readmit the Jews to England in 1656. In 1655, Menasseh ben Israel, a leader of the Jewish community in Amsterdam, came to England to persuade Cromwell to readmit the Jews. In December of that year, a conference of lawyers, merchants, and theologians met in Whitehall to discuss the issue, but failed to reach a verdict.

While Cromwell never officially readmitted Jews, a small colony of Sephardic Jews living in London was identified in 1656 and allowed to remain.

Although Cromwell did not actually change British policy toward Jewish immigration, the discussion reflected a fundamental rethinking of the importance of the Jews to prophetic Scripture. This was, therefore, one of the many factors that contributed to changing Western thinking about the Jews and their role in God's plan.

During the Cromwellian period, interest in Jewish matters increased for two reasons. The pragmatic reason was based on the international trade and commercial connections of the Amsterdam Jewish community. But the doctrinal reason was the belief among many Protestants, including Cromwell, that the conversion of the Jews to Christianity would hasten Christ's second coming. Indeed, many thought 1656 might be the year in which this would happen.

The Fifth Monarchists were one of those groups who believed, according to Daniel 2 and the dream of Nebuchadnezzar, that there would be four world empires (Babylonia, Persia, Greece, and

Rome). The final empire of history, the Monarchists concluded, would be established by Jesus as King of Kings and Lord of Lords, who would reign with His saints on earth for a thousand years. The Fifth Monarchists saw themselves as saints in the coming millennial kingdom. Interest in the Jews and helping to facilitate their conversion were important aspects of the Fifth Monarchist vision and passion.[371]

The focus of the Puritans on the Jews and Jewish conversion marked a significant shift in Protestant thinking about eschatology. Lutheran and Calvinist Reformation thinkers followed Augustine, who argued that the prophecies relating to Israel were fulfilled in the church (i.e., the church was the new Israel). But English Puritans and some Continental theologians (e.g., Johann Alsted) interpreted the prophetic passages regarding Israel literally. They looked to the restoration of the Jews to their land and to their ultimate conversion. Converted Jews would be a part of Christ's millennial kingdom. When Puritans migrated to the New World, they took these prophetic ideas with them.[372]

Napoleon Bonaparte and the Jews

The French Revolution, which began in July 1789, deteriorated into ghastly revolutionary violence under the Jacobins during the Reign of Terror in 1793–4. A conservative reaction under the Girondists ended when Napoleon Bonaparte seized power and made himself emperor. From 1804–12, his military genius resulted in the conquest of much of Europe, but ended with the calamitous failure of his invasion of Russia in 1812. His widespread reforms produced legal, religious, and political changes, some of which are still in effect today. Most important for this study was his reform program that impacted the Jews of Europe.

In 1798, Napoleon began his conquest of Egypt, which he hoped would gain him control of the Mediterranean and cut off British access to India. At the Battle of the Pyramids, he defeated the

Ottomans, but his navy was destroyed by Admiral Horatio Nelson of Great Britain. Seemingly trapped in Egypt, Napoleon needed to conquer Palestine to secure Syria and defeat the Ottomans on land.

So, in February 1799, he invaded Palestine, advancing on Jaffa and coming to within three miles of Jerusalem. He captured Jaffa and Haifa, and then marched toward Acre, laying siege to the city in March 1799. Defeating the Ottoman armies at the Battle of Tabor Mountain, Napoleon issued his famous "Proclamation to the Jews" from "General Headquarters, Jerusalem, 20 April 1799": "Bonaparte, Commander in Chief of the Armies of the French Republic in Africa and Asia, to the rightful heirs of Palestine—the unique nation of Jews who have been deprived of the land of your fathers by thousands of years of lust for conquest and tyranny. Arise then with gladness, ye exiled, and take unto yourselves Israel's patrimony. The young army has made Jerusalem my headquarters and will within a few days transfer to Damascus so you can remain there [in Jerusalem] as ruler."[373]

Unable to conquer Acre, Napoleon retreated toward Egypt and eventually back to France. Napoleon had failed in his grand vision for the eastern Mediterranean, but, in Montefiore's words, he "had made the Levant fashionable."[374] He signaled the growth of European involvement in the Ottoman Empire and especially in Israel. Napoleon's campaign was the first substantial contact between Palestine and the West since the destruction of the Crusaders at Acre in the 1290s.

Napoleon significantly altered the status of Jews within France and major portions of Europe itself. For example, he abolished laws that had restricted Jews to ghettos. Within France, he recognized Judaism as a legitimate faith, together with Catholicism, Lutheranism, and Reformed Protestantism. For many European Jews, Napoleon was greeted as "the continental emancipator of Jews, the demolisher of ghetto walls."[375] Wherever his armies went, Jews greeted them as liberators.

On 6 October 1806, the Assembly of [Jewish] Notables, convened by Napoleon, issued a proclamation to all the Jewish communities of Europe, inviting them to send delegates to the Great Sanhedrin, to convene on 20 October. This proclamation, written in Hebrew, French, German, and Italian, spoke of the importance of this revived institution to the Jewish people.

While the actions of Napoleon garnered hope among Europe's Jews, others objected forcefully. The first to object to the creation of the Great Sanhedrin was the Russian czar, Alexander I. He vehemently denounced the liberties given to the Jews and referred to the emperor in a proclamation as "the Anti-Christ" and the "Enemy of God."

The Great Sanhedrin, which consisted of twenty-six laymen and forty-five rabbis, addressed a proclamation to all European Jews that, among other things, regulated worship in the synagogues, marriage practices, and the charging of interest for loans (usury).[376]

Benjamin Disraeli, Prime Minister of England (1868, 1874–80)

Benjamin Disraeli (1804–81) was raised a Jew, but converted to Anglicanism and was baptized at age twelve. Yet he remained proud of his Jewish heritage. He once said, "Yes, I am a Jew, and when the ancestors of the right honorable gentleman were brutal savages in an unknown island, mine were priests in the temple of Solomon." His 1831 tour of the Middle East was one of the most formative events of his life. He spent a week in Jerusalem, reflecting on his Jewishness. He wrote of Jerusalem, "I was thunderstruck. I saw before me apparently a gorgeous city. Nothing can be conceived more wild, and terrible, and barren than the surrounding scenery, dark, stony, and severe ... Except Athens I never saw anything more essentially striking; no city except that, whose site was so pre-eminently impressive."[377]

As a Jewish Christian, he saw himself as a completed Jew, for he seemed to blur the differences between Judaism and Christianity.

To be a Jew was to be a proto-Christian; to be a Christian was to see Judaism completed.[378] His 1831 visit convinced him that Britain must play a role in the Middle East. Indeed, by 1851, he believed that "restoring the Jews to their land, which could be bought from the Ottomans, was both just and feasible."[379]

As prime minister, his foreign policy saw the fulfillment of his vision for Britain's role in the Middle East. In 1869 the Suez Canal was completed, financed largely by French money. The majority of shares in the canal were held by the Khedive of Egypt (the Ottoman minion). By 1875, the Khedive needed £4 million to avoid bankruptcy. In despair he began negotiations with French businessmen, trying to sell them his shares. A journalist passed on the news to Disraeli, who saw that the security of the British Empire's hold on India depended on Britain acquiring a controlling interest in the canal. He convinced Lionel de Rothschild to lend Britain the money to purchase the controlling interest.

The security of the Suez Canal, as the pathway to India, now became the major focus of British foreign policy. Further, in 1878, Disraeli attended the Congress of Berlin, which he dominated. Among many other things, the congress ceded Cyprus to Britain from the Ottoman Empire.[380] Great Britain (a Christian European nation) now controlled the Suez Canal and the most important single island in the eastern Mediterranean. Islamic Turkish control of this part of the world was slipping away.

Lord Palmerston and the Earl Of Shaftesbury: British Evangelicals and the Jews

Under the leadership of Lord Palmerston (1784–1865), as foreign secretary and as prime minister, Great Britain maintained that by supporting the Jews it would advance British power in the eastern Mediterranean. For him it was a pragmatic issue, not a theological conviction.

It was his colleague, Anthony Ashley Cooper, Earl of Shaftesbury (1801–85), who advanced the cause of the Jews from an evangelical perspective. A devout Christian, Shaftesbury believed that the Bible was God's Word, "written from the very first syllable down to the very last."[381] Influenced by Puritan millennial ideas, Shaftesbury believed that Christ's return and the conversion of the Jews would create "an Anglican Jerusalem and the Kingdom of Heaven." In a memorandum he prepared for Palmerston, he wrote, "There's a country without a nation and God in his wisdom and mercy directs us to a nation without a country."

Shaftesbury also argued in 1839 that the Jews must return to Palestine before Christ's return. Therefore, he saw to it that Great Britain opened a consulate in Jerusalem, and the consul was instructed to guard the interests of the nearly ten thousand Jews living there under Ottoman rule. In fact, a Colonial Office officer in 1845 maintained that a Jewish nation in Palestine under the protection of England would "place [England] in a commanding position in the Levant ... to overawe our enemies and, if necessary, to repel their advance."[382]

Under Shaftesbury's leadership, the London Society for Promoting Christianity among the Jews, founded in 1808 by members of the Clapham Sect (e.g., William Wilberforce and Charles Simeon), thrived. Its goals represented the connection British evangelicals were making between the evangelization of the Jews, their regathering in their homeland in Palestine, and the second coming of Christ:

- Declaring that Jesus is the Messiah, to the Jew first and also to the non-Jew
- Endeavoring to teach the church its Jewish roots
- Encouraging the physical restoration of the Jewish people to Eretz Israel—the Land of Israel
- Encouraging the Hebrew Christian/Messianic Jewish movement

As Montefiore argues, Shaftesbury and the British evangelical movement reflected a belief "in the divine providence of the British Empire and the Jewish return to Zion. The righteousness of evangelical zeal and the reborn passion of Jewish dreams of Jerusalem dovetailed to become one the Victorian obsessions."[383]

American Revivalism and Biblical Prophecy

The Puritans who migrated to the New World in the early 1600s were overwhelmingly premillennial; that is, they believed that Christ would return and then establish his thousand-year kingdom on earth. Indeed, Increase Mather (1639–1723) and his son, Cotton Mather (1663–1728), preached in Puritan New England that America would play a strategic role in Christ's coming kingdom and would be "the seat of the Divine Metropolis" in the millennium.[384] Cotton Mather preached that Christ's kingdom would usher in economic justice, social harmony, and the end of all dishonest merchants and politicians. The Mathers exemplified that curious blend of eschatology, American patriotism, and virtual date-setting that would often characterized American Protestantism.

During the First Great Awakening, especially in the person of Jonathan Edwards, a significant shift from premillennialism to postmillennialism occurred. Edwards believed that the awakening sweeping through the colonies was the beginning of the millennium, which he reasoned might actually begin in America: "And if these things are so; it gives us more abundant reasons to hope that what is now seen in America, and especially in New England, may prove the dawn of that glorious day: and the very uncommon and wonderful circumstances and events of this work, seem to me strongly to argue that God intends it as the beginning or forerunner of something vastly great."[385]

For Edwards, that millennium would precede Christ's second coming, which he speculated would be around AD 2000. Before Christ's return, nearly everyone would turn to Christ, "the wolf shall dwell with the lamb," there would be a "vast increase in knowledge," and "all heresies and false doctrines shall be exploded." This kingdom would be "an event unspeakably happy and joyous." He also concluded that "since the overwhelming majority of all humans that ever lived would live during the millennium and virtually all of those would be redeemed, the percentage of humans damned would be tiny."[386] Indeed, in his notebooks that outlined his projected opus, the "History of Redemption," he posited seven great eras of history, with the sixth being "The Overthrow of Judaism, Mahometanism, and Heathenism throughout the World."[387] For Edwards there was little interest in the Jews returning to their homeland. His interest was in what God was doing in America, the key to the postmillennial return of Christ.

This postmillennial optimism permeated early nineteenth century America and fed the fury and enthusiasm of the Second Great Awakening, deepening the conviction that God had chosen the United States to usher in the kingdom. Postmillennialism joined with the doctrine of perfectionism—the notion that Christians could be completely sanctified while on earth—to energize the reform of American society.

For evangelical Christians in America, then, the millennial kingdom was within reach through the dual agencies of revival and social reform. America must end slavery, introduce temperance, grant rights to women, and foster utopian societies as the foundation for the new era. By the mid-1830s, evangelical leaders were declaring that "the millennium is at the door" and "if the church will do her duty, the millennium may come in this country in three years."[388] The revivalist Charles G. Finney (1792–1875) epitomized this connection between postmillennialism, perfectionism, and the reform of American society.[389]

As America approached the Civil War and especially in the years immediately after the war, postmillennialism was waning within evangelicalism. Although small, premillennialism as a movement remained alive during the heyday of postmillennialism. It was perhaps William Miller (1782–1849) and his followers who best represented antebellum premillennialism. Through his study of biblical prophecy and a complicated mathematical formula he constructed, Miller predicted that Christ would return in 1843. Utilizing tracts, prophecy conferences, and tent services, Miller saturated the North with his ideas. When Christ did not return in 1843, Miller recalculated his prediction to 22 October 1844. When that failed, Miller was humiliated, but his followers helped birth Seventh-Day Adventism.

Premillennialism experienced a significant resurgence through the theological system known as dispensationalism. The touchstone of this system was not the number of dispensations in God's program or distinctions between the kingdom of heaven and the kingdom of God. At the vital center of dispensationalism was the conviction that Israel and the church are distinct. The church is not the "new Israel," and all of God's promises to ethnic, national Israel will be fulfilled. The biblical covenants, especially the Abrahamic and the Davidic covenants, created the framework for understanding God's redemptive and eternal plan.[390]

Theologian Charles Ryrie is certainly correct when he argues that dispensational ideas were evident in early church leaders such as Justin Martyr (110–65), Irenaeus (130–200), Clement of Alexandria (150–200), and even Augustine (354–430). Modern scholars such as Pierre Poiret (1646–1719) and the hymn writer Isaac Watts (1674–1748) also evidenced early dispensational ideas.[391] But it was indisputably the Plymouth Brethren and John Nelson Darby (1800–1882) who helped systematize the dispensational approach to Scripture.

Darby traveled widely in England, Ireland, and America between 1859 and 1877, and his efforts stimulated resurgence in premillennialism and interest in the regathering of the Jews to their land. This resurgence was further energized by Gilded Age evangelists such as Dwight L. Moody, William Bell Riley, James Brookes, Reuben Torrey, and Arno Gaebelein.

Dispensational premillennialism reached its early modern apex with Cyrus Scofield (1843–1921), who came to faith due to the influence of James Brookes. In 1882 Scofield became pastor of Dallas's First Congregational Church. He traveled widely across America and edited the famous *Scofield Reference Bible*, published in 1909, which more than any other work solidified dispensational premillennialism.[392]

The resurgence of premillennialism between 1865 and 1920 dovetailed with other cultural developments and foreign policy concerns. Historian Paul Boyer summarizes the widespread appeal of these ideas. For example, an 1891 memorial to President Benjamin Harrison, written by premillennialist William Blackstone, urged support for a Jewish homeland in Palestine and was signed by 413 prominent Americans, including Cyrus McCormick, J. P. Morgan, and John D. Rockefeller. The memorial urged such action "to further the purposes of God concerning His ancient people" and "to restore them to the land of which they were so cruelly despoiled by our Roman ancestors."[393] Two oilmen from California, Lyman and Milton Stewart, funded the publication and distribution of *The Fundamentals*, which defended the tenets of premillennialism, among other things, against the growing theological liberalism of the mainline churches. Dispensational premillennialism attracted and was supported by some of the most influential and wealthy leaders of America during this period. Together with England, America was becoming the energized hub for a premillennial theology that advocated a Jewish homeland in Palestine.

The Crimean War, 1853–56

By the nineteenth century, the nation of Russia, its czar, Nicholas I, and the Russian Orthodox Church believed that Russia's divine mission was to liberate Orthodox Christians from the Islamic Ottoman Empire and restore Constantinople as the center of

Eastern Christianity. Indeed, Czar Nicholas I envisioned a Russian Orthodox empire stretching from Siberia to Jerusalem.[394] As Montefiore concludes about the Crimean War, "Even though most of the fighting was far away in the Crimea, this war placed Jerusalem at the center of the world stage, where she has remained ever since."[395] This is necessary background for understanding the Crimean War, the most important war before World War I. The Crimean War profoundly changed the Middle East.

A religious quarrel began the Crimean War. In 1853, Czar Nicholas I demanded the right to protect Christian holy sites in Jerusalem, then part of the Ottoman Empire. Nicholas believed that he was "engaged in a religious war to complete Russia's providential mission in the world."[396] As a first step, Nicholas moved his troops into the Turkish Balkans. The Turkish sultan, counting on the support of Britain and France, refused the czar's demands and declared war on Russia. Britain feared that Russia, if it controlled Constantinople, would cut off British access to India. So Britain, joining with France, also declared war on Russia. Russia was driven from the Balkans and suffered immeasurable losses around the Black Sea. After it lost Sevastopol, Russia accepted a humiliating peace.

The Crimean War was fundamentally a religious war, with the fault line between Russian Orthodoxy and Islam fueling the conflict. Every nation involved, especially Russia, was certain that God was on its side. As Orlando Figes argues, the Crimean War "opened up the Muslim world of the Ottoman Empire to Western armies," and "sparked an Islamic reaction against the West which continues to this day."[397]

Although the Ottomans were victorious, their victory was at a terrible cost. Their Islamic domain had been saved by Christian soldiers from Britain and France. The Ottoman Empire was now increasingly dependent on Western Europe, which preferred a weak Ottoman Empire as a check on Russia. The Turkish sultan was forced to decree absolute equality for all religious minorities and permit the Europeans a degree of liberty in Jerusalem that would once have been thought inconceivable. Christian buildings were built in Jerusalem, and Western Christians became an important part of Jerusalem. France, especially the Franciscans, protected Roman Catholic interests and holy sites, while Russia protected Eastern Orthodox sites. Great Britain protected Protestant interests as well as the increasing presence of Jews in Palestine.

Western Europe's presence in Palestine increased after the Crimean War. After Prime Minister Disraeli acquired controlling interest in the Suez Canal in 1875 and acquired Cyprus in 1878, British interests turned to controlling all of Egypt. In 1882, Britain invaded Egypt, which, although ostensibly still Ottoman, was then occupied by Britain. Conflict and military skirmishes between the Ottomans and Britain continued until an important agreement was reached on 1 October 1906, fixing the border between the Ottoman Empire and Egypt at a line stretching from the Mediterranean to the Gulf of Aqaba. This would remain a fixed border for the rest of the twentieth century, and is today the border between Israel and Egypt. The British also founded the Palestine Exploration Fund to survey the land and begin archeological digs.

Germany also showed interest in the land. German members of a Christian sect called the Templars built colonies in Israel. The Austro-Hungarian emperor Franz Joseph visited, as did the German emperor Wilhelm II in 1898. In fact, by the end of the nineteenth century, Germany was probably the most influential European group in Israel. Christian pilgrims from all over Europe and also from America were flooding into Israel, visiting the holy sites and traversing the land. Even the American writer Mark Twain visited Israel in 1867.

Theodore Herzl and the Zionist Movement

By the mid to late nineteenth century, Diaspora Jews, especially those who settled in Western Europe, believed that they could assimilate into European culture. Most of the European democracies had granted Jews citizenship, facilitating this cultural accommodation. But this was not the case in Eastern Europe and Russia, where Jews were segregated into ghettos and regularly experienced the violence of *pogroms*—anti-Semitic, government-sponsored violence against the Jews. Accommodation in the West and pogroms in the East threatened the survival of the Diaspora Jews.

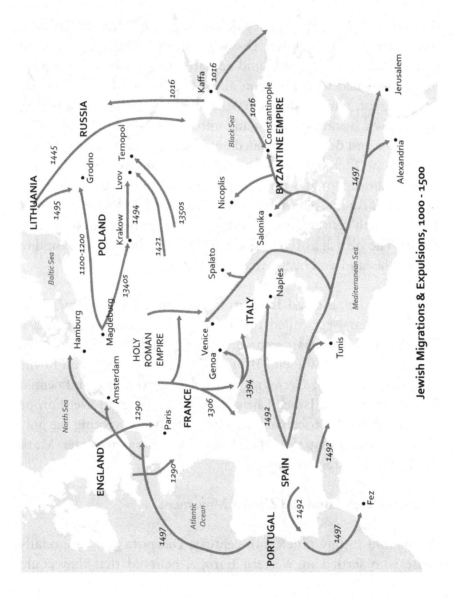

This was thus the context for the birth of Zionism. A Sephardic rabbi from Belgrade, Judah Alkalai (1798–1878), and an Ashkenazi rabbi from Poland, Zvi Hirsch Kalischer (1795–1874), both proclaimed that the only hope for the Jewish people was to return to their land. Since Scripture stated that the Messiah would come to the Jews in Zion, they needed to be there when He came, they reasoned. In addition, the secular Jewish leader Moses Hess (1812–75), a friend of Karl Marx, also argued that Jews must return to the land of Israel as the only means of survival in the face of the anti-Semitism permeating European civilization.[398]

Thus, between 1882 and 1903, small agricultural settlements in Israel emerged, supported by the "Lovers of Zion" movement in Europe and America and financed in part by the Rothschild family of France. These first settlers, numbering about 25,000, became the first wave of immigrants, the *aliyah*, who today are often referred to as the "pioneers."

In 1895, a Jewish officer on the French general staff, Captain Alfred Dreyfus, was convicted of spying for Germany and sent to Devil's Island. Despite obvious evidence demonstrating his innocence, the general staff refused to act. Anti-Semitic riots broke out, and a purge of all Dreyfus sympathizers ensued in the French army and government.[399] Although Dreyfus was pardoned in 1899, European Jews concluded that assimilation was now impossible.

A Hungarian Jew and literary critic from Vienna named Theodore Herzl (1860–1904) reacted to the Dreyfus affair in 1896 by publishing his famous book, *Der Judenstaat (The Jewish State)*. Herzl argued that the Jews were a distinct people but without a state—and this was the root cause of anti-Semitism and violence against Jews throughout much of history. The only solution, therefore, was for the Jews to establish a state that would guarantee their survival and endurance as a distinct people. Although at first he did not specify where the state would be, he quickly became convinced that only in the land of Israel should the new Jewish state be established.

"Palestine is our ever-memorable home. The Maccabees will rise again. We shall live at last as free men on our own soil and die peacefully in our own homes."[400] To that end, he formed the World Zionist Organization.

In 1897 the first Zionist Congress was held in Basel, Switzerland, and Herzl was elected president, a position he held until his death in 1904. For the rest of his life, he engaged in significant diplomatic initiatives with European leaders to build support for a Jewish state.

At first he believed that Germany under Kaiser Wilhelm would be his advocate, but Wilhelm's self-elevating arrogance quickly dispelled that idea. Next, Herzl turned to England, which initially offered him Uganda as a homeland. Herzl and the Zionists quickly rejected that idea. Re-energized pogroms in Eastern Europe and Russia in 1903 and 1905 led to a second wave of immigrants to Israel (the second *aliyah*) from Russia. Among those immigrants was David Ben-Gurion, who, at eleven years of age, regarded Herzl as "the Messiah who would lead the Jews back to Israel."[401]

As the twentieth century began, the idea of a Jewish homeland in Israel was no longer a distant, unimaginable dream. Although few in number, Jews were returning to their land. Herzl's vision was internalized by a dynamic, energized group of Eastern European Jews, who were farming a once-barren land, draining the swamps of Galilee, and reclaiming what was lost in AD 70. But the world community was not yet ready to accept this idea of a Jewish home-land. World War I and its subsequent events would produce that acceptance.

Chapter 15

The Regathering of the Jews, Israel as a Nation-State, and the Struggle for Survival

W orld War I (1914–8) produced the dismemberment of the Ottoman Empire, established the British Mandate, and set the stage for the creation of the nation-state of Israel in 1947. To survive since 1947, the nation of Israel has fought four major wars and numerous smaller but deadly conflicts with the PLO, Hamas, and Hezbollah. Israel is still the only functioning democracy in the Middle East, and now boasts the largest concentration of Jews in the world, even exceeding the Jewish population residing in the United States. Due to its six desalination plants, Israel is self-sufficient in terms of meeting its water needs, and, as a result of the recent discovery of natural gas off its northern shore (called the "Leviathan"), is now self-sufficient in its energy needs. It is an exporter of agricultural products, is the world's leading producer of diamonds, and is often called the "Silicon Valley" of the Middle East. It is a modern miracle. This chapter chronicles that miracle.

World War I and the Balfour Declaration

World War I, often called the Great War, began on 28 July 1914 and ended on 11 November 1918. It involved the world's leading powers, assembled in two opposing alliances: the Allies (based on the Triple Entente of the United Kingdom, France, and Russia) and the Central Powers (originally the Triple Alliance of Germany, Austria-Hungary, and Italy). These alliances reorganized (Italy eventually fought for the Allies) and expanded as more nations entered the war. The Ottoman Empire sided with Germany. Ultimately more than 70 million military personnel, including 60 million Europeans, were mobilized. More than 9 million combatants were killed, largely because of enhanced military technology (e.g., tanks, gas warfare, airplanes, machine guns, etc.). It was the sixth-deadliest conflict in world history, and forever changed the Middle East. Its impact paved the way for the creation of a homeland for the Jewish people.

Before the outbreak of the war, a cohesive and well-organized Jewish community in Israel (known as the *Yishuv* or new settlers) had grown to nearly 100,000 people. Along with agricultural settlements, the Yishuv founded new village communities and laid the foundation for a thriving Jewish presence in Israel. About half of the Jewish population lived in Jerusalem, with the other half in the rural areas and in urban communities growing in Jaffa and Haifa. The Yishuv founded Tel Aviv in 1909 as the first modern Hebrew city. The resurgence of Hebrew as a modern spoken language was the work of Eliezer Ben-Yehuda (1858–1922), and by World War I Hebrew was becoming the national language of this flourishing Jewish population.[402]

The Ottomans had organized the area of Palestine into the Ottoman province of Beirut in the north and the district of Jerusalem in the south. Since the Ottomans had sided with Germany in the Great War, the Germans assumed protection of the Jews in Palestine. Under Ahmet Jemal, the Ottomans recruited both Jews and Arabs into their army to fight the Allies. Because he feared collaboration with the British, Jemal expelled many foreigners who did not have Ottoman citizenship. Between 12,000 and 15,000 Jews fled Israel, including David Ben-Gurion.

Jemal forced both Christians and Jews into labor battalions to build roads and fortify Jerusalem. The Ottomans destroyed much of the land of Israel during the war, confiscating livestock, trees, crops, and property for their war effort. The suffering was intense. In fact, within Jerusalem, due to starvation, disease, and deportation, the total Jewish population dropped by 20,000.[403]

The British Empire hoped to drive the Ottomans from Palestine and secure a safe route to its prized possession of India, while creating a buffer to protect the Suez Canal in Egypt. Field Marshal Lord Kitchener, the secretary of state for war in London, believed that aligning the Arabs with Britain was the key to defeating the Ottoman Turks in Palestine. Kitchener therefore opened discussions with the Sharif of Mecca, Hussein ibn Ali (1854–1931) of the Hashemite family (direct descendants of Muhammad), to launch an Arab revolt against the Ottomans. Kitchener ordered Sir Henry McMahon, high commissioner in Egypt, to do whatever he could to keep the Arabs on Britain's side in the war.

Hussein, as a price for leading the Arab Revolt, demanded that Britain grant him an empire that included Arabia, Syria, Palestine, and Iraq. On 24 October 1915, McMahon replied to Hussein, granting him his request for an "empire," but clearly excluding Palestine and Jerusalem. The so-called McMahon–Hussein Correspondence, an exchange of letters between 14 July 1915 and 30 January 1916, was interpreted by Hussein as a promise that Britain would give him Palestine once the war had ended. The British government has always disputed this interpretation. Indeed, in 1922 McMahon declared, "It was as fully my intention to exclude Palestine as it was to exclude the more northern coastal tracts of Syria." He also stated "that Palestine was not included in my pledge was clearly understood by Hussein."[404] Nonetheless, many Arabs today still charge Britain with a "shameless betrayal of its wartime pledges."[405]

Meanwhile, from November 1915 through March 1916, Britain and France were engaged in secret negotiations on the future of the Middle East. The result was the Sykes–Picot Agreement, named after the principal negotiators, Sir Mark Sykes of Britain and Francois Georges-Picot of France. The agreement was concluded in May 1916. As Efraim Karsh argues, the agreement was a commitment by Britain and France "'to recognize and protect an independent Arab State or a Confederation of Arab States—under the suzerainty of an Arab chief' stretching over the vast territory from Aleppo to Rawandaz and from the Egyptian-Ottoman border to Kuwait. This commitment represented a clear victory for Britain's championing of Arab independence and unity over French opposition."[406] The agreement also provided for the internationalization of Jerusalem. The spheres of influence of both France and Britain, detailed in the agreement, provided a framework for what would become the French and British Mandates after the war.

In London, another remarkable agreement was being negotiated. The conversations in 1914 were initially between Arthur Balfour, the British foreign secretary, and Dr. Chaim Weizmann, a Russian-born scientist, a professor of chemistry at the University of Manchester, and a committed Zionist. Balfour listened as Weizmann presented his case for a Jewish homeland in Israel. Weizmann made a similar appeal to David Lloyd George, who became a committed Zionist as well.

In 1917, the minister of munitions, Winston Churchill, summoned Weizmann, then the director of the British Admiralty laboratories, to London to explain Britain's need for acetone, a key component in the manufacture of munitions. Weizmann had developed a new process for extracting acetate from horse chestnuts, which provided abundantly for Britain's munition needs.[407] (Chaim Weizmann would later become the first president of the State of Israel.)

In December 1916, Lloyd George became prime minister, and he named Arthur Balfour as his foreign secretary. As a part of the war effort, Lloyd George and Balfour agreed to issue the Balfour Declaration. In a letter addressed to Lord Rothschild on 2 November 1917, Balfour proclaimed, "His Majesty's Government views with favour the establishment in Palestine of a national home for the Jewish people, and will use their best endeavors to facilitate the achievement of this object, it being clearly understood that nothing shall be done which may prejudice the civil and religious rights of existing non-Jewish communities in Palestine or the rights and political status enjoyed by Jews in another country."[408] Science and Zionism"[409] had combined to produce the first modern affirmation that the Jews were entitled to a homeland in their ancient land.

The new British commander, Sir Edmund Allenby, arrived in Cairo on 28 June 1917 to begin his conquest of Palestine. He amassed an infantry of 75,000, with cavalry support totaling 17,000. He promised the British people that he would give them Jerusalem as a Christmas present. He kept his promise. On 11 December 1917, the Ottoman Empire surrendered Jerusalem to the 60th Infantry Division of the British army.[410]

For the first time in 1,200 years (except for the brief Crusader rule), Muslim rule of Jerusalem had come to an end. General Allenby entered Jaffa gate into the Old City of Jerusalem on foot, stating emphatically that no Christian should enter Jerusalem, where Jesus died, in an arrogant or pompous manner. By September 1918, Allenby had driven the Germans and the Ottomans completely out of Israel. Israel was now in the hands of the British Empire.

The end of World War I produced the dismemberment of the Austro-Hungarian Empire, the Russian Empire, and the Ottoman Empire. At the 1919 Versailles Peace Conference, the ideal of national self-determination (largely the vision of US president Woodrow Wilson) was widely endorsed but not applied either consistently or fairly.

For our purposes, the dismemberment of the Ottoman Empire through the 1920 Treaty of Sevres was a watershed. In Article 95 of that treaty, the principles of the Balfour Declaration were adopted:

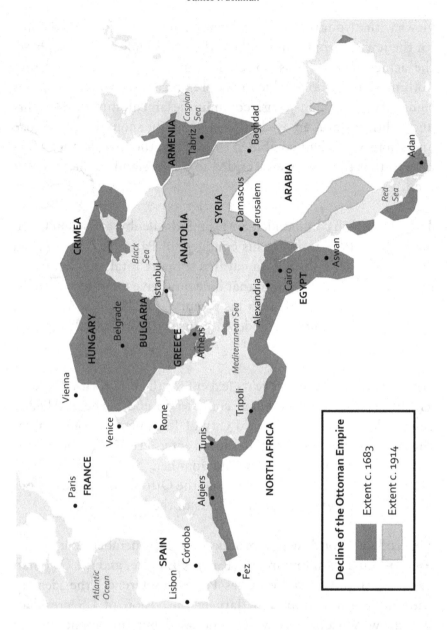

The High Contracting Parties agree to entrust, by application of the provisions of Article 22, the administration of Palestine, within such boundaries as may be determined by the Principal Allied Powers, to a Mandatory to be selected by the said Powers.

The Mandatory will be responsible for putting into effect the declaration originally made on November 2, 1917, by the British Government, and adopted by the other Allied Powers, in favour of the establishment in Palestine of a national home for the Jewish people, it being clearly understood that nothing shall be done which may prejudice the civil and religious rights of existing non-Jewish communities in Palestine, or the rights and political status enjoyed by Jews in any other country.[411]

The subsequent 1923 Treaty of Lausanne led to the international recognition of the sovereignty of the new Republic of Turkey. Turkey gave up all claims to the remainder of the Ottoman Empire, and in return the Allies recognized Turkish sovereignty within its new borders.

The British Mandate, 1918–48

On 24 April 1920, at the San Remo Conference, David Lloyd George accepted the British Mandate to rule Palestine. Since Britain firmly controlled Israel, it was logical to give to the British the responsibility to assist the Jewish people in developing the land and preparing for their independence.

Since nothing was said of a homeland for Palestinian Arabs, they demanded recognition as a separate nation as well. Fearing violence, the British created the Supreme Muslim Council, which principally dealt with religious affairs, not politics. Nonetheless, the Arabs consistently claimed that the British had betrayed them, especially in how they understood the McMahon-Hussein letters of 1915–6. That sense of betrayal framed many of the Arab-British disagreements during the Mandate period.

The Arabs of Palestine strongly opposed the increase in Jewish immigration. Between 1919 and 1923, over 40,000 Jews (known as the third *aliyah*), largely fleeing the Bolsheviks of Russia, arrived in Israel, settling particularly in the Tel Aviv region.[412] Violence by Arab-instigated mobs and riots ensued in Jaffa and Jerusalem, where hundreds of Jews were beaten and several dozen killed. Great Britain was largely ineffectual in controlling the growing Arab-Jewish violence in the British Mandate territory.

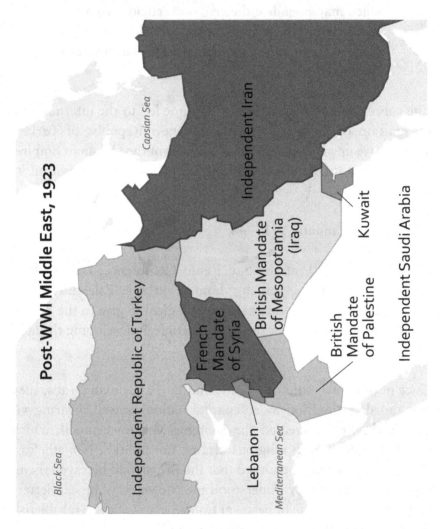

In the spring of 1921, Winston Churchill, the secretary of state for colonial affairs, arrived in the Middle East, together with his aide and friend, Lawrence of Arabia. Churchill called the Cairo

Conference, which dramatically changed the geography of the Middle East.

First, Churchill gave control of Iraq to Prince Faisal, the son of Sharif Hussein. He made Haj Amin el-Hussein the mufti of Jerusalem. Finally, he created the new Arab kingdom of Transjordan (basically today's Jordan) and gave it to the other son of Sharif Hussein, Abdullah. West of the Jordan River to the Mediterranean would be ruled by Britain, with a commitment to continued Jewish immigration.[413]

But, as Karsh correctly observes, an unintended consequence was that Faisal and Abdullah "had talked the largest empire on earth into enthroning them in newly created Iraqi and Transjordanian states, thus making them key figures in the post-war Middle East and the natural contenders for the realization of the Arab imperial dream."[414]

Jewish immigration to Israel accelerated. Between 1924 and 1928 (the fourth *aliyah*) over 70,000 Jews arrived, many of them from Poland. The Jews of Palestine, now living under the British Mandate, formed their own national council and a militia, called the Haganah, to defend themselves against growing Arab violence.

In 1929 the mufti of Jerusalem charged that Jews sought to seize the Al-Aqsa mosque on Temple Mount. Riots ensued, killing 135 Jews and wounding another 350. The Jews in Hebron were especially targeted, with 67 of them killed.[415] To investigate the causes of this bloodshed, the British formed the Shaw Commission of Inquiry. The commission concluded that Jewish purchase of land and immigration were the causes of the violence. The recommendation was to slow down immigration and end Jewish land purchases. Thus, the British government issued the 1930 White Paper of Colonial Secretary Lord Passfield, restricting Jewish immigration to Israel and retracting the intent of the Balfour Declaration.

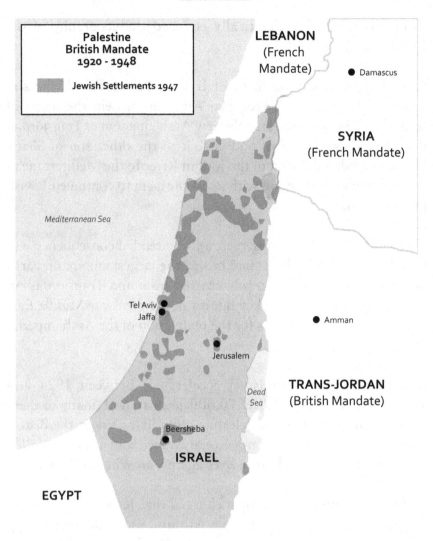

The effects of the white paper were dramatic. The Zionist movement had depended on Chaim Weizmann, whose in turn counted on Britain fulfilling its promise in the Balfour Declaration of a Jewish homeland. Although Weizmann convinced Prime Minister Ramsay MacDonald to renounce the white paper and reopen Jewish immigration, Weizmann lost his role as Zionism's president.

David Ben-Gurion emerged as Zionism's new leader, and the Haganah militia began arming itself. In addition, a more militant

Zionist militia, the Irgun, was founded. Finally, the Mufti al-Husseini emerged as the Arab nationalist leader, even holding meetings of the 1931 World Islamic Conference on Temple Mount in Jerusalem. His aim was to bring an end to Jewish immigration and to see Arabs dominate the Mandate area. The cleavage between Jew and Arab in Israel was widening and becoming more violent.[416]

As Hitler consolidated his power as chancellor of Germany in 1933, he began to reveal his anti-Semitic policies. Jewish immigration to Israel thereby quickened. In 1933, 37,000 Jews arrived in Israel; 45,000 arrived in 1934. In what is often called the fifth *aliyah*, over 120,000 Jews, principally from Germany and Poland, emigrated to Israel.

Most of these immigrants were better educated, bringing industrial and professional skills that dramatically affected the development of the Jewish communities. Between 1931 and 1939, major industrial development increased by 150 percent, as did the availability of electrical power. Haifa Bay became a trading center. Finally, the new immigrants enhanced the development of the arts—museums, theaters, and opera houses. The total Jewish population in Israel was approaching 400,000, while the Arab population was nearly 1.25 million.[417]

The Arab Revolt, 1936–45

As 1935 ended, violence between Jews and Arabs intensified. In early 1936, the Mufti al-Husseini of Jerusalem formed the Higher Arab Committee, which called a national strike against the British that turned quite violent. The mufti then declared this violent outbreak a sacred one and labeled his forces the Holy War Army. It attracted armed Arab groups from Syria, Iraq, and Transjordan to fight the Jews and the British. The Arab Revolt had begun. Hundreds of Jews were wounded and dozens killed.[418]

The British government responded to the revolt by forming a commission led by Lord William Robert Peel. After spending two months in Israel and meeting with the various groups, Jew and Arab, he published his report in July 1937. Peel was critical of Great Britain for violating the original meaning of the Mandate by not assisting the Jews in forming their own homeland. Further, he criticized Britain for permitting thousands of Arabs to cross the interior borders unchallenged. Finally, he recommended a partition of the land into two independent states—Jewish (about 20 percent of the Mandate) and Arab (about 70 percent). He also advocated the transfer of about 300,000 Arabs from the Jewish area and that Jerusalem remain under British control. The Zionists in Israel accepted the idea; the Arabs did not.[419]

The Jewish militia, the Haganah, responded to the revolt in an aggressive manner. A British military officer, Orde Wingate, an evangelical Christian, became a passionate advocate for the Jews in Israel. In fact, he once declared, "Everyone's against the Jews, so I'm for them." In March 1938, the British commander, Sir Archibald Wavell, ordered Wingate to train the Haganah and deploy them as special night forces against the Arab rebels. Montefiore says of the importance of Wingate's efforts, "During the Revolt and later during the Second World War, the British trained 25,000 Jewish auxiliaries, including other commando units led by Yitzhak Sadeh, a Russian Red Army veteran, who became Haganah's chief of staff. 'You are the sons of the Maccabees,' Wingate told them. 'You are the first soldiers of a Jewish Army!' Their expertise and spirit later formed the basis of the Israel Defense Forces."[420]

In March 1939, Major General Bernard Montgomery, British divisional commander, condensed the increasingly bitter Arab-Jewish violence into this prophetic statement: "The Jew murders the Arab and Arabs murder the Jews and it will go on for the next 50 years in all probability."[421]

The Jewish-Arab violence once again exploded, and an additional concern emerged for the British—a seemingly imminent conflict with Adolf Hitler's Germany. To address these concerns, British Colonial

Secretary Malcolm MacDonald published another white paper on 17 May 1939. MacDonald proposed severely limiting Jewish land purchases, restricting Jewish immigration to 15,000 people annually for five years (after which Arabs would have a veto), and calling for the establishment of an independent Arab state, but no Jewish state. It was an outright repudiation of the Balfour Declaration.

Amazingly, the mufti of Jerusalem rejected the British proposal, while the Jews in Israel followed the counsel of David Ben-Gurion, now the undisputed leader of the Zionist cause: "We must assist the British in the war as if there were no White Paper, and we must resist the White Paper as if there were no war."[422] Thus, nearly 40,000 Jews from Israel volunteered to serve with the British. At the behest of Winston Churchill, a Jewish brigade fought in Italy.[423]

When World War II erupted, the situation in Israel changed dramatically. Most Arabs in Israel did not support the British but temporarily ceased terrorist activities against the British and the Jews. The mufti of Jerusalem traveled to Germany in 1941 to meet with Hitler, hoping to form a common alliance against their common enemies—the British and the Jews. The mufti willingly embraced not only Hitler's strategic opposition to the British, but also his virulent racial anti-Semitism. In his memoirs, the mufti admitted that he was told of the Nazi extermination of at least three million Jews already, and he boasted that "if Germany had carried the day, no trace of the Zionists would have remained in Palestine."[424]

By 1944–5, the horrors of the Nazi Holocaust were becoming clear. Nazi conquest had brought over nine million Jews under their control, and the "final solution" resulted in two-thirds of them being killed—men, women, and children.

Adding to this unspeakable horror was British policy. The British crackdown on Jewish immigration detailed in the 1939 White Paper meant that British troops were turning back shiploads of frantic Jews seeking refuge from Hitler's terror.

The combination of the Arab Revolt, the "final solution," and MacDonald's white paper led many Zionists to the conclusion that only focused violence would force Great Britain to once again embrace the idea of a Jewish state in Palestine. The catalyst for that violence was Menachem Begin and Irgun.

As soon as the war ended, the British people voted Winston Churchill out of office, replacing him with Clement Attlee as prime minster. Attlee chose Ernest Bevin as his foreign secretary. Worldwide sympathy for the Jewish plight increased, and pressure on the British to end the immigration blockade mounted. Even the new American president, Harry Truman, appealed to Attlee to allow 100,000 displaced Jews into Israel.

Attlee refused. Incredibly, many Jews who had survived Hitler's concentration camps now found themselves in displaced person camps organized and run by the British. The most famous of these was on the island of Cyprus.

Understandably, violence between the British and the Jews increased. David Ben-Gurion's Haganah joined with Begin's Irgun and a smaller, more radical group called Lehi (or the Stern Gang) to form the United Resistance Command to smuggle into Israel European Jews from the British camps and to coordinate attacks on British facilities in Israel.

Without the support of Ben-Gurion, Begin and Irgun focused on the King David Hotel in Jerusalem, the administrative center of the British Mandate. On 22 July 1946, Irgun blew up an entire wing of the hotel, killing ninety-one people. Ben-Gurion withdrew from the United Resistance Command, and the British retaliated severely and ruthlessly.

Defying British law, illegal immigration to Israel continued. The most famous example was the *Exodus 1947* ship, which set sail in the summer of 1947 from France, filled with Jewish immigrants.

British foreign secretary Bevin refused to accept the immigrants and sought to return them to France on prison ships. The immigrants refused to disembark, and the French refused to support the British. Bevin then brought them to Hamburg, Germany, where the immigrants were forcibly removed.

Images of Holocaust survivors being forced off the ship filled the world's newspapers and newsreels. Worldwide opinion turned decisively against the British, and sympathy for the Jews increased. By now, Great Britain had over 100,000 troops in Palestine, but it could not contain the violence or restrict Jewish immigration. The British Mandate had become an unmitigated disaster, turning into what Churchill called this "senseless squalid war with the Jews."[425] In April 1947, Prime Minister Attlee therefore asked the newly formed United Nations to form a special commission on Palestine (UNSCOP) to resolve the question of Palestine.[426]

The Creation of Israel and the War for Independence, 1948–51

During the summer of 1947, UNSCOP commissioners researched the situation in Palestine, holding meetings with Jewish leaders but finding no cooperation from Arab leaders. In fact, the Arab leaders completely boycotted all UNSCOP meetings and requests for information. In August, the commissioners published their report and presented it to the UN General Assembly. UNSCOP recommended partitioning the land into a Jewish state and an Arab state. The Arabs rejected any solution that did not call for a completely Arab state in Palestine.

On 29 November 1947, the UN General Assembly voted on UNSCOP's recommendations. Thirty-three nations voted in favor of the plan, while thirteen voted against it and ten nations abstained. The Partition Plan (known as UN Resolution 181) declared the following:

1. The British Mandate in Palestine would terminate no later than 1 August 1948.

2. Two states would be established, a Jewish state and an Arab state.
3. An international tribunal would govern Jerusalem.
4. A UN committee of five members would assume power from Britain and transfer it to the new Israeli and Arab governments.

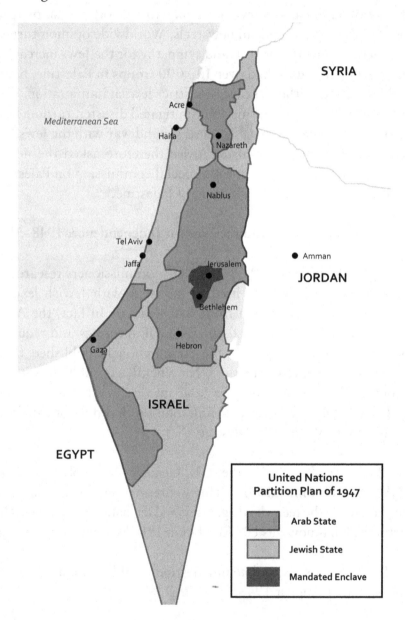

Resolution 181 defined the Jewish state as encompassing the coastal plain, western Galilee, and the Negev Desert. The proposed Arab state would encompass eastern Galilee, the central part of Palestine on the West Bank of the Jordan River, and the Gaza Strip.[427]

Immediately, the Jewish Agency under David Ben-Gurion accepted Resolution 181. The Palestine Arab Higher Committee and the Arab League rejected it. The British accepted the resolution but made it clear that Britain would play no role in implementing it.

Between December 1947 and May 1948, a terrorist war led by the various Arab factions against the Jews ensued. Haganah, Irgun, and the Stern Gang responded in kind. With the certain threat of war from Arab nations, on 14 May 1948, David Ben-Gurion, standing under Theodore Herzl's portrait, read Israel's Declaration of Independence. Rydelnik summarizes the substance of the declaration: "Citing the historic Jewish ties to the land, the Balfour Declaration, the UN Partition resolution, Jewish suffering during the Holocaust, and Zionist sacrifices for the land, Ben-Gurion declared, 'by virtue of our natural and historic right and the strength of the United Nations General Assembly [resolution], we hereby declare the establishment of a Jewish state in Eretz-Israel, to be known as the state of Israel.'"[428]

The declaration also encouraged Jewish immigration to Israel, promised equal rights to all Israeli citizens (including Arabs), and called for peace with its Arab neighbors.

Within minutes of Ben-Gurion's declaration, United States president Harry Truman recognized the new state of Israel.[429] The Soviet Union followed soon thereafter.

The Arab response to the declaration was immediate. Egypt, Jordan, Iraq, Syria, and Lebanon invaded Israel with the express purpose of liquidating the Jews in Israel. Indeed, the secretary of the Arab League, Azzam Pasha, declared, "This will be a war of extermination and a momentous massacre which will be spoken of like the Mongolian massacres and the Crusades."[430] This was a jihad against the Jews. Half of the Egyptian forces were members of the Muslim Brotherhood, including the young Yasser Arafat.

From 15 May to 11 June 1948, Israel primarily fought a defensive action against the invaders. The Arab siege of Jerusalem was starving the city, causing Jewish leaders to go on the offensive to break the blockade. A turning point in the first phase of the war, the offensive ensured a continued supply of food and water to Jerusalem. A brief ceasefire (11 June–8 July) permitted Israel to gain much needed military supplies.

The Independence War, nonetheless, continued. Between 8 and 18 July 1948, Israel launched a ten-day offensive to drive out the Arab League invaders. Amazingly, the Jewish military was successful in defeating the Egyptian forces in the south, driving the Jordanians into the West Bank, pushing the Lebanese army to the northern border, and capturing the city of Nazareth. The Egyptians, however, still controlled the Negev Desert.

The final phase of the Independence War lasted from 22 December 1948 to 8 January 1949, with Israel pushing Egypt out of the Negev into the Sinai. The Jews were not successful in conquering the Old City of Jerusalem, however. It remained in Jordanian hands.

Israel had won the war against enormous odds, even slightly enlarging its territorial boundaries. In the words of Ralph Bunche, the UN peace negotiator, Israel was now "a vibrant reality."[431] Israel signed ceasefire agreements with Egypt, Lebanon, Syria, and Jordan, but Iraq refused to sign any such agreement.

The Independence War had two immediate effects. First, the creation of the nation-state of Israel created the Arab refugee problem. For many complex reasons, Arabs in the Jewish state fled Israel, most settling in refugee camps set up in Jordan, Lebanon, and

Syria. Some were forced to leave (e.g., the town of Lydda), but most fled because of the propaganda coming from the Arab states, which created fear and panic.

Once the war ended, David Ben-Gurion was not open to the return of these refugees. The descendants of these refuges today demand a "right of return" to Israel, claiming that the land is their land. This demand remains one of the most difficult issues separating the Palestinian people and the Jewish state of Israel.

The second effect of the victory was the flood of refugees that poured into the new state of Israel. In fact, the Israeli parliament, the Knesset, enacted the "law of return," which gave any Jewish person or any person with a Jewish parent or grandparent the right to come to Israel and be granted immediate citizenship.[432] Within three years, over 300,000 Holocaust survivors came to Israel, with an additional 400,000 coming from hostile Arab nations (e.g., Yemen, Iraq, Syria, Tunisia, Libya, etc.). The state of Israel tripled in size.

Israel's Wars: The Fight for Survival, 1956–82

Since no Arab nation was interested in a permanent peace treaty with Israel, the effect was an ongoing state of war. After the armistice, Egypt, under Gamal Abdel Nasser (1918–70), emerged as the leader of the Arab imperial dream.[433] Nasser insisted on pan-Arab unity, and he saw the 1948 defeat by Israel as a piercing lesson for the Arab world: "There was no Arab unity and no line for concerted Arab action. There was no plan for a unified Arab objective … The Arab countries were defeated because there were seven countries fighting against one country, namely Israel … In order that we may liberate Palestine, the Arab nation must unite, the Arab armies must unite, and a unified plan of action must be established."[434]

Nasser therefore supported Palestinian raids against Israel, led by the *fedayeen*, a terrorist group equipped and trained by Egypt. He also blockaded the Straits of Tiran, Israel's primary supply route with Asia. The dream of Arab unity also informed his decision to nationalize the Suez Canal in 1956. The jurisdiction, revenues and administration of the canal would be under Nasser's control.

Nasser's actions threatened the British and French empires, but they needed a pretext for military action. Both nations secretly approached Israel with a plan: Israel would attack Egypt in the Sinai, and then Britain and France would invade Egypt, ostensibly to separate the two warring nations. Israel accepted the plan, for its goals were to open the Straits of Tiran and to end *fedayeen* terrorism.

On 29 October 1956, Israel attacked Egypt, seized the entire Sinai Peninsula, and opened the Straits of Tiran. Britain and France lacked the power for any sustained military campaign, so the United States aggressively intervened, demanding that Israel withdraw from the Sinai. Israel reluctantly agreed. The United States assured Israel that the Straits of Tiran would remain open. It sponsored a UN resolution that provided a peacekeeping force in the Sinai to prevent *fedayeen* terrorists from entering Israel and that kept the Suez Canal and the Straits of Tiran open to international trade. The 1956 crisis marked the end of British involvement in any significant manner in the Middle East and the rise of the United States as the key regional player.[435]

In 1959, Yasser Arafat founded the militant terrorist organization called Fatah (meaning "conquest") to engage in small terrorist raids into Israel. Over time, his "pistol-packing, khaki-clad, *keffiyeh*-wearing" demeanor became the symbol of the Palestinian cause.[436] In 1964, the Arab League, under Nasser's strong leadership, founded the Palestine Liberation Organization (PLO), with a twofold purpose—the right of return to Israel for Palestinian Arabs and the annihilation of the state of Israel through "armed struggle and resistance."[437]

Although Arabs who lived in Israel possessed the right to vote and serve in the Knesset, few were active in Israeli political life. So in

1966 Israel removed the military rule it had imposed on Israeli Arabs and began to invest heavily in Arab communities, hoping to integrate them into the life of Israel. Despite such initiatives, Israeli Arabs remained largely sympathetic to the PLO.

In 1958, Nasser announced the formation of the United Arab Republic (UAR), which was an attempt to integrate Egypt and Syria into one Arab supernation. It was a disaster, ending in a Syrian military coup in 1961. Nasser then threw his entire pan-Arab ambition into laying the groundwork for a decisive confrontation with Israel. He hoped this would unite the Arab world under Egypt.

But in early May 1967, the Soviet Union warned of a large-scale Israeli troop buildup along the border with Syria. (Israel was doing no such thing.) In addition, during the previous month, the Israeli Air Force had shot down six Syrian fighter jets. Syria demanded Egyptian military support based on the 1966 defense pact between the two nations.

Therefore, in direct violation of the 1956 UN resolution, on 14 May Egypt moved two armored divisions into the Sinai Peninsula. Nasser also ordered the UN Emergency Force (UNEF) to withdraw from the Sinai, and he again closed the Straits of Tiran to Israeli shipping. Nasser declared that if hostilities were to break out, "our main objective will be the destruction of Israel" and "Allah will certainly help us to restore the status quo of before 1948."[438] Nasser's fervor was contagious, for Jordan and then Iraq joined in a defense pact with Egypt. Expeditionary forces from Saudi Arabia, Syria, and Iraq were all gathering against Israel.[439]

Israel, a nation that was only eleven miles wide at its center, was now terribly vulnerable. In Chaim Herzog's words, Israel was "ringed by an Arab force of some 250,000 troops, over 2,000 tanks and some 700 front line fighter and bomber aircraft."[440] Israel therefore made a pivotal decision to launch a preemptive strike against its enemies. On 1 June, Moshe Dayan was named

Israeli defense minister. On 5 June 1967, the Israeli Air Force
attacked the Egyptian Air Force, destroying over 300 planes on
the ground. Israel thereby attained complete air superiority in the
region. The Israeli Air Force likewise struck key Syrian areas in the
north, and Dayan ordered Israeli troops into the Sinai.

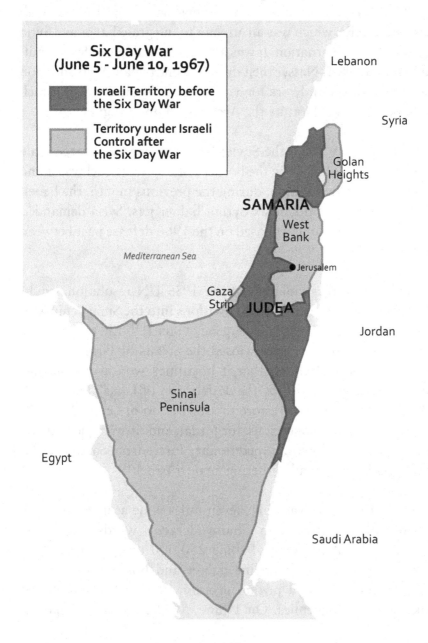

Through the United States, Israel pleaded with King Hussein of Jordan to stay out of the conflict, but he refused. Instead, he ordered his artillery to begin shelling West Jerusalem. The Israeli Air Force responded by destroying the Jordanian air force and half of the Syrian air force.

Over the next five days, Israel captured the Old City of Jerusalem, including Temple Mount and the Western "Wailing" Wall. Israel likewise took the entire West Bank of the Jordan River, the Golan Heights, and the Sinai Peninsula. It was the most humiliating defeat the Arab world had experienced—and a triumph for the young Jewish state. Israel had tripled its size and had reunited Jerusalem, making it the capital of the nation.

Since 1967, the results of this important war have framed the developments, politics, and foreign policy decisions of the Middle East and much of the world.

1. One of the more difficult issues for Israel was what to do with Temple Mount in Jerusalem. Ten days after the war, Moshe Dayan met with the Muslim leaders at the al-Aqsa mosque on Temple Mount. He explained that Israel now controlled Jerusalem and it had no intention of returning it; it would be Israel's capital. However, he stated that the Muslim Foundation, known as the *Waqf*, would control Temple Mount. Further, he declared, Jews would not be encouraged to pray on Temple Mount.[441] Some of the most sacred symbols of Islam, the Dome of the Rock and al-Aqsa, would be respected. In addition, Christians would have access to Temple Mount as well. It was an extraordinarily magnanimous act on the part of Israel.

2. After the 1967 War, Israel hoped that the Arab nations would now desire a permanent settlement of their differences with Israel. However, that hope was dashed at an August 1967 Arab meeting in Khartoum, Sudan. Nasser and the other Arab leaders boisterously proclaimed their

famous "Three Nos" to Israel—no peace with Israel, no negotiations with Israel, and no recognition of Israel.[442] No peace; only an ongoing state of war.

3. On 22 November 1967, the United Nations Security Council unanimously adopted Resolution 242, perhaps the most important UN resolution on the Middle East. The resolution's preamble refers to the "inadmissibility of the acquisition of territory by war and the need to work for a just and lasting peace in the Middle East in which every State in the area can live in security." It also "affirms that the fulfillment of [UN] Charter principles requires the establishment of a just and lasting peace in the Middle East which should include the application of both the following principles:

   • Withdrawal of Israel armed forces from territories occupied in the recent conflict;
   • Termination of all claims or states of belligerency and respect for and acknowledgment of the sovereignty, territorial integrity and political independence of every State in the area and their right to live in peace within secure and recognized boundaries free from threats or acts of force."

On 1 May 1968, the Israeli ambassador to the UN expressed Israel's position to the Security Council: "My government has indicated its acceptance of the Security Council resolution for the promotion of agreement on the establishment of a just and lasting peace. I am also authorized to reaffirm that we are willing to seek agreement with each Arab State on all matters included in that resolution." The resolution is controversial and has been subject to numerous interpretations, but it has formed the basis of a policy Israel has followed since 1967—"land [the first principle] for peace [the second principle]." If an Arab nation is willing to recognize Israel as a legitimate nation and as a homeland for the Jewish people, Israel has demonstrated its willingness to return all land gained in 1967. It has done so with Egypt and Jordan.[443]

4. Terrorism against Israel increased. As mentioned above, under Nasser's leadership, the Arab League sponsored the formation of the PLO, which became the vehicle for sustained attacks on Israeli citizens. Well into the 1980s, the PLO spearheaded acts of terror. Numerous hijackings of planes, the murder of schoolchildren, and other nefarious acts of terrorism followed. The most famous occurred in June 1976 when PLO terrorists hijacked an Air France jet traveling from Paris to Tel Aviv and forced it to fly to Uganda, a nation that supported the PLO. Israel refused to negotiate the release of the eighty-three Israeli passengers. Instead, the Israeli special forces engaged in a spectacular rescue mission at Entebbe, the Ugandan airport. The terrorists were killed and most of the hostages freed. Israel's resolve against terrorism remained steadfast.

Because the PLO maintained Jordan as its primary base of operations, the growth of the PLO actually began to threaten the stability of King Hussein of Jordan. So, in 1970, in what was called "Black September," King Hussein made war on the PLO, in effect expelling them from his country. Yasser Arafat relocated to Lebanon and began an international campaign to reinvigorate the demoralized PLO. Perhaps the most brazen illustration of this strategy occurred at the 1972 Munich Olympics, when the PLO murdered eleven Israeli athletes.

Israel's astonishing success in the 1967 War lulled the political and military leaders of Israel into a degree of complacency mixed with some arrogance. When Nasser died in September 1970, he was replaced by Anwar Sadat, who had a grand vision of restoring Egypt to a position of Middle Eastern supremacy. In 1971, he announced the formation of an Egyptian-Syrian-Libyan federation and began to lay plans to regain the Sinai Peninsula from Israel. Through the

UN, he informed Israel of his willingness to negotiate, but Israel questioned his sincerity and rejected the offer.

On 6 October 1973, while millions in Israel were observing the high holy day of Yom Kippur, Israel experienced its most devastating attack since 1948. Egypt launched an offensive from the south and Syria from the north. Syria's impressive column of 1,400 tanks advanced deep into Galilee, and an Egyptian column of 2,000 tanks crossed the Suez Canal deep into the Sinai.

Over the next eighteen days, Israel, with the help of airlifted military supplies from the United States, drove the Egyptians back across the Suez Canal, surrounding the entire Third Army of Egypt. Egypt's capital at Cairo was now vulnerable. At enormous cost, Israel also recaptured the Golan Heights from Syria, advancing to within sight of Damascus. The ceasefire restored the status quo on the Golan and along the Suez Canal.

But the 1973 Yom Kippur War was a watershed, altering the course of Middle Eastern history.

1. The seeming invincibility of Israel was shattered. As Karsh comments, "The Arabs were elated. For many of them the war was a moment of treasure, a glorious break with a painful past, redemption of lost pride and trampled dignity, 'a new era of unity of ranks and purpose.'"[444] For Sadat, the war gave him an improved bargaining position when it came to Israel.
2. Anwar Sadat reached a fundamental conclusion about the Middle East—there was no military solution to the feud with Israel. "Israel was in the Middle East to stay and the Arabs had better disavow their unrealistic dream of a unified regional order and follow Egypt's lead in rolling back to the 1967 borders."[445] He was willing to travel to Jerusalem and address the Israeli Knesset as the first step in peace negotiations.

3. The war altered the political culture of Israel. A special committee, formed to investigate the lack of military preparedness, placed virtually all blame on the military leaders and none on the political leaders. But, after weeks of popular demonstrations, Golda Meir's government resigned. Due to the political residue from the war, plus numerous financial scandals within the Labor Party, the May 1977 elections resulted in the election of Menachem Begin and the Likud Party, ending the Labor Party's continuous rule since Israel's founding in 1948. Therefore, when Sadat proposed coming to Jerusalem, Begin issued the invitation to Sadat in November 1977. Sadat stayed in the King David Hotel, prayed at the al-Aqsa mosque, visited Yad Vashem (the Holocaust Museum in Jerusalem), and delivered an address of peace before the Knesset.[446]

In September 1978, after thirteen days of negotiations at Camp David in the United States, Anwar Sadat and Menachem Begin signed two agreements—the "Framework for Peace in the Middle East" and the "Framework for the Conclusion of a Peace Treaty Between Egypt and Israel" (the Camp David Accords). Then on 26 March 1979, in Washington, DC, Sadat and Begin signed the peace treaty in which Israel promised to evacuate the Sinai Peninsula, with the establishment of open borders. In addition, the two nations agreed to exchange ambassadors, establish embassies, and encourage trade and tourism. Egypt had recognized Israel's right to exist—the first Arab nation to do so—on the basis of "land for peace."

Although Menachem Begin was willing to make peace with Egypt, he remained stalwart about Israel's identity and security. For example, he refused to call the territory gained in the 1967 War "the West Bank," calling it instead Judea and Samaria. He also was an unrelenting advocate of building Jewish settlements in this territory.

Further, in 1981, when it became evident that Iraq's Saddam Hussein was building a nuclear reactor, Israeli fighter jets leveled the reactor. Finally, because Syria showed no signs of negotiating a peace treaty with Israel, Begin annexed the Golan Heights in December 1981, providing security for the entire region of Galilee from the threat of Syrian artillery.

As a result of "Black September" in 1970, the PLO was firmly entrenched in southern Lebanon, from which it bombed and shelled northern Israel. Thus, in June 1982, Begin ordered his defense minister, Ariel Sharon, to invade Lebanon with the goal of eliminating the PLO's grip. Allied with Christians and Shiite Muslims, Israel defeated the PLO by September, driving them out of Beirut, breaking Syria's stranglehold on Lebanon and in-stalling a Christian-dominated government. Yet Syria's influence remained, and Israel continued its occupation in an increasingly unpopular war.

The war's unpopularity, especially after the 1982 Lebanese Christian massacres at the Palestinian refugee camps of Sabra and Shatila, eventually caused Begin's resignation and the birth of the Lebanese militia, Hezbollah. Hezbollah would become a powerful terrorist group allied with Syria and Iran. Finally, in May 2000, Israel withdrew from Lebanon.

The Oslo Accords and the Changing Face of Islamic Terrorism, 1983–Present

Because of the peace treaty with Israel, a radical Egyptian Muslim group led by Ayman al-Zawahiri, called the Organization of the Jihad, assassinated Anwar Sadat on 6 October 1981. (Zawahiri would later become a leader of al-Qaeda). Sadat's assassination was an early sign of a new power rising in Islam—radical Islamic fundamentalism.

In addition, Hamas, a branch of the Muslim Brotherhood, which had been a part of Egyptian Islam for years, surfaced in Gaza. "Hamas" is an Arabic acronym for the Islamic Resistance

Movement. It adopted the slogan, "Allah is [Hamas's] goal, the Prophet its model, the Qur'an its Constitution, Jihad its path and death for the cause of Allah its most sublime belief." Hamas combined the goal of extinguishing the state of Israel with the lofty goal of spreading the message of Allah.[447] The issue of Palestine was no longer a dispute about territory, it was now a holy war involving worldwide Islam: "When our enemies usurp some Islamic lands, Jihad becomes a duty binding on all Muslims." Hence, "the land of Palestine has been an Islamic trust (*waqf*) throughout the generations and until the Day of Resurrection, no one can renounce it or part of it, or abandon it or part of it."[448]

The most formidable example of this fundamental shift in Islam was the Islamic Republic of Iran, created in 1979 by the religious Shiite radical Ayatollah Ruhollah Khomeini. For Khomeini, history was a struggle between the house of Islam and everyone else. Since World War I especially, the Western powers had sought to keep Muslim communities in a state of ignorance, fragmentation, and oppression, Khomeini argued. Muslims were therefore obliged "to overthrow the oppressive governments installed by the imperialists and bring into existence an Islamic government of justice that will be in service to the people." Khomeini's goal was "an Islamic world order [that] would see the territorial state transcended by the broader entity of the umma [Islamic community]."[449]

A further illustration of the changing dynamic of Islam was the Intifada ("uprising"), which began in Gaza in 1987 and spread quickly to Jerusalem. At first spontaneous, the Intifada involved Palestinian teens throwing rocks, Molotov cocktails, and even grenades. As it developed, Yasser Arafat, now in Tunisia, began directing the uprising, calling for "days of rage" among the Palestinians. As Israel dealt with the Intifada, its image in the world was affected. These were no longer murderous PLO hijackers killing Israeli children; these were Palestinian teens using slingshots against uniformed, armed Israeli soldiers. Israel was losing the propaganda war.

When Saddam Hussein invaded Kuwait in 1990 and the West responded with the Gulf War of 1991, Yasser Arafat and the PLO supported Saddam. When Saddam fired Scud missiles into Israel in a futile attempt to draw Israel into the conflict, Palestinians cheered. Wisely, Israel did nothing.

As the conflict ended, Arafat was humiliated and thereby lost significant credibility throughout the world. The PLO was now vulnerable as the legitimate representative of the Palestinian people; Hamas was a viable alternative. And, with the defeat of Saddam in the Gulf War, the United States was now a much more decisive player in the Middle East.

Thus, on 30 October 1991, a major peace conference was convened in Madrid, Spain. For the first time since Israel's independence in 1948, Israel sat at a table with Syrians, Jordanians, and Palestinians, joined by the United States, Russia, the European Union, and representatives of the United Nations. The primary subject was the Arab-Israeli conflict. Although no agreement was reached, it provided necessary momentum for further discussions. All of these developments provided the context for the Oslo Accords of 1993.

The new Israeli government under Yitzhak Rabin, the hero of the 1967 war, was elected in 1992 with a clearly defined peace platform. Rabin expressed a willingness to talk with the PLO, even though the PLO had not yet abandoned its dedication to Israel's total destruction. Hence, secret talks began in Oslo, Norway, between Israel and the PLO.

These talks culminated on 13 September 1993 with the signing on the White House lawn of the "Declaration of Principles on Interim Self-Government Arrangement." It was an extraordinary agreement based on the premise that each party would agree on simpler issues, leaving the more difficult issues (e.g., Jerusalem, borders, and refugees) for future negotiations. It provided for Palestinian self-rule in the entire West Bank and Gaza for a transitional period not to exceed five years, during which time Israel and the PLO would negotiate a permanent peace.

Although there was understandable euphoria over the Oslo Accords, the reality was that Arafat was not really embracing a two-state solution. Rather, he was achieving what the PLO had failed to attain after years of violence and terrorism. Karsh summarizes Arafat's objective:

> As early as August 1968, Arafat had defined the PLO's strategic objective as 'the transfer of all resistance bases' into the West Bank and the Gaza Strip, occupied by Israel during the 1967 war, 'so that the resistance may be gradually transformed into a popular armed revolution.' This, he reasoned, would allow the PLO to undermine Israel's way of life 'preventing immigration and encouraging emigration ... destroying tourism ... weakening the Israeli economy and diverting the greater part of it to security requirements ... [and] creating and maintaining an atmosphere of strain and anxiety that will force the Zionists to realize that it is impossible for them to live in Israel ....' Indeed the prominent PLO leader Faisal Husseini famously quipped, Israel was willingly introducing into its midst a 'Trojan Horse' designed to promote the PLO's strategic goal of a 'Palestine from the [Jordan] River to the [Mediterranean] Sea'—that is, a Palestine in place of Israel.[450]

In fact, as Karsh also observes, until September 2000, when Arafat launched his second Intifada, he consistently was schizophrenic in his public statements about the Oslo Accords. "Whenever addressing Israeli or Western audiences he would habitually extol the 'peace of the brave' he had signed with 'my partner Yitzhak Rabin,' while at the same time denigrating the peace accords to the Palestinians as a temporary measure to be abandoned at the first available opportunity, and indoctrinating his people, and especially the youth, with an abiding hatred of the state of Israel, Jews, and Judaism."[451]

As the Oslo Accords were implemented, the euphoria turned to harsh reality. In May 1994 Israel withdrew from Jericho and Gaza City, the first step in the agreement. Jordan embraced the spirit of Oslo and signed a peace treaty with Israel on 26 October 1994. Foreign donors, many from the Persian Gulf states, began channeling vast sums of money to the PLO, ostensibly to help in the construction of roads, schools, and other infrastructure and social improvements. Little of that money went to such projects, however; instead, much of it went to fund the nepotism and growing corruption of the PLO.

In addition, terrorism against Israel did not subside. Homicide bombings increased. While initially this was thought to be a result of the disorganization of the PLO, quickly it became apparent that Arafat had no intention of honoring the Oslo Accords. Arafat refused to disarm Hamas and other militant groups, such as Islamic Jihad, as required by the accords. He created a far larger Palestinian army than the accords allowed.

Many Israelis blamed Prime Minister Rabin for the increased terrorism and the noncompliance of Arafat. Tragically, after speaking at a Tel Aviv rally on 4 November 1994, Rabin was assassinated by a right-wing Israeli extremist, Yigal Amir. A stunned nation looked inward, trying to make sense of what was happening.

By September 2000, the Palestinian Authority (PA) had gained control of about 40 percent of the West Bank, including Hebron, Bethlehem, and Jericho. Both the Israelis and the Palestinians were frustrated by the absence of significant progress in serious negotiations on the next phase of the Oslo Accords—the more acute issues dealing with the borders and the status of Jerusalem. But with the 1999 election of the former Israeli Defense Force chief of staff,

Ehud Barak, hope increased in Israel, for Barak proposed a peace strategy that included a final status agreement with the Palestinians and the settlement of the ongoing Lebanon crisis.

Israel had occupied southern Lebanon since 1982, initially to protect northern Israel from continued shelling from Lebanon. Tragically, it had turned into a guerilla war led by Hezbollah ("Party of God"), a Shiite Muslim terrorist militia heavily financed and armed by Syria and Iran. Since Israeli casualties remained frustratingly high, on 24 May 2000 Israel completely withdrew from Lebanon. Hezbollah championed this as a decisive defeat for Israel and set up bases and rocket launching sites all over southern Lebanon—in private homes, bunkers, and schools. Today, Hezbollah remains a formidable threat to Israel in the north.

In the summer of 2000, President Bill Clinton of the United States summoned Ehud Barak and Yasser Arafat to Camp David for the express purpose of negotiating a final settlement to the Israeli-Palestinian conflict. After marathon negotiations, Barak agreed to recognize a Palestinian state in the Gaza Strip and to give the PA about 95 percent of the West Bank, even agreeing to dismantle many Israeli settlements. He also agreed to allow up to 100,000 Palestinian refugees to return to Israel and to financially compensate other Palestinian refugees who had lost land when Israel was created in 1948. Amazingly, Barak also agreed to share sovereignty over Jerusalem with the PA.

Arafat's position evidenced no desire for compromise. He demanded the right of return for all Palestinian refugees. He demanded that Israel return to its pre-1967 borders, and he insisted on total sovereignty over Jerusalem. During the negotiations, Arafat rejected any notion that Jerusalem had ever been the site of the Jewish temple—"a modern invention," he insisted. In fact, Arafat personally banned Palestinian historians and archeologists from admitting that there had ever been a Jewish temple on Temple Mount.[452] The negotiations failed.

A typical Palestinian commentator placed this in a Palestinian historical context: "If time constitutes the [criteria of] existence, then Israel's temporary existence is only fifty-two years long while we, the Palestinian Arabs, have lived here for thousands of years, and we, the indigenous population, will eventually expel the invaders, however long it takes."[453]

From 2000 to 2003, violence exploded across Israel in what has been called Intifada II. It has also been called the Al-Aqsa Intifada because, in September 2000, Ariel Sharon, the leader of the Likud Party in Israel, visited Temple Mount in Jerusalem, which incited a massive, violent response from the Palestinians. The violence was dreadful, for it included numerous homicide bombings that killed dozens of Israeli citizens.

Seeking to kill or capture the terrorist leaders, Israel retaliated in what was known as Operation Defensive Shield. Israel invaded Palestinian cities, refugee camps, and other terrorist hideouts. Israel even blockaded Arafat's compound in Ramallah. In addition, the new prime minister, Ariel Sharon, implemented a different strategy: the physical separation of Palestinians and Israelis. An immense security fence, in some sections a wall, was built during 2003–4—and the terrorist violence and homicide bombings ended. Further, Sharon ordered the Israeli evacuation of the Gaza Strip, turning it over completely to the PA in the summer of 2005.

In 2006, elections in Gaza were held, and Hamas won a resounding victory. Today, Palestinian control of the disputed territory is divided between the Palestinian Authority (the West Bank) and Hamas (Gaza). The PA continues to negotiate with Israel; Hamas refuses to do so.

Yasser Arafat died in November 2004 and was succeeded by Mahmoud Abbas, who has orchestrated a reduction in the violence against Israel. His enemy is also Hamas, which seeks to destabilize his rule over the West Bank areas the PA controls. Negotiations with Israel for a final settlement continue, but Benjamin Netanyahu, Israel's current prime minister, faces the growing threat of Iran, which is on the verge of nuclear weapon capability.

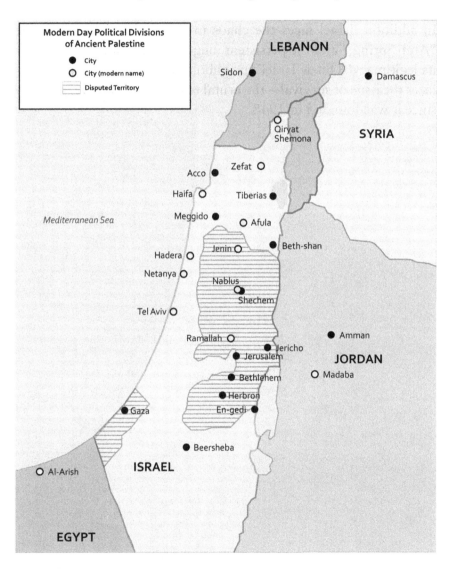

So this is Israel in the early twenty-first century: a lethal enemy to its north (Hezbollah), with which it fought a deadly but short conflict in 2006, and a terrorist state to its west (Hamas), which remains bent on its annihilation. Further to its north is Syria, which as of this writing is engaged in a civil war that could lead to its dismemberment. And, of course, to Israel's east is Iran and its nuclear project.

In addition, Israel faces the chaos in the Arab world called the "Arab Spring," and the persistent, ongoing Palestinian rejection of its legitimacy. This is Israel's neighborhood, one in which it daily faces the issue of survival—the brutal reality of this amazing nation since it was founded in 1948.

Conclusion

Senior columnist for the Israeli newspaper *Haaretz*, Ari Shavit, has written that the twentieth century was "the most dramatic century in the dramatic history of the Jews. In its first half, we lost a third of our people. But the second half of the century was miraculous. In North America, we created the perfect diaspora, while in the land of Israel we established modern Jewish sovereignty. The Jews of the 21st century have today what their great-grandparents could only dream of: equality, freedom, prosperity, dignity. The persecuted people are now emancipated. The pitiful people are now proud and independent ... [Israel] is the demography of hope: an almost extinguished people renewing itself."[454]

Shavit also documents the staggering success of the Zionist movement in Israel: "In 1897, approximately 50,000 Jews lived here. Now the Jewish population exceeds six million ... In 1897, Jews living in Palestine represented only 0.4 percent of world Jewry. In 1950 we accounted for 10.6 percent. In 1980, 25.6 percent. Now we make up almost 45 percent. The historic project that aimed to congregate most of the world's Jews in the Promised Land has had mind-boggling success. Today, the Jewish community in Israel is one of the two largest in the world. Given current trends, by 2025 the majority of the world's Jews will be Israelis."[455]

How do we explain this—Jews once again in their Promised Land? It was certainly the vision of Theodore Herzl and the Zionist movement to transfer people from one continent where they were being persecuted, almost extinguished, to their ancient homeland. And it was their goal to reestablish the state of Israel with its revived language of Hebrew—all in the land of their forefathers.

This book has documented the historic events that effected the realization of these goals.

Yet this book has also argued that there is a supernatural explanation for the miracle called Israel. It is God fulfilling His promises, first detailed in the Abrahamic covenant and reiterated continuously throughout the major and minor prophets of the Old Testament. The birth of the modern nation-state of Israel is not only an event of history; it is the fulfillment of prophecy.

Ezekiel 36:16–38 is one the most important passages in Scripture, envisaging the restoration of the Jewish people to their land. As this event is accomplished, Ezekiel exclaimed, the nations will be silent in their amazement of what God has done (vv. 33–36). I believe quite strongly that in the twenty-first century, we are witnessing that restoration.

But the other dimension of Ezekiel's prophetic claim is the spiritual restoration of the Jews. That is detailed in Ezekiel 36:22–32 and 37:15–28. God will put His Spirit in them, they will obey Him, and they will walk with Him forever. The fulfillment of God's covenantal promises to Abraham (land, seed, and blessing) and to David (an eternal throne, kingdom, and dynasty), and the new covenant of spiritual renewal are foretold in 37:24–28. The Jewish people will be united as one people, secure in the land God promised them, renewed spiritually and with their Davidic King ruling in their midst. We await that fulfillment.

Are the Jewish people in Israel and throughout the world looking for their Messiah? Thomas Friedman argues that there are four distinct groups of Jews within modern Israel (and the world). The first and largest are the secular and nonobservant Jews who built the modern state of Israel. Many of them are secular Zionists who came to Israel in part as a rebellion against their grandfathers and Orthodox Judaism. For these secular Jews, being in the land, erecting a modern society and army, and observing the Jewish holidays as national holidays all substitute for religious observance and faith.

The second group is the religious Zionists, who are traditional or modern Orthodox Jews. They fully support the secular Zionist state but insist it is not a substitute for the synagogue. The creation of the Jewish state is a religious, "messianic" event.

The third group is the religious or messianic Zionists, who see the rebirth of the Jewish state as the first stage in a process that will culminate in the coming of the Messiah.

The final group is the ultra-Orthodox, non-Zionist Jews, who do not regard the Jewish state as important. In fact, many view the modern state of Israel with disdain and scorn. Only when the personal Messiah returns, they believe, and the rule of Jewish law is complete will the true Jewish state be created.

Thus, except for messianic Jews, most Jews today reject the teaching that Jesus is the Messiah. Excluding the ultra-Orthodox and some messianic Zionists, even the idea of a personal Messiah who will establish a kingdom of peace, righteousness, and justice is usually rejected. The messianic idea is politicized, associated with the modern state of Israel, or rejected as an aspect of an antiquated belief of a dead form of Judaism.[456]

However, three important scriptural passages, among many others, demonstrate that one day the Jewish people will embrace Jesus as their Messiah:

- Matthew 23:39: Jesus had just finished His lament over Jerusalem (vv. 37–38); His people were rejecting Him as their Messiah. But He envisioned a time when the Jewish people would embrace Him as their Messiah and Savior. He quoted Psalm 118:26, "Blessed is he who comes in the name of the Lord"—the same thing they proclaimed as He entered Jerusalem on Palm Sunday. When will that be?

- The Old Testament prophet Zechariah helps us understand that the events surrounding the second coming of the Messiah, Jesus (see Zechariah 14 and Revelation 19) will result in a profound change in the hearts of the Jewish people: "They will look upon him whom they pierced and mourn" (Zechariah 12:10). This will be followed by a time of spiritual renewal and restoration of the Jewish people.
- Romans 11:26 is the key New Testament marker; it stipulates a time when "all Israel will be saved." In the context of Romans 9–11 and in light of all the biblical passages in which God promises salvation for His people, Paul's claim can only refer to the salvation of Israel at the end of history, when Jesus returns as the Messiah, defeats His enemies, and rescues Israel. The Jews alive at that time will look upon Jesus and believe.

This book has presented God as a covenant-making, covenant-keeping God. He made a series of promises to Abraham and King David, promises that center on the people of Israel. God also promised a time of national restoration and spiritual renewal for the people of Israel, the new covenant. All three of these covenantal promises are to be fulfilled in Jesus Christ.

Nearly seven hundred years before His incarnation, the prophet Isaiah spoke of Jesus in that majestic prophecy, Isaiah 9:6–7, which George Frideric Handel put to music in his oratorio *Messiah*. Arguably, Handel's majestic oratorio is one of the greatest pieces of music ever written. Part 1 gives focus to the Old Testament prophet Isaiah and the "Prophecy of Christ's Birth": "For unto us a child is born, unto us a son is given." In fact, Handel constructed scene 3 around Isaiah's entire prophecy in 9:6–7 so that this child, whom the New Testament affirms is Jesus, would be worshipped and adored. This child, a Son and a King, would rule forever.

Further, the names that Isaiah used to describe this child and Son are all names for God:

- "Wonderful Counselor." The term "wonderful" is never used in Scripture of a human being, only of God, who resolves the unsolvable problems of humanity. This child would have insight and wisdom into how to rule.
- "Mighty God." This child would have the resources of God to effect the salvation of His people and rule the world.
- "Eternal Father." This means "my Father forever," as the one who cares for, nurtures, and provides. As Jesus declared in John 14:9, "Since you have seen me, you have seen the Father." Jesus is the revelation of God.
- "Prince of Peace." This child would establish peace on earth "and of His peace there will be no end," Isaiah declares. The Hebrew word for peace is *shalom*, which conveys not so much the absence of conflict as the notion of positive blessing, of a healthy relationship with God. It also suggests the fullness of well-being, a freedom from anxiety, and goodwill and harmony in human relationships. The New Testament teaches that Jesus provides peace with God through His cross, which then produces the peace of God as a quality of life. It also teaches that His return will bring true global peace, which humanity has sought for over five millennia. In fact, Isaiah 2:4 prophesies that at that time, the nations "will hammer their swords into plowshares, and their spears into pruning hooks. Nation will not lift up sword against nation, and never again will they learn war."

As Isaiah 9:7 declares, this child is the Davidic King, whose throne of justice and righteousness would be established forever.

Handel's *Messiah* reminds us that the primary message of the Bible is one of hope, encouragement, and fulfillment. God's care for His world is best evidenced by what happened on Christmas morning. All eyes that day were on Rome with its power, majesty, and glory.

But in that small village a few miles south of Jerusalem, God "showed up." His plan to establish His peace on earth began with this child, His Son, whose kingdom would one day be established. For two thousand years, Christians have proclaimed that the hope of humanity is not in political, economic, or financial power. It is in the power manifested by that child who grew to be a man and who offered salvation to the world through His cross and His resurrection.

The history of Israel, God's covenant people, is a history of God keeping His covenant. Since the creation of Israel in 1948, regardless of what occurs in the United States, in China, or in Russia, the Middle East has remained the center of international concern. That will not change, for God is ordering events for the return of his Son, the Lord Jesus Christ. We long for that day; we pray for that day—for in that day "every knee shall bow and every tongue confess that Jesus Christ is Lord" (Philippians 2:10–11).

In that day as well, the Jewish people will embrace Him as their Messiah, and He will rule over them and over the whole world from Jerusalem, the capital of His Kingdom. In that day, God's irrevocable covenantal promises to the Jewish people will be finally fulfilled. So we echo a prayer from the early church: may He come—and may He come quickly!

Endnotes

1. An excellent atlas on Israel and its geography is Thomas V. Brisco, *Holman Bible Atlas* (Nashville, Tenn.: Holman, 1998), 12–24.
2. Eugene H. Merrill, *Kingdom of Priests: A History of Old Testament Israel* (Grand Rapids, Mich.: Baker, 1987), 31.
3. Merrill, p. 26; see also Allen P. Ross, *Creation and Blessing: A Guide to the Study and Exposition of Genesis* (Grand Rapids, Mich.: Baker, 1988), 258.
4. Ross, *Creation and Blessing*, 312.
5. Merrill, *Kingdom of Priests*, 34–35.
6. Brisco, *Holman Bible Atlas*, 46.
7. Ross, *Creation and Blessing*, 324–25.
8. Ross, *Creation and Blessing*, 331–33.
9. Merrill, *Kingdom of Priests*, 31.
10. Ross, *Creation and Blessing*, 380.
11. Merrill, *Kingdom of Priests*, 31.
12. Ross, *Creation and Blessing*, 441, 553.
13. Ross, *Creation and Blessing*, 553-556.
14. Ross, *Creation and Blessing*, 558.
15. Merrill, *Kingdom of Priests*, 49.
16. Merrill, *Kingdom of Priests*, 50; Brisco, *Holman Atlas*, 49–50.
17. Merrill, *Kingdom of Priests*, 48; Brisco, *Holman Atlas*, 50–51.
18. For a helpful discussion of this issue, see Leon J. Wood, *A Survey of Israel's History*, rev. ed. (Grand Rapids, Mich.: Zondervan, 1986), 65–69.
19. For a helpful and succinct summary of the two positions on the Exodus, see the *ESV Study Bible* (Wheaton: Crossway, 2008), 33; Thomas V. Brisco, *Holman Bible Atlas* (Nashville: Broadman and Holman, 1998), 63–64; and Wood, 69–86.
20. Eugene Merrill, "Numbers," in *The Bible Knowledge Commentary*, ed. John F. Walvoord, Roy B. Zuck (Wheaton: Victor, 1985), 216–17.
21. Eugene H. Merrill, *Kingdom of Priests: A History of Old Testament Israel* (Grand Rapids: Baker, 1987), 60.
22. Merrill's account of Moses and Thutmoses is quite helpful, see pp. 61–62 in his *Kingdom of Priests*; also see Wood, 91–95.
23. Merrill, *Kingdom of Priests*, 63.

24. See Brisco, *Holman Atlas*, 43, 51–53, 57; Merrill, *Kingdom of Priests*, 52–55.

25. John J. Davis, *Moses and the Gods of Egypt* (Grand Rapids: Baker, 1971), 54–55 and *ESV Study Bible* (Wheaton: Crossway, 2001), 146.

26. Davis, *Moses*, 55–56.

27. Margaret Bunson, *A Dictionary of Ancient Egypt* (New York: Oxford, 1991), 152.

28. Henri Frankfort, *Ancient Egyptian Religion* (New York: Harper and Row, 1948), 86–87.

29. Bunson, *Dictionary*, 205–7.

30. Bunson, *Dictionary*, 189-191, 197–98.

31. Bunson, Dictionary, 225-26.

32. Bunson, *Dictionary*, 19–21.

33. John D. Currid, *Ancient Egypt and the Old Testament* (Grand Rapids: Baker, 1997), 115.

34. Currid, *Ancient Egypt*, 108–13.

35. Currid, *Ancient Egypt*, 121.

36. Currid, *Ancient Egypt*, 134–36.

37. Merrill, *Kingdom of Priests*, 66.

38. Currid, *Ancient Egypt*, 136–37.

39. Bruce K. Waltke, *An Old Testament Theology* (Grand Rapids: Zondervan, 2007), 407.

40. Waltke, 409.

41. Waltke, 409–11.

42. Waltke, 411.

43. Waltke, 413.

44. Waltke, 413.

45. Brisco, *Holman Atlas*, 70.

46. Eugene Merrill, *Kingdom of Priests: A History of Old Testament Israel* (Grand Rapids: Baker, 1987), 99. This section is dependent on Merrill's helpful summary, 93–99.

47. See the helpful article by Kenneth A. Kitchen in *The New Bible Dictionary*, ed. J.D. Douglas (Grand Rapids: Eerdmans, 1962), 183–86.

48. Kitchen, 186 and Jack Finegan, *Myth and Mysteries: An Introduction to the Pagan Religions of the Biblical World* (Grand Rapids: Baker, 1989), 123–27.

49. See Merrill's helpful discussion, *Kingdom of Priests*, pp. 100–108, and Nadav Na'aman, "The Trowel vs. the Text: How the Amarna Letters Challenge Archeology," *Biblical Archeology Review* (January/February 2009), 52–56, 70–71.

50. *Kingdom of Priests*, 104.
51. Originally published in 1958, an English edition by Eerdmanns contains a valuable introductory essay by Ben Ollenburger: Gerhard von Rad, *Holy War in Ancient Israel* (Grand Rapids: Eerdmanns, 1991).
52. Bruce Waltke, *An Old Testament Theology* (Grade Rapids: Zondervan, 2007), 519.
53. See the most helpful essay in *The ESV Study Bible* (Wheaton: Crossway, 2008), 390–91; Waltke, 518–19, 522–23; and Peter C. Craigie, *The Problem of War in the Old Testament* (Grand Rapids: Eerdmans, 1978), 33–44.
54. Waltke, 517.
55. Waltke, 517.
56. Waltke, 517.
57. Waltke, 518–19.
58. See Merrill, *Kingdom of Priests*, 116–18; Waltke, pp. 522–23; Brisco, *Holman Atlas*, 78–79, 81.
59. Waltke, 523.
60. Waltke, 523–24.
61. Brisco, *Holman Atlas*, 83.
62. Leon J. Wood, *A Survey of Israel's History*, rev. ed. (Grand Rapids: Zondervan, 1986), 157–63; and D.A. Hubbard in the *New Bible Dictionary*, 1028–34.
63. Allen P. Ross, *Holiness to the LORD: A Guide to the Exposition of the Book of Leviticus* (Grand Rapids: Baker, 2002), 79.
64. Ross, 79.
65. Ross, 80.
66. Ross, 80.
67. Ross is excellent for this entire section on the offerings made in ancient Israel; see especially 79–80.
68. Ross, 80–81.
69. Bruce Waltke, *An Old Testament Theology* (Grand Rapids: Zondervan, 2007), 588–89; and Eugene Merrill, *Kingdom of Priests: A History of Old Testament Israel* (Grand Rapids: Baker, 1987), 162.
70. Gleason Archer, *A Survey of Old Testament Introduction* (Chicago: Moody, 1974), 276–77. Also see Merrill, 146–51.
71. Waltke, 589–91.
72. Waltke, 613–17.
73. Waltke, 591.
74. Thomas Brisco, *Holman Bible Atlas* (Nashville: Holman, 1998), 92.
75. Waltke, 597.
76. Merrill, *Kingdom of Priests*, 161–63.

77. Merrill, 164.
78. Waltke, 600.
79. Waltke, 600–601.
80. Waltke, 601.
81. Waltke, 166.
82. Merrill, *Kingdom of Priests*, 169.
83. Waltke, 604.
84. Waltke, 601.
85. Merrill, *Kingdom of Priests*, 173.
86. Merrill, 173.
87. See Brisco for a helpful summary of the Sea Peoples, *Holman Atlas*, 76-77; 94-95.
88. Merrill, *Kingdom of Priests*, 174.
89. Waltke, 613, where he is quoting Barry Webb's commentary on Judges.
90. Waltke, 612.
91. Waltke, 612-613.
92. Merrill, 178–88. He calls these texts in Judges and Ruth "The BethlehemTrilogy."
93. Merrill, 187–88.
94. Waltke, 862–63.
95. Bruce Waltke, *An Old Testament Theology* (Grand Rapids: Zondervan, 2007), 624.
96. Waltke, 634.
97. Eugene H. Merrill, *Kingdom of Priests: A History of Old Testament Israel* (Grand Rapids: Baker, 1987), 194. Paul stated that Saul reigned for forty years (Acts 13:21).
98. Merrill, 210.
99. Waltke, 638.
100. Waltke, 640.
101. Merrill, *Kingdom of Priests*, 213.
102. Merrill, 226–28.
103. The chronology of David's life in this chapter is dependent on Merrill, 243–48.
104. Thomas V. Brisco, *Holman Bible Atlas* (Nashville: Holman, 1998), 105.
105. Brisco, 105.
106. Brisco, 105.
107. Waltke, 660.
108. Waltke, 660.
109. Merrill, *Kingdom of Priests*, 275.
110. Weights as computed by Merrill, *Kingdom of Priests*, 278.

111. Leon J. Wood, *A Survey of Israel's History*, rev. ed. (Grand Rapids: Zondervan, 1986), 227–30. This section has an excellent summary of David's administrative initiatives. Also see Merrill, *Kingdom of Priests*, 281–84.

112. Waltke, 666.

113. Waltke, 666.

114. Waltke, 671.

115. Waltke, 674.

116. Waltke, 677.

117. Waltke, 678.

118. Waltke, 708.

119. Merrill, *Kingdom of Priests*, 308–9.

120. See Brisco for a helpful summary of Solomon's' economic exploits, *Holman Atlas*, 107–9.

121. *ESV Study Bible* (Wheaton: Crossway, 2008), 754.

122. See Merrill, *Kingdom of Priests*, 303–7.

123. Merrill, 300–302.

124. Brisco, *Holman Atlas*, 108–9.

125. See Brisco, 109; and Merrill, *Kingdom of Priests*, 296–98.

126. See *ESV Study Bible* notes on 1 Kings 7:1–12, 607.

127. Brisco, *Holman Atlas*, 111.

128. See the reference note on this verse in the *ESV Study Bible*, 603.

129. Waltke, 709.

130. This description of the temple is a combination of Brisco, *Holman Atlas*, 113–14 and *ESV Study Bible* notes on 604–5.

131. The dating of the kings of the divided kingdom is notoriously difficult. For a summary of the differences, see Thomas V. Brisco, *The Holman Bible Atlas* (Nashville: Holman, 1998), 116–17. This book follows the slightly different chronology of Eugene H. Merrill, *A Kingdom of Priests: A History of Old Testament Israel* (Grand Rapids: Baker, 1987), 320.

132. Bruce Waltke, *An Old Testament Theology* (Grand Rapids: Zondervan, 2007), 714.

133. The chart is dependent on data, dates, and information gleaned from Willem VanGemeren, *The Progress of Redemption: The Story of Salvation from Creation to the New Jerusalem* (Grand Rapids: Zondervan, 1988), 252; Brisco, *Holman Atlas*, 117; Merrill, *Kingdom of Priests*, 320; *ESV Study Bible*, (Wheaton: Crossway, 2008), 622-623; and the dates offered in Waltke, 712–37.

134. Brisco, *Holman Atlas*, 115.

135. Brisco, 115.

136. Brisco, 124–25; Merrill, *Kingdom of Priests*, 329–31; John Bright, *A History of Israel*, 2d ed. (Philadelphia: Westminster, 1972), 239–41.

137. Brisco, 131–36; Bright, *History of Israel*, 246–53; 267–74.

138. Merrill, *Kingdom of Priests*, 340.

139. Brisco, 126–27; Leon Wood, *A Survey of Israel's History*, rev. ed. (Grand Rapids: Zondervan, 1986), 262–63.

140. Bright, *History of Israel*, 238; Brisco, *Holman Atlas*, 126.

141. Merrill, *Kingdom of Priests*, 345.

142. Brisco, 128.

143. Thomas R. Schreiner, *The King in His Beauty: A Biblical Theology of the Old and New Testaments* (Grand Rapids: Baker, 2013), 179; Bright, *History of Israel*, 243.

144. Merrill, *Kingdom of Priests*, 346.

145. Schreiner, *The King*, 180.

146. Schreiner, 183–84; Merrill, *Kingdom of Priests*, 380.

147. Wood, *A Survey*, 265.

148. Bright, *History of Israel*, 250.

149. Bright, 251.

150. This is the only surviving representation of an Israeli king.

151. So suggests Bright, 253.

152. Merrill, *Kingdom of Priests*, 372.

153. Merrill, 375.

154. Wood, *A Survey*, 276–77; Bright, *History of Israel*, 254–55.

155. Merrill, *Kingdom of Priests*, 378–82; Waltke, *Old Testament Theology*, 805–49.

156. VanGemeren, *Progress of Redemption*, 269.

157. See Waltke, 828–33.

158. Merrill, *Kingdom of Priests*, 388.

159. Bright, *History of Israel*, 263.

160. Wood, *A Survey*, 280; Merrill, *Kingdom of Priests*, 395–96; Bright, *History of Israel*, 269–70.

161. Bright, *History of Israel*, 271–73; Merrill, *Kingdom of Priests*, 396–97; Wood, *A Survey*, 280–81.

162. Bright, 273–74.

163. See Merrill, 401.

164. Willem Van Gemern, *The Progress of Redemption: The Story of Salvation from Creation to the New Jerusalem* (Grand Rapids: Zondervan, 1988), 264–65.

165. Van Gemeren, 265.

166. John Bright, *A History of Israel*, 2d ed. (Philadelphia: Westminster, 1972), 229–30; *ESV Study Bible* (Wheaton: Crossway, 2008), 628.

167. The chronology of Asa's reign is complicated. See Eugene H. Merrill, *A Kingdom of Priests: A History of Old Testament Israel* (Grand Rapids: Baker, 1987), 332–34, for a most helpful discussion and resolution to the problems.

168. Bright, *History of Israel*, 231; *ESV Study Bible* notes, 761.

169. Merrill, 335.

170. This included a three-year coregency with his father Asa. See Merrill, *Kingdom of Priests*, 341.

171. G.T. Manley, "High Places," in *The New Bible Dictionary*, ed. J.D. Douglas (Grand Rapids: Eerdmans, 1978), 525–26.

172. Bright, *History of Israel*, 248.

173. Bright, 248.

174. Merrill, *Kingdom of Priests*, 353–54; *ESV Study Bible* notes, 771.

175. Merrill, *Kingdom of Priests*, 360.

176. See a defense of this date in Merrill, *Kingdom of Priests*, 372, note 30.

177. Merrill, *Kingdom of Priests*, 370–73; Bright, *History of Israel*, 253–54; *ESV Study Bible* notes, 776–77.

178. On the complexities of these coregencies, see Wood, *A Survey*, 298–99, and Merrill, 375–76.

179. Bright, 254–55; Merrill, 376.

180. Merrill, *Kingdom of Priests*, 376–77; Bright, *History of Israel*, 254–55.

181. Merrill, 377.

182. See *ESV Study Bible* notes, 778, and Merrill, 377.

183. VanGemeren, 266.

184. The complexities of these coregencies are summarized in Wood, *A Survey*, 300, and Merrill, *Kingdom of Priests*, 405.

185. Bright, *History of Israel*, 275.

186. See VanGemeren, *Progress of Redemption*, 269-270; Bright, *History of Israel*, 278.

187. Bright, *History of Israel*, 282; Merrill, *Kingdom of Priests*, 412.

188. Bright, 280.

189. *Archaeological Study Bible* (Grand Rapids: Zondervan, 2005), 659.

190. Bright, *History of Israel*, 284-86; Merrill, *Kingdom of Priests*, 413–17.

191. Merrill, *Kingdom of Priests*, 435; Bright, *History of Israel*, 313.

192. Bright, 313; *ESV Study Bible* notes, 792–93.

193. Merrill, 435.

194. Merrill, *Kingdom of Priests*, 436.

195. Bright, *History of Israel*, 312–21; Merrill, *Kingdom of Priests*, 436–41.

196. Wood, *A Survey*, 318; Merrill, *Kingdom of Priests*, 451–52.

197. Merrill, *Kingdom of Priests*, 453.

198. Willem VanGemeren, *The Progress of Redemption: The Story of Salvation from Creation to the New Jerusalem* (Grand Rapids: Zondervan, 1988), 283.

199. John Bright, *A History of Israel*, 2d ed. (Philadelphia: Westminster, 1972), 344.

200. Leon J. Wood, *A Survey of Israel's History*, rev. ed. (Grand Rapids: Zondervan, 1986), 321–24; Thomas V. Brisco, *Holman Bible Atlas* (Nashville: Holman, 1998), 158–60; *ESV Study Bible* (Wheaton: Crossway, 2008), study notes, 1474.

201. Bright, 344.

202. Bright, 346–47; Brisco, 160.

203. Bright, *History of Israel*, 346-47; Brisco, *Holman Atlas*, 160; Wood, *A Survey*, 328–30.

204. Eugene H. Merrill, *Kingdom of Priests: a History of Old Testament Israel* (Grand Rapids: Baker, 1987), 475–78; Wood, *A Survey*, 324–26; Bright, *History of Israel*, 361.

205. Bright, 36–361; Merrill, 478–80.

206. Merrill, 491–92; Wood, 334; Bright, 361–62. In addition to the possible influence of Daniel, the ancient Jewish historian, Josephus, suggests that Cyrus had read Isaiah and was moved to fulfill what the text said about him. See *ESV Study Bible* notes, 1322.

207. Edwin M. Yamauchi, *Persia and the Bible* (Grand Rapids: Baker, 1990), 65–278; Wood, *A Survey*, 331–33; Brisco, *Holman Atlas*, 165–67.

208. Merrill, *Kingdom of Priests*, 492–93; Bright, *History of Israel*, 363–64, 366; Brisco, *Holman Atlas*, 168–69.

209. Thomas R. Schreiner, *The King in His Beauty: A Biblical Theology of the Old and New Testaments* (Grand Rapids: Baker, 2013), 210–11.

210. Merrill, *Kingdom of Priests*, 495–96.

211. Merrill, 501.

212. *ESV Study Bible*, notes on 856.

213. *ESV Study Bible*, 501–2.

214. Schreiner, *The King*, 225.

215. Bright, *History of Israel*, 387. Beginning with Cyrus, Persia generally supported local religious practices, so Ezra's appointment was consistent with this practice.

216. Bright, 381.

217. Schreiner, *The King*, 210.

218. See *ESV Study Bible*, notes on 819.

219. Bright, *History of Israel*, 382–83; Merrill, *Kingdom of Priests*, 507–9.

220. Bright, 383; Merrill, 509–10.

221. Bright helpfully summarizes Nehemiah's opposition in *History of Israel*, 384.

222. Brisco, *Holman Atlas*, 172.

223. Schreiner, *The King*, 219.

224. VanGemeren, *Progress of Redemption*, 297–99; Schreiner, *The King*, 423–27.

225. Willem Van Gemern, *The Progress of Redemption: The Story of Salvation from Creation to the New Jerusalem* (Grand Rapids; Zondervan, 1988), 314.

226. John Bright, *A History of Israel*, 2d ed. (Philadelphia: Westminster, 1972), 411–12.

227. Bright, 413–14.

228. Bright, *History of Israel*, 419.

229. Bright, *History of Israel*, 418–19; Thomas V. Brisco, *Holman Bible Atlas* (Nashville: Holman, 1998), 174–76.

230. Bright, 416–17; Brisco, 175–78.

231. Leon Wood, *A Survey of Israel's History*, rev. ed. (Grand Rapids: Zondervan, 1986), 354; Brisco, 179–180; Bright, 416.

232. Brisco, *Holman Atlas*, 180.

233. Bright, *History of Israel*, 417; Brisco, 180–81.

234. Bright, 417–18.

235. Bright, 422.

236. Bright, 422.

237. Bright, *History of Israel*; Wood, *A Survey*, 355.

238. Bright, 424.

239. Wood, *A Survey*, 357–58; Bright, *History of Israel*, 426–28.

240. Brisco, *Holman Atlas*, 184–85; Wood, *A Survey*, 360–61.

241. Wood, 363–64. The name "Hasmonean" comes from the great-grand-father of Mattathias Maccabeus (called Hashmon); see Bright, *History of Israel*, 428 note.

242. For the paragraphs on the Hasmoneans, see Wood, *A Survey*, 365–68; Brisco, *Holman Atlas*, 185–88; F.F. Bruce, *New Testament History* (New York: Doubleday Anchor, 1969), 4–13; and E. Mary Smallwood, *The Jews Under Roman Rule* (Leiden: Brill, 1981), 1–20.

243. David O'Brien in Wood, *A Survey*, 371. O'Brien added the last chapter in the revision of Wood's classic text.

244. Bruce, *NT History*, 77.

245. Bruce, 69–73.

246. In Wood, *A Survey*, 373.

247. Wood, 373; Bruce, *NT History*, 74–78.

248. Philip R. Davies, George J. Brooke, and Philip R. Callaway, *The Complete World of the Dead Sea Scrolls* (London: Thames and Hudson, 2002), 54–58; Bruce, *NT History*, 82–92. Also see Hershel Shanks, *The Mystery and Meaning of the Dead Sea Scrolls* (New York: Vintage, 1998), 82–105.

249. Schreiner, *The King*, 428.

250. Willem VanGemern, *The Progress of Redemption: The Story of Salvation from Creation to the New Jerusalem* (Grand Rapids: Zondervan, 1988), 323.

251. Thomas R. Schreiner, *The King in His Beauty: A Biblical Theology of the Old and New Testaments* (Grand Rapids: Baker, 2013), 433.

252. Michael Grant, *History of Rome* (New York: Scribner's, 1978), 8–156; Michael Grant, *The World of Rome* (New York: Meridian, 1987), 21–38.

253. E. Mary Smallwood, *The Jews Under Roman Rule* (Leiden: Brill, 1981), 21–27.

254. Smallwood, *The Jews*, 28–30.

255. Smallwood, 38–43.

256. Smallwood, 49–59.

257. Harold W. Hoehner, *Herod Antipas* (Grand Rapids, 1980), 5–11; Smallwood, 60–70, 86–88.

258. Silvia Rozenberg and David Mevorah, Ed., *Herod the Great* (Jerusalem: The Israeli Museum), 96

259. Simon Sebang Montefiore, *Jerusalem: The Biography* (New York: Knopf, 2011), 92.

260. On Herod's building projects, see the wonderful summaries in Thomas V. Brisco, *The Holman Bible Atlas* (Nashville: Holman, 1998), 201–6, 231.

261. Smallwood, *The Jews*, 98–104; Hoehner, *Herod Antipas*, 10–11; Brisco, 201.

262. Hoehner, 18–33.

263. Smallwood, 105–14; 144–48.

264. Smallwood, *The Jews*, 114–17.

265. Hoehner, 239–49; 169–71; 251–62.

266. Schreiner, 499.

267. F.F. Bruce, *New Testament History* (New York: Doubleday anchor, 1972), 164–67.

268. See Harold W. Hoehner, *Chronological Aspects of the Life of Christ* (Grand Rapids: Zondervan, 1977), 13–27 for a helpful discussion on the challenges in dating Jesus' birth.

269. Brisco, *Holman Atlas*, 218.

270. Smallwood, *The Jews*, 144–56.

271. Smallwood, *The Jews*, 171.

272. Smallwood, 160–74.

273. Bruce, *NT History*, 93–100.

274. The details and the evidence for this chronology are found in Hoehner, *Chronological Aspects*, 45–63.

275. See Hoehner, *Chronological Aspects*, 95–139 and the *ESV Study Bible* (Wheaton: Crossway, 2008), 1809–10, for a defense of these dates.

276. James P. Eckman, *Exploring Church History* (Wheaton: Crossway), 10.

277. Eckman, 9–10.

278. Eckman, 11–13.

279. James P. Eckman, *The Truth About Worldviews* (Wheaton: Crossway, 2004), 62–64.

280. E. Mary Smallwood, *The Jews Under Roman Rule: From Pompey to Diocletian* (Leiden: Brill, 1976), 175.

281. Smallwood's account of Caligula's plan is most helpful. See 174–80.

282. Smallwood, *The Jews*, 194–95.

283. Smallwood, *The Jews*, 200

284. Smallwood, *The Jews*, 257–72; F.F. Bruce, *New Testament History* (New York: Anchor, 1972), 338–46.

285. Smallwood, 276.

286. Smallwood, 284–92; Bruce, *NT History*, 377–80; Simon Sebag Montefiore, *Jerusalem: The Biography* (New York: Knopf, 2011), 116–29.

287. Smallwood, *The Jews*, 293.

288. Bruce, *NT History*, 381.

289. Smallwood, 298–301.

290. Josephus, Flavius: *The Jewish War*, trans. G. A. Williamson (New York, Penguin, 1981), 24. Also see Frederic Raphael, *A Jew Among Romans: The Life and Legacy of Flavius Josephus* (New York: Random House, 2013), a creative and very helpful biography of Josephus.

291. On the crushing of the Jewish Revolt see Smallwood, *The Jews*, 293-326; Bruce, *NT History*, 379-382; Thomas V. Brisco, *Holman Bible Atlas* (Nashville: Holman, 1998), 258-262.

292. Smallwood, 327.

293. Quoted in Montefiore, *Jerusalem*, 136.

294. Smallwood, *The Jews*, 333, 339.

295. Bruce, *NT History*, 389–90; Smallwood, 372, 374.

296. Bruce, *NT History*, 385.

297. Bruce, 384–85.

298. Bruce, 385–89.

299. Smallwood, *The Jews*, 351–52.

300. On the trustworthy details of this not well documented revolt, see Smallwood, 389–427.

301. Quoted in Montefiore, *Jerusalem*, 139.

302. Smallwood, *The Jews*, 436.

303. Brisco, *Holman Atlas*, 275.

304. Smallwood, *The Jews*, 457–66.

305. Simon Sebag Montefiore, *Jerusalem: The Biography* (New York: Knopf, 2011), 144.

306. E. Mary Smallwood, *The Jews Under Roman Rule: From Pompey to Diocletian* (Leiden: Brill, 1981), 467–75.

307. Smallwood, 476.

308. Smallwood, 342, 488–92.

309. James P. Eckman, *Exploring Church History* (Wheaton: Crossway, 2002), 30, 39; and "Constantine: The Reign of Mixed Blessings," *Confident Living* (December 1991), 25–28.

310. Montefiore, *Jerusalem*, 154.

311. Peter J. Leithart, *Defending Constantine: The Twilight of an Empire and the Dawn of Christendom* (Downers Grove: InterVarsity, 2010), 138-139. Leithart's study brings a balanced perspective to the study of Constantine. He argues for the legitimacy of Constantine's Christianity and for a shrewd ruler who tried to balance all of the complexities of a pluralistic empire.

312. Leithart, *Constantine*, 132.

313. Montefiore, *Jerusalem*, 156–57; Leithart, 132–33.

314. James Carroll, *Constantine's Sword: The Church and the Jews* (Boston: Mariner, 2001), 216–17.

315. Alister E. McGrath, *Christian Theology: An Introduction* (Malden: Blackwell, 1998), 461–62.

316. The Origen and Lactantius quotations are from Michael Vlach, "Replacement Theology: Has the Church Superseded Israel as the People of God?" The William R. Rice Lecture Series, Detroit Baptist Theological Seminary (17 March 2010).

317. The quotations from Augustine and Chrysostom are from Michael Rydelnik, *They Called Me Christ Killer* (Grand Rapids: RBC Ministries, 2005), 7–8.

318. Rydelnik, *They Called Me*, 9–10.

319. Norman Davies, *Europe: A History* (New York: Oxford, 1996), 239–40.

320. Davies, *Europe*, 224.

321. Peter Brown, *The World of Late Antiquity* (New York: Norton, 1989), 66.
322. Brown, 67.
323. Brown, 82.
324. Brown, *The World*, 96-110.
325. Davies, *Europe*, 246. See also Steven Runciman, *Byzantine Civilization* (Cleveland: Meridian, 1967).
326. Brown, *The World*, 104, 106); A.H.M. Jones, *The Later Roman Empire, 284–602: A Social Economic and Administrative Survey*, 2 vol. (1964, reprinted 1986), 208-216. Also see Noel Q. King, *The Emperor Theodosius and the Establishment of Christianity* (1960).
327. Davies, *Europe*, 242-245; Brown, 150-157; Charles Diehl, *Byzantium: Greatness and Decline* (New Brunswick: Rutgers, 1957), 6-8, 177-179.
328. Montefiore, *Jerusalem*, 169.
329. Montefiore, 167; Runciman, 105.
330. Montefiore, 168.
331. Montefiore, 168.
332. Patrick O. Cate, *Understanding and Responding to Islam* (Dallas: Dallas Theological Seminary, 2001), 12-14.
333. This entire introduction to the history and theology of Islam is based on James P. Eckman, *The Truth About Worldviews: A Biblical Understanding of Worldview Alternatives* (Wheaton: Crossway, 2004), 75–84.
334. Norman Davies, *Europe: A History* (New York: Oxford, 1996), 257.
335. Davies, 258; and Robert Lopez, *The Birth of Europe* (New York: Evans and Lippincott, 1967), 80.
336. Steven Runciman, *History of the Crusades*, as quoted in Ibid., 253.
337. Moshe Sharon, "Islam on the Temple Mount," *Biblical Archeology Review* (32:4: July/August 2006), 38–39.
338. Sharon, 45.
339. Sharon, 47.
340. Simon Sebag Montefiore, *Jerusalem: The Biography* (New York: Knopf, 2011), 191.
341. Montefiore, 193; Albert Hourani, *A History of the Arab Peoples* (Cambridge: Belknap Press, 1991), 27–28.
342. Montefiore, 195; Michael Rydelnik, *Understanding the Arab-Israeli Conflict* (Chicago: Moody, 2004), 56.
343. Montefiore, 198.
344. Montefiore, *Jerusalem*, 212; Jonathan Phillips, *Holy Warriors: A Modern History of the Crusades* (New York: Random House, 2009), xxiii–xxiv.

345. Efraim Karsh, *Islamic Imperialism: A History* (New Haven: Yale, 2006), 69-70.

346. Karsh, 70.

347. Marcus Bull, "Origins", in *The Oxford Illustrated History of the Crusades*, ed. Jonathan Riley-Smith (New York: Oxford, 1995), 22.

348. Bull, 33.

349. Phillips, *Holy Warriors*, 6-7.

350. Both quotations are from Phillips, 9–10.

351. Dan Jones, *The Plantagenets: The Warrior Kings and Queens Who Made England* (New York: Viking, 2012), 272.

352. Jones, 273–74.

353. Montefiore, *Jerusalem*, 217–25; Karsh, *Islamic Imperialism*, 70; Robert G. Clouse, Richard V. Pierard, and Edwin M. Yamauchi, *Two Kingdoms: The Church and Culture through the Ages* (Chicago: Moody, 1993), 199.

354. Karsh, *Islamic imperialism*, 72.

355. Phillips, *Holy Warriors*, 166.

356. Phillips, 167–95.

357. Efraim Karsh, *Islamic Imperialism: A History* (New Haven: Yale, 2006), 84–86.

358. Karsh, 88.

359. Karsh, 89.

360. Karsh, 89.

361. Simon Sebag Montefiore, *Jerusalem: The Biography* (New York: Knopf, 2011), 304, 305.

362. Montefiore, 308.

363. Quoted in Karsh, *Islamic Imperialism*, 93–94.

364. Karsh, 90.

365. Karsh, 90.

366. Karsh, 91.

367. Karsh, 91.

368. Michael Rydelnik, *Understanding the Arab-Israeli Conflict* (Chicago: Moody, 2004), 57.

369. Montefiore, *Jerusalem*, 306-7.

370. Montefiore, 307–8. Also see James Carroll, *Constantine's Sword: The Church and the Jews* (New York: Mariner Books, 2002), 352–62.

371. Christopher Hill, *The World Turned Upside Down: Radical Ideas During the English Revolution* (London: Penguin, 1991), 71–72, 87–106, 171–73; Barbara Coulton, "Cromwell and the 'Readmission' of the Jews to England, 1656," *Journal of Cromwell Association* (2001), 1–21.

372. Paul Boyer, *When Time Shall Be No More: Prophecy Belief in Modern American Culture* (Cambridge: Harvard, 1994), 181–83.
373. Quoted in Montefiore, *Jerusalem*, 331.
374. Montefiore, 333.
375. Carroll, *Constantine's Sword*, 418.
376. Georges Lefebvre, *Napoleon* (London: The Folio Society, 2009), 423-424.
377. Both quotations are in Robert Blake, *Disraeli* (New York: St. Martins, 1967), 67.
378. Blake, 204.
379. Quoted in Montefiore, *Jerusalem*, 340.
380. Blake, *Disraeli*, 641–54.
381. The quotations in this paragraph are from Montefiore, 347–48.
382. Quoted in Boyer, *When Time Shall Be No More*, 184–85.
383. Montefiore, *Jerusalem*, 348–49.
384. Boyer, *When Time Shall Be No More*, 68–69, 70.
385. Quoted in George M. Marsden, *Jonathan Edwards: A Life* (New Haven: Yale, 2003), 264.
386. Quoted in Marsden, 335.
387. Marsden, *Jonathan Edwards*, 485.
388. Ronald G. Walters, *American Reformers, 1812-1860* (New York: Hill and Wang, 1978), 23–35. Quotations are from Timothy P. Weber, *Living in the Shadow of the Second Coming, 1875–1982* (Grand Rapids: Zondervan, 1983), 14.
389. See Keith J. Hardman, *Charles Grandison Finney, 1792–1875* (Grand Rapids: Baker, 1990), 254–55,324–49.
390. See Charles C. Ryrie, *Dispensationalism*, rev. ed. (Chicago: Moody, 1995), 39–40; and Craig A. Blaising and Darrell L. Bock, *Progressive Dispensationalism: An Up-to-Date Handbook of Contemporary Dispensational Thought* (Wheaton: BridgePoint, 1993), 46–54.
391. Ryrie, 62–67; Boyer, *When Time Shall Be No More*, 87–89.
392. See Boyer, 90–99.
393. Boyer, 100, 186; Weber, *Living in the Shadow*, 139.
394. Orlando Figes, *The Crimean War: A History* (New York: Metropolitan Books, 2010), 9–26.
395. Montefiore, *Jerusalem*, 359.
396. Figes, 36–37.
397. Figes, xxiii.
398. Michael Rydelnik, *Understanding the Arab-Israeli Conflict* (Chicago: Moody, 2004), 63–65.

399. On the details of the Dreyfus affair, see Carroll, *Constantine's Sword*, 450–64.

400. Quoted in Montefiore, *Jerusalem*, 392.

401. Quoted in Montefiore, 399.

402. Efraim Karsh, *Islamic Imperialism: A History* (New Haven: Yale, 2006), 136.

403. Simon Sebag Montefiore, *Jerusalem: The Biography* (New York: Knopf, 2011), 412–16; and Karsh, 136.

404. Martin Gilbert, *Churchill and the Jews: A Lifelong Friendship* (New York: Holt, 2007), 48.

405. Karsh, 137.

406. Karsh, *Islamic Imperialism*, 188.

407. Gilbert, *Churchill and the Jews*, 26–27.

408. Montefiore, *Jerusalem*, 433.

409. Montefiore, *Jerusalem*, 430.

410. Montefiore, 427, 435–41.

411. "The Treaty of Sèvres, 1920," *Treaties of Peace 1919-1923,* vol. 2 (New York: Carnegie Endowment for International Peace, 1924).

412. Michael Rydelnik, *Understanding the Arab-Israeli Conflict* (Chicago: Moody, 2004), 72.

413. Gilbert, *Churchill and the Jews*, 52–56.

414. Karsh, *Islamic Imperialism*, 193.

415. Rydelnik, *Understanding*, 73.

416. Montefiore, *Jerusalem*, 458–59; Gilbert, *Churchill and the Jews*, 93–96, 102.

417. Gilbert, 108, 111; Montefiore, 460; Rydelnik, *Understanding*, 74.

418. Montefiore, 468–69; Rydelnik. 74.

419. Montefiore, *Jerusalem*, 468–69.

420. All Wingate quotations in this paragraph are from Montefiore, 472.

421. Montefiore, 474.

422. Montefiore, *Jerusalem*, 474; Rydelnik, *Understanding*, 76.

423. Gilbert, *Churchill and the Jews*, 216–18.

424. Montefiore, 476.

425. Gilbert, *Churchill and the Jews*, 264.

426. Rydelnik, *Understanding*, 81–82; Montefiore, *Jerusalem*, 488.

427. Rydelnik, *Understanding*, 82–83.

428. Rydelnik, 85.

429. See Michael Beschloss, *Presidential Courage: Brave Leaders and How They Changed America, 1789–1989* (New York: Simon and Schuster, 2007), 196–234. Beschloss tells the story of how Truman's Jewish friend from Kansas City, Eddie Jacobsen, and Clark Clifford helped

shape Truman's understanding of the importance of a Jewish homeland in Palestine.

430. Montefiore, *Jerusalem*, 498.
431. Quoted in Rydelnik, *Understanding*, 89.
432. Rydelnik, 93.
433. Karsh, *Islamic Imperialism*, 144.
434. Quoted in Karsh, 157.
435. Karsh, 152; Rydelnik, *Understanding*, 95–97; Montefiore, *Jerusalem*, 511.
436. Montefiore, 512.
437. Karsh, *Islamic Imperialism*, 179-182.
438. Quoted in Karsh, *Islamic Imperialism*, 161.
439. On the details behind Nasser's ambitions and Israel's subsequent actions, see Karsh, 154–64; and Michael B. Oren, *Six Days of War: June 1967 and the Making of the Modern Middle East* (New York: Presido Press, 2003), 42–169.
440. Quoted in Rydelnik, *Understanding*, 98.
441. Montefiore, *Jerusalem*, 519.
442. Rydelnik, *Understanding*, 100.
443. All quotations in section 3 are from *United Nations Security Council Official Records* (Twenty-Second Year, 1382nd Meeting), 22 November 1967.
444. Karsh, *Islamic Imperialism*, 169.
445. Karsh, 170.
446. Montefiore, *Jerusalem*, 526.
447. Karsh, *Islamic Imperialism*, 213–14.
448. Quoted in Karsh, 214.
449. Khomeini quotations in this paragraph are from Karsh, 216–17.
450. Karsh, *Islamic Imperialism*, 180-181.
451. Karsh, *Islamic Imperialism*, 181.
452. Montefiore, *Jerusalem*, 530–31; Rydelnik, *Understanding*, 23–25.
453. Quoted in Karsh, *Islamic Imperialism*, 182.
454. Ari Shavit, "The Real News From Israel," *Wall Street Journal* (30 November–1 December 2013), C-3.
455. Ari Shavit, *My Promised Land: The Triumph and Tragedy of Israel* (New York: Spiegel and Grau, 2013), 387.
456. Thomas Friedman, *From Beirut to Jerusalem* (New York: Anchor Books, 1989), 285–88; James P. Eckman, *The Truth About Worldviews* (Wheaton: Crossway, 2004), 63–73.